Penguin Books

Heddy and Me

Susan Varga was born in Hungary in 1943 and came to Australia with her mother, Heddy, her sister and her stepfather in 1948. She has a Masters degree in English Literature and a law degree. She has worked as a teacher, in film and video, as an arts administrator, journalist and lawyer. She now writes full time. *Heddy and Me* was awarded the FAW Christina Stead Award.

Heddy and Me

Susan Varga

Penguin Books

Penguin Books Australia Ltd
487 Maroondah Highway, PO Box 257
Ringwood, Victoria 3134, Australia
Penguin Books Ltd
Harmondsworth, Middlesex, England
Viking Penguin, A Division of Penguin Books USA Inc.
375 Hudson Street, New York, New York 10014, USA
Penguin Books Canada Limited
10 Alcorn Avenue, Toronto, Ontario, Canada M4V 3B2
Penguin Books (N.Z.) Ltd
182–190 Wairau Road, Auckland 10, New Zealand

First published by Penguin Books Australia, 1994
10 9 8 7 6 5 -
Copyright © Susan Varga, 1994

Typeset in 11/13½ Sabon by Midland Typesetters, Maryborough, Victoria
Made and printed in Australia by Australian Print Group, Maryborough, Victoria

National Library of Australia
Cataloguing-in-Publication data:

Varga, Susan.
Heddy and me.

ISBN 0 14 023767 4.

1. Varga, Heddy. 2. Varga, Susan. 3. Varga family. 4.
World War, 1939–1945 – Jews – Hungary – Biography. 5.
Jews – Australia – Biography. I. Title.

940.531503924

Contents

A Guide to Hungarian Pronunciation

Hungarian	English	Hungarian	Phonetic English

Vowels

a	=	short o	Kató	Kotto
á	=	aa	Náci	Naatsi
e	=	e	Heddy	Heddy
é	=	air	néni	nairni
u	=	oo	Gyuszi, Pubi	Jooci, Poobi
o	=	o	Robi	Robbie
ó	=	or	Hódmezövásárhely	Hordmezovaashaarhey

Consonants

c	=	ts	Náci	Naatsi
cs	=	ch	Jancsó	Yoncho
j	=	y	Jutka	Yootka
gy	=	j	Gyuszi	Jooci
s	=	sh	Budapest	Boodapesht
sz	=	s	Szeged	Seged
zs	=	zh	Zsuzsi	Zhoozhi

Two easy rules:
* Vowels with an accent over them are pronounced long.
* The emphasis is invariably on the first syllable.

The Family

Náci Bleier Heddy's father
Kató Bleier Heddy's mother
Pali Heddy's brother
Pubi (Henrik) Hiekisch her elder half-brother
Baba (Richard) Hiekisch her other half-brother
Feri Schwimmer Heddy's first husband
Jutka their older daughter
Zsuzsi their younger daughter (me)
János and Margit Schwimmer Feri's brother and sister-in-law
Mária Schwimmer Feri's mother
Gyuzsi Weiss (later Varga) Heddy's second husband
Jóska and Klára Gyuzsi's brother and sister-in-law
Little Zsuzsi their daughter

Part I
Budapest

'Violets on Sundays'

Chapter One

Why am I getting interested in my father now – now that I've lived longer than he did, and almost everyone who knew him is dead? His brother in America is dead, his nephew in America doesn't remember him. There are no relatives of his in Hungary, that I know of.

Over the years I've had many chances to learn more about him but I never did. Him, Feri, my father – what do I even call him? I was six months old when he last saw me. He was dead before I was eighteen months old.

I was just over three years old when a replacement father came. He was cuddly and loving and my loyalties went out to him immediately. He'd come just at the right time to make our lives more normal again. I knew from the start that while he could not be consoled for the loss of his two sons in the War, acquiring two golden-haired small girls was almost like God making amends, ameliorating the senseless-ness of it, a little.

I sat on his lap the first time we met, and within a couple of months we were a reconstituted family unit. Such was the need in those times to recreate order and re-establish continuity.

I thought it almost traitorous to our new lives to show any interest in the father who'd conceived me, and who'd let us down by not surviving the Holocaust. He was dead and part of an era best forgotten, except for special emotional moments when the icons of memory were brought out and held aloft, then put away for another year or two.

From these times I learned that my father was bookish, conscientious, shy, delicate in health, somewhat over-protected, and that he adored my mother, who was fond of him.

I learned these things when I was old enough to be curious. In photos he looked innocent and grave, gazing at us children as if his fathership of us was a miracle. He wasn't handsome but he looked nice. At the time that was enough. I concentrated on the here and now, living in Australia in the 1950s.

At times though, during my teens, when I felt different from everyone, dropped into my family from another planet and making a poor pretense of being a normal adolescent, I'd wonder if there might have been a fellow feeling with him. I might have felt part of a line, or a family type, instead of some weird dead end. I'd wonder if he might have lent me books, or silent sympathy. I liked it when my mother said we held a teacup in the same way.

★

My mother and I are sitting in her long dining room, she facing the arched windows, I opposite a large Japanese screen. We've been sitting like this, with a small tape-recorder between us, once a week, every week, for about six months. I've come to know that screen well – there's a delicate scene of an old man crossing a bridge just in front of me. The room itself is imposing, with its long oak table and chairs covered in embossed velvet. Imposing but not unfriendly, which is very much Mother's style.

I switch on the tape-recorder. She talks, I listen. She doesn't need much prompting; she's telling me her life story, which she knows will be raw material for a book. In the past when people have said to her, 'Heddy, you should tell your life story,' she has said, 'I'm waiting for Susan.'

I've told her it won't be her life story, not properly. It will be filtered through my reactions and thoughts, my second generation eyes.

People tell her she's brave. What might I do? All kinds of distortions are possible. She replies that she's getting old, she's got nothing to lose, she wants to tell her life.

So we've been sitting in the dining room with the tape-recorder through spring and summer, and now it's early autumn, with a different light filtering through the windows and onto her face. It's still a handsome face, animated, the features strong and even. The eyes have lost only the edge of the brilliant dark blue that has made them famous among her acquaintance. Her light olive skin is wrinkled, but not much, considering she's seventy-three. Her voice is passion-ate, insistent; she rarely hesitates. Only when she breaks into English does it take on a forced note.

We both know it's a risky enterprise, this interviewing. We love each other, of course, but we haven't always liked each other. She finds me evasive and disappointing. I find her intensity both invasive and disarming; she often infuri-ates me with her dogmatism. But she can be colourful, warm and intuitive. And she is always lively.

She's been talking about our early years in Australia. Sud-denly she leaps ahead almost forty years, to a return trip to Hungary, timed especially for the fiftieth anniversary of her matriculating high school class.

'It was the fifty-year reunion of all the girls I'd matricu-lated with in 1934 – can you imagine it? After dinner, each person was asked to recount her life briefly, in three minutes. You can tell a life in three or four minutes, although some of the girls took advantage and took much longer. But I stuck to the three minutes. Do you know what I said? It crystallised within me after thirty-eight years away. I said to them, "As you know, I first married in Hungary and had my two children here, but unfortunately through certain events of history, I lost my husband." (The room was full of Christian girls, too, and I didn't want to hurt anyone or to use a vengeful tone. We'd all come together, everyone was very nice to me, everyone was glad to see me, so I wasn't going to bring in that tone.) I said, "After that, tragedies followed upon one another. Everyone knows what happened, I don't need to go into it. After the War, I stood there at the age of twenty-eight, widowed, with two small children. I was alone; my husband had died a tragic martyr's death ... In the end, I met my second husband, Gyuszi, who you see sitting here beside me. He had lost his wife and two children in Auschwitz. Coming together with that tragic background, we decided to begin a new life. The first step was to leave everything behind and not feel bitterness about what had happened. We thought, let's forget everything, and start a new life together, supporting each other.

"So this wouldn't happen again to my children, we decided to emigrate to Australia, and the emigration itself was, emotionally, culturally and intellectually, a shock. We had to struggle with it. But from the first moment I knew it was worth it because I felt myself free. An equal citizen in society."

'Oh, and I also said, "That feeling of freedom helped me put down roots in an alien world."'

She looks at me, face alight. I am at once embarrassed and moved, and try not to show either.

When I was growing up, I never let myself think about my father too much, because it was dangerous territory. Was I like him, a weakling who had no stomach for what he was witness to, who turned his face to the wall and died? In the hierarchy of suffering, he hadn't even got to concentration camp level. He suffered less than a year before he gave up.

In 1944, Feri, my father, was taken to the Hungarian border, to a labour camp called Fertörákos. There he suffered hunger and cold, was worked like a beast and humiliated like one. One morning he asked the man in the next bunk to deliver a message to us if he got the chance.

'Tell my wife and children that I loved them very much but that I died.'

With what mixed emotions I turned that phrase over in my mind. I was living among a band of survivors with heroic tales to tell. They seemed to have survived with a combination of luck and grit. If they ever thought about whether they actually wanted to live, they banished the thought as a waste of crucial energy and got on with survival full throttle. That energy still lingers about them. Having vanquished death, the survivors in my family don't namby-pamby with life.

I wasn't like my mother or grandmother, handsome hardy women gusting through like strong winds, nor was I like my new father, quick-thinking, wily, the ultimate pragmatist. Then I must be like *him*, the shameful one, who turned his back on it and gave up.

Still, I had a curious respect for my father's last words: 'Tell them that I loved them very much but that I died.'

Perhaps saying that, then doing it, took great courage. I liked someone who didn't want life at any price. Who chose a private way of saying 'No', and didn't wait.

I admired my mother's way and secretly dreaded and respected my father's. I didn't want to crumple in a crisis, yet I wanted always to be able to make a choice of dignity as I hoped my father had done.

When war was brewing in Europe, my mother and father's early reactions showed how they would deal with what was to come. In 1938 they honeymooned in Italy. My father had a Budapest paper sent to him. He was sitting up in bed reading it in an elegant hotel in Capri (he was a man of simple tastes who liked a few good things; well-cut suits and good hotels), when he saw an article announcing the first anti-Jewish laws. He read it carefully, then put the paper down. Tears came to his eyes and fell down his cheeks.

'That I have lived to see this day,' he said.

Two years later, the war in Europe already under way, they went to Italy again. My mother smuggled out some diamonds in a chocolate box as a first move in the battle to come. She did it alone, judging her husband too anxious and honest for the task.

Which one of them was I? Neither and both of course. And I am only just beginning to realise that it probably never mattered, and certainly doesn't matter any more.

★

In 1990, when Mother and I met up in Budapest, we went together to see the flat in Isabella Street where she was living when she first met my father.

It's a stone building from the 1890s with iron railings running around the inner courtyard. The arched windows have ladies' faces carved over the porticos. The fading blue woodwork is peeling, and skinny wooden poles, themselves rotting, hold up some of the balconies. If the place ever gets fixed up, it will be lovely again.

Isabella Street is a grimy street full of buildings like this one. Yet to me, these decaying apartment buildings, with unexpected glimpses of plane trees and children playing and women gossiping in their courtyards, are Budapest's charm. Even Heddy looks at them with a new eye. But in 1937 that flat on the first floor represented a new aspect of misery, the worst flat the family had lived in.

We enter the dingy courtyard. Mother pauses like a pointer dog, sniffs the air and turns decisively right.

'Up there, first floor, the corner flat, yes that's it.'

Not bad, I think, after fifty-three years.

'I remember watching Feri from my room when he was coming to see me; I saw him crossing the courtyard before he came up the stairs.'

Heddy met Feri one evening at the Belvárosi coffee house. She was only there to keep her friend Zsuzsi company. Zsuzsi had organised herself an introduction to Feri because she had heard he was available, amiable and rich.

The Belvárosi was a plush place; polished wood, chandeliers, dancing at night. All that evening Zsuzsi worked on Feri; she chattered and beamed at him, 'cooked' him, Heddy says. He was a tall awkward man, already in his thirties, clumsy in his mannerisms, straightforward, rather quiet. As they were leaving he said, 'Heddy, you were the prettiest woman in the room – you don't make yourself up.'

'That was the beginning of your father's role in my life,' Heddy says. 'We started to go out, here and there, to the theatre and the opera, and after we'd been going out for a couple of weeks, he said he wanted to introduce me to a classmate of his. He seemed quite excited about it. There was nothing much yet, no great confidences or anything. Anyway, one night at the opera this woman and a man were coming towards me, and he said, "Here she is, my classmate! I want to introduce you to my sister-in-law Margit and my brother János." (He and Margit really had been in the same class together in Hódmezövásárhely.) I went home to report everything to Mother, and I said to her, "Hey, this fellow Schwimmer's taking things seriously. His brother and sister-in-law were there; it was all pre-arranged so that they could meet me." '

Feri paid court quietly and methodically. There were no passionate declarations, yet there was an extra dimension in everything he did, like the time they went to an exhibition at the Ernst Museum:

'It was a retrospective of the artist Pólya. We were comparing the paintings we liked, and he said, "Which one do you like best?" and I said, "That one, the barnyard scene with the rooster," and he went up to the gallery owner and made an offer on the price and he bought it. I went home again to Mother and said, "Something serious really is afoot because he bought the painting I liked." '

When I was in Budapest in 1990, before meeting Heddy there, I'd already come across some locations of their courtship. I'd peered into the windows of the Belvárosi coffee house (it was closed and being renovated as a casino) and oohed and aahed over its chandeliers and panelled walls, but I didn't realise it was the coffee house where they'd met. And I'd already come across the Ernst Museum. I walked past it all the time, a two-storey building with magnificent bronze doors redolent of the thirties. I had wondered whether this was where Feri bought the Pólya picture as a first declaration of his love.

Of the scraps of information I have about my father, I like this the best. To buy the picture she liked most but not to say a word about it. Only later, when he put the ring on her finger, he said, 'And you know, we already have a child in common.'

I've always loved the Pólya picture. Now that Mother is old enough to talk occasionally about who will inherit what, and for me to let her do it, she asks, 'What picture do you like most?'

'The Pólya,' I say instantly. 'I don't care about the others, but leave me the Pólya.'

I like the painting as much as the story behind it, or maybe I can't separate the two. It's of a farmyard scene in the snow; the main colour is white. A farmhouse is in the background, dashing and substantial, its woodwork in acid blues and orange reds. There's a big cockerel in the foreground, pecking at scraps, brilliant in the same colours. It's a cheerful big picture; it's the Hungarian countryside buried somewhere deep in my memory.

My father must have known such scenes all through his childhood. When I went to Hódmezővásárhely, his home town on the Great Hungarian Plain south of Budapest, I visited the street where he was born. His house had been pulled down but next door the gate opened to a scene from the Pólya painting: chooks and horses in the courtyard, the very smell I had imagined from that scene.

The old ladies across the road remembered my father. One gazed at me mournfully, and said, 'Your father walked with his head down, looking at no one, because he knew what would happen. He could see the future and didn't like it. He was no fool, Feri Schwimmer.'

No one knows much about Feri, not even my mother. They were married only five years before he was sent away. And he was not outgoing, even in childhood. All the Schwimmers kept themselves to themselves.

The Schwimmer family settled in Hódmezővásárhely in 1848, after fleeing the Serbs in another part of the Austro-Hungarian Empire. Feri's father Lajos was a feather merchant, as his father had been before him. He built his wealth slowly and steadily in his lifetime, buying feathers from the local farmers and smallholders, storing them in a big storehouse-barn at the back of the yard, then selling them to the feather merchants of Budapest. Lajos was respected by the peasants for driving a fair bargain and keeping his word. They got to know him better than they did most Jews, for he liked a drink and a game of cards. Otherwise he was a man of few words.

His wife was also quiet, devoted to her three sons. When the middle son died young she turned her attentions obsessively to the frail and sickly Feri. In his teens, he developed tuberculosis and spent much of his youth in various sanitaria, being nursed, reading and dreaming. In the family's scheme of things, János was to conquer the world; Feri was to do his duty, when he was well enough.

Once the Schwimmers moved to Budapest, they began to amass a serious fortune. When their father died, János looked after the business side, and Feri did the administration and the buying from the country feather merchants such as they had once been. He became expert at assessing the quality and weight of feathers.

But his real life was elsewhere. He would sit for hours in his room in his mother's flat, reading, making notes in the margins of books. The room was his haven; he had furnished it himself in modern black lacquer, a style quite different from his mother's heavy brown Biedermeier. He had a favourite wrought-iron reading lamp, which has become mine.

His mother continued to pamper and coddle him. He went dutifully to the office. He played bridge a little, there was an occasional outing with a woman, nothing serious. He turned thirty-four. His mother was beginning to despair.

'We couldn't believe it,' the old ladies from Hódmezővásárhely said, 'when we heard he got married, and to such a pretty girl!'

★

It is grey and rainy when I arrive at Mother's house. A soft light trails through the windows. She is looking miraculously young; the blue eyes have regained their intensity of colour, the face structure is still perfect behind the wrinkles.

She retells a tale I already know, only this time I listen with a different attention.

1940. The Anschluss was old news. Heddy was twenty-three, two years married to Feri. Feri's brother was already in America and urging them to come out. They hesitated, both loath to leave their parents behind.

Nonetheless, moves had to be made to guard against an uncertain future. Heddy needed an exportable skill. She began a course in confectionery making at the renowned Ruszwurm coffee house where, in 1940, they were teaching a handful of well-heeled young women in the kitchens. (Ruszwurm is still there; a tiny place, all dainty Biedermeier furniture.)

Heddy would get up early, leaving the maid to wake Feri for breakfast. By 6.30 she'd be heading across the river to the Castle district. The streets were already busy; the milk-men were out, the bread carters, the early workers. They'd whistle and joke as she passed.

She liked the course, although she hoped never to have to use it seriously. She bought the metal cones and wired shapes so that she could practise at home, and made trays of elaborately shaped savouries when her friends came to tea.

And she thought of an immediate use for her new skill. At a classy jeweller's in Váci Street, she and Feri bought some diamonds. Then she bought a box of the famous Stühmer bonbons. At home, she unwrapped a few and put the wrappings aside. She made up some chocolate marzipan, covered the diamonds in the chocolate and rewrapped them, arranging them in the bottom row of the gorgeous box.

The box was to go with them to San Remo in Italy. (Hungarian Jews holidaying in Italy in 1940! Were they mad, was half of Europe still asleep? Yet Primo Levi said he felt no danger, was still preoccupied with his everyday concerns, so who were they I suppose?)

Heddy sent Feri ahead. She would take a later train, with the chocolates.

'Of the two of us, I can lie better. You're too honourable; your face will give us away.'

He obeyed her. At the border he was searched down to the soles of his shoes. He rang her from the platform.

'Everything is okay. They searched me on the train and found nothing of course.' That meant, ABANDON PLANS. LEAVE THE DIAMONDS AT HOME.

Two nights later, she boarded the sleeper with the chocolates in her overnight bag. She remembers the name of the woman who shared the sleeper – a Mrs Horváth, a professor's wife. She offered Mrs Horváth the lower bunk. To test her nerve, she passed down the box of chocolates.

'Do have some. They're Stühmer chocolates; I can't resist them.'

Mrs Horváth took one, then two. Heddy ate a couple herself. The sleeping car attendant came around to collect the passports. She waited for the border and the guards.

She woke to hear voices, Slav voices. Dear God, was it possible? She had fallen asleep!

The train was stationary. Minutes passed. No one came. No one checked the bags.

She stayed a night in Trieste with her Aunt Rózsika. Rózsika and her family had fled from their home in Vienna in 1939, then again from Budapest. Trieste, too, was temporary till they worked out where on earth to go.

It was a gay reunion. Heddy offered the chocolates around in triumph. What a coup!

'Eat some more! Go on! But if you eat the wrong one, I won't be leaving till you shit it out!'

'We nearly died laughing,' she says to me. 'I was young then and could laugh from the heart. And Rózsika and I could always laugh together. We had a lovely day, and then I got on the train to San Remo and arrived in the afternoon, to meet up with your poor father.'

She found Feri in the hotel, sitting up in bed, swathed in a white mosquito net, being, as he often was, a little careful of his health. He was just emerging from his afternoon nap.

'You understood my message,' he said. 'It was far too dangerous to bring anything.'

'Yes, yes, I understood,' she said, impatient, 'but everything's here!' And she glowed with girlish glee, just as she does now, telling me about it.

From Italy they went to Paris, where they sold the jewels to Cartier.

'I must be one of the few women to sell something to Cartier, rather than buy.' She grins, enjoying her own joke.

The money from the sale went to America, care of János. Nine years later, en route to Australia, she collected it.

'And that's how we found the deposit for the first house in Chatswood,' she says, triumphant.

We both sit back, satisfied.

Chapter Two

Heddy adored her father, Náci, even in the years when he lied to Kató constantly, kept going to the races and losing until there was no bread on the table. There is a different tone in her voice when she talks of him, a softness as absolute as his love for her.

'My father and I never quarrelled,' she says, 'never.'

Since then, men have always been of a different moral order for her. They are to be forgiven. Women are to be tested. And found wanting.

Náci was a good-looking man in a soft way, with a fine straight nose and benign eyes. When he and Kató, dressed to go out, showed themselves off to the children, Heddy was proud of them: her mother firm-backed, large-bosomed, arresting; her father substantial but not corpulent, almost distinguished.

Náci died when I was a few months old. When I look at photos of him bending over us as babies, I see a wholly masculine givingness, an enveloping mildness. How often Heddy has told me of sitting in his lap, even when she was a married woman, and stroking the baby fineness of his hair, smelling the barber's cologne from his daily shave. I can see why Náci charmed his womenfolk. I can see (but only just) how Kató – my momentous grandmother – would have bent her will to his, just once, and given up the opera stage for him.

Náci and Kató met when he was supervising the building of the new People's Opera, built to supplement the ornate Opera House on Andrássy Avenue and to sate Budapest's lust for opera and operetta.

Náci was attentive to Madame-the-Artiste's every whim as to her dressing room and amenities; it was a love match from the start. In 1912, in conservative Budapest, he did not care that she was a separated woman, or that she had two boys under ten. He offered to take the boys on. He defied his father, an Orthodox Jew. Old Bleier was scandalised that Kató had been married not only to a Christian, but to an orchestra conductor known around town as a libertine.

Náci put one condition on the marriage. Normally the mildest of men, he feared the stage as other men might fear a sexual rival. He made her promise to burn her costumes. She was not to read the theatrical magazines. She was to sing only for guests at home, or for him and the children. Then he was very proud of her. Much later, when Heddy was ten and Kató was safely transmuted into a bourgeois matron with four children, Náci allowed her, for the child's sake, to take out opera subscriptions. So they went on Friday nights, *en famille*, and Heddy wept over Mimi's fate and Madam Butterfly's fair-haired little boy.

In 1916, when Heddy was born, Budapest was just beginning to feel the effects of war. The city was enjoying an extraordinary efflorescence still clinging to it from the turn of the century, when it had burst upon Europe as a thriving metropolis whose cultural life, some said, surpassed that of Vienna. There were even those who claimed that Budapest was the more beautiful: 'the Paris of the East'.

Hungary was belatedly shaking off feudalism. The twin cities of Buda and Pest on either side of the broad Danube were sleepy towns until the flat side, Pest, took off in the building and cultural boom of the 1880s. Between 1900 and 1914, a new, predominantly Jewish bourgeoisie flourished, especially in Pest. At the turn of the century, one fifth of the city was Jewish. Vienna's mayor, Karl Lueger, who hated the Hungarians even worse than the Jews, nicknamed it 'Judapest'. The assimilation and penetration of Budapest's Jews gave the city a different flavour from that even of Vienna or Prague. In 1900, sixteen Jews were members of Parliament. Forty per cent of Budapestians entitled to vote were Jewish.

The old aristocracy found such Jews useful for the development of the country; these were thoroughly Magyarised and genuinely patriotic Jews, sophisticated, well-educated and prosperous. The 'Christian middle class', meaning simply the non-Jewish, emerged far more slowly. Among them were the newly urbanised 'petty' gentry who mostly whiled away their time in the public service, resentful of the prominence of the Jews.

Budapest was an exuberance of styles and influences, pomp and show; of opera and cakes, comfort and conservatism, combined with a formidable intellectual and artistic life. Arthur Koestler grew up in Budapest, György Lukács was writing his first books there, Kodály and Bartok were already composing, and Hungary's great avant-garde poet, Ady, was in his prime. For the more conventional bourgeoisie, there was the world of opera, theatre, good food and 'fine literature'.

Defeat and the Treaty of Trianon hit Hungary worse than any other German ally. The Austro-Hungarian Empire was gone forever, and with it two thirds of Hungary's prewar territory. Millions in population went to her victorious neighbours: Czechoslovakia, Romania, Yugoslavia and Russia.

From the postwar chaos emerged the first Communist

dictatorship in Europe, a brief, confused and bloody regime, led by the Jew Béla Kun. In 1920, when Kun and his Commissars fled, Admiral Horthy rode into Budapest on a white horse, was elected Regent, and remained in power for over twenty years. His Prime Minister, Bethlen, headed a rightist regime that was saved from outright Fascism only by the old-fashioned 'decent' conservatism of Bethlen himself and the old ruling class.

The new industrial workers lived in misery. In the country, despite a few reforms, the peasants continued largely landless and desperately poor.

Thirty-two of the forty-five Communist Commissars had been Jewish; Lukács himself had been the Commissar for Culture. During the White Terror that followed, the words 'Jew' and 'Socialist' became synonymous and thousands of Jews, socialists and industrial workers were massacred.

Little of this intruded on Heddy's childhood. She heard much later that a relative on Kató's side had been part of the Kun Government; he was hanged when the Rightists regained power. Two of her Bleier uncles had served in the Great War and Uncle Béla had been injured. Postwar, Náci had avoided involvement in the huge building scandals that ruined many of Budapest's bourgeoisie. His little brood was secure.

'When I think about my childhood,' Heddy says, 'especially the outings, it's just like those early films.'

She so relishes talking about it, and I enjoy listening; I am seduced by her images as much as I am suspicious of them. I know, and I think even she suspects these days, that we are talking of a complacent, class-bound, doomed world.

Heddy's childhood was filled with Pali. Pali was her brother, eighteen months older than she, handsome and good. They were always together. The older boys, Pubi and

Baba (Henrick and Richard outside the family) were already adolescents and had quite different pursuits.

On Sundays, Náci would take the younger children on special outings; Heddy in her best pink satin, high white boots and snowy socks, Pali in his sailor suit with the wide white trousers. Each Sunday the same fiacre with the same driver would be waiting at the corner of Rákoczi Street. Sometimes Pali was allowed to sit beside the driver and to hold the reins as they drove down towards the Körút, the circular promenade that rings central Budapest.

On the corner of the Körút was the National Theatre where the balloon and flower sellers stood. Náci would buy them a bright balloon each and a posy of violets to take home to Kató. Sometimes, instead of violets, there was spring mimosa brought in from Italy.

The promenade would end in the glory of a visit to Hauer's. Among the city's renowned coffee houses, Hauer's was arguably the best, if not the most elegant.

'Mr Hauer, the proprietor, would be waiting at the door in his tall white hat and impeccable white apron,' Heddy says. 'He was always there to greet his best clients. And he'd address my father as Sir-The-Esteemed-Architect and enquire after Kató – "Gracious Madame", he called her. Pali and I had to be polite and respectful to "Hauer-bácsi". The Hauers were of good family. The business had been in the family for generations and they were proud of their reputation. The greeting at the door was part of the ritual.'

At the tiny gilt tables under the chandeliers, Heddy and Pali stuffed themselves on kuglof and mignons or the little savouries in aspic that were a house specialty. Náci took particular pleasure in watching his children eat. Later, when they left Pest to live at Rózsadomb, he made regular excursions across the river to bring home the best cold meats, the latest delicacies, the richest patisserie.

Some Sundays he took them to Margaret Island, a spacious pleasure garden in the middle of the Danube. All Budapest went there. Heddy and Pali liked the little train pulled by ponies, the puppet kiosks in summer, and, when they were older, the fiacres pulled by plumed horses down the park's shaded laneways.

In the summer of 1990, one of the first things I did to escape the overheated city was to go to Margaret Island. You can walk across Margaret Bridge to it, from either Buda or Pest. It is a green expanse, less formal than a Paris park, but more organised and full than an Australian one. There are tennis courts, two swimming pools, a hotel, tricycle and fiacre rides. And so many people. Yet it is quiet, uncrowded, immensely civilised.

I was five when I left Hungary and have virtually no memories – but I knew that the smell of the grass, the pleasure in those flowers, was the pleasure of being three or four years old, of being safe and warm. I had been there as a child, as surely as my mother had.

While Náci was the king of the Sunday outings, Kató officiated at home, high priestess to her twin deities, music and food. She still sang for the family from time to time in the evenings, mostly Schubert and Schumann lieder. She accompanied herself on the Bösendorfer Grand, around which hung six heavy oil portraits of the Great Composers, or those who were considered great at the time: Beethoven, Mendlessohn, Meyerbeer, Gluck ... Heddy has forgotten the other two. The oils were a precious memento; a gift from old Hiekisch, Kató's music professor and father of her first husband, whom she had married when she was just eighteen.

Kató was now queen of the kitchen as once she had been queen of the stage. The maid took care of breakfast – coffee, and fresh white bread rolls delivered daily to the door – but then Kató took over. At 10 o'clock, her voice would ring peremptorily through the courtyard.

'Heddy, Pali, lángos!'

The lángos was a kind of fried bread, still hot and dripping fresh oil, with a clove of garlic rubbed on it. Or there might be scrambled eggs sprinkled with paprika, and bread and butter.

But this was just a small rehearsal for lunch. Every day was a production, a storm of preparation, until the soup hit the table at the very moment the lift bearing Náci reached the fifth floor. Kató prided herself on her timing. The maid was merely the stage hand, cleaning up after the grand performance.

In the evenings, when they had just a cold supper and tea, Uncle Béla, who lived almost next door, would shuffle over, already in his slippers, bearing a hunk of rye bread with chicken fat and a slice of capsicum, and Heddy and Pali would vie with each other for a bite.

Heddy was Uncle Béla's favourite, and she loved him because he was kind and funny. Once a year the six Bleier brothers, all apostates in their father's eyes, gathered in his dim flat for Passover. Heddy and Pali always made sure they sat next to Béla. He winked at them when they threw the bitter herbs under the table, and he only pretended to read the Hebrew words of the service, making up funny Hungarian words instead to make them laugh. Grandfather Bleier would point his snowy goatee at them severely but he never caught on.

Although Uncle Béla lived in the same apartment block, his flat was not as good as theirs. It only had two main rooms facing the dim courtyard, whereas theirs had three rooms, with two facing the street. (Budapestians estimate the size of their flats by the number of rooms that can actually be lived in, and don't count kitchens and bathrooms.) The difference between a three-room and a two-room flat could tell a whole life story for the Budapest bourgeoisie; among other things that Náci was a successful architect-builder and destined to be more so, and that Béla was an employee in a leathergoods firm and without brilliant prospects. It could also mean the difference between a live-in maid and a daily, the most telling social and economic difference of all.

In the flat in Rákoczi Street where the family lived until Heddy was ten, their three rooms accommodated the six of them. The younger children shared the marital bedroom; the older boys' room doubled as the family day room.

This was a normal kind of arrangement in apartment houses throughout Central Europe. But I think about the proximity of it all, with the parental bedroom full, the growing boys sharing their bedroom with the daily life of everyone else, all of them trooping through the tiny maid's room which was a thoroughfare to the kitchen, the washing hauled up on racks to drip on my grandmother's neck as she cooked, the kids getting underfoot in the hall already crowded with storage cupboards. Such different notions as to what constitutes a good life from the Sydney suburbs where I grew up. Lack of space was not a difficulty. Good food and opera tickets were the priorities – and domestic help, made possible by the extreme poverty of the working class. Families of even moderate income could afford a live-in maid who worked long hours and, if she was lucky, was treated as a second-rate member of the family.

Anything important in the flat happened in the dining room, which was crammed with a long table, twelve portentous leather-embossed chairs, two vitrines loaded with the good china and lace, the upright radio, a divan, and three very important objects: the palm, the piano and the clock. The palm was enormous, and Kató's pet; its maintenance was surrounded by solemn rituals. It sat by the bay window overlooking the street, and flourished year after year. The grand piano, the Bösendorfer, stood cool and shiny, its rear end draped in Gobelin lace.

The clock was Heddy's favourite object. It was a large musical clock, black and gold, sitting on top of an ebony and gold vitrine. By the time she was six or seven, she was allowed to get up on a chair and pull a little wire in the clock base which made the music go.

I have ended up owning the clock. It's a bizarre piece, the clock-face almost incidental to the design, with its columns, cupolas and statues of ancient Greeks playing the lyre and angels holding trumpets. In the middle of the base sits a bust of Joseph the Second of the Austro-Hungarian Empire, and at the top broods a gilded eagle.

When I show it to my friends, they often stare in fascinated horror. But when I start playing the clock's music box, the same look of dreamy delight comes over their faces as came over mine as a child, for out of this grandiose monster come six tinkling eighteenth-century tunes of great sweetness and delicacy.

When Kató forsook the stage and threw herself into being a bourgeois housewife with the same energy and pride she'd put into the opera, the clock was an important early purchase and an enduring symbol. It was never sold when times were bad. It survived the War. Finally it came out to Australia with my mother for safekeeping, until Kató managed to escape Hungary to rejoin it, and us.

I don't remember much about the clock when I was little. Later, in Killara, when Kató (Granny by then) was in her final illness, it stood tall on the unused piano in her stale-smelling room. I went in often – though it got more difficult as the room smelt more of decay – and listened to its tunes.

I liked the whirr and clank it made as the music stopped almost as much as the music itself.

★

Kató had musical ambitions for all her children. All four of them sang and played the piano. 'But none of us,' Heddy says, 'had her God-given natural gift, or her confidence.' Pubi, the eldest, had the best voice, and the looks and dash for the stage, but in the end nothing came of it. Baba had his mother's gusto and could be devastatingly funny, but he didn't have her drive. Pali, her first-born by Náci, was her favourite – a young god-king in her eyes, graceful and serious, with a talent for Rachmaninoff but no temperament for the stage.

Finally, with her last-born, Kató had a little girl to dress and dream for. She taught Heddy piano, but the lessons always ended in tears. She would pull the frightened child's plaits and yell, 'No, no, false, can't you hear it you donkey? Again!'

Outside teachers had to be brought in. There was a fair-haired Christian lady, wafting perfume, then a wan woman from downstairs who smelled of her musty flat.

Kató listened for Heddy's voice, which was warm and bell-like. She dragged the terrified twelve-year-old along to audition with her former colleague, Mária Basilides, who was mildly encouraging. Then to a formidable professor at the Music Academy, scene of her own triumphs as a girl. Heddy sang for him, her voice cracking in fear.

'A pretty voice my dear Madame,' said the Professor, 'charming, but a chamber voice at best; that's all it will ever be.'

In the end, Kató gave up. It never occurred to her that

her energetic ambitions might contribute to a shyness and shrinking in Heddy. Self-consciousness was not a word in Kató's vocabulary.

As the family grew, and the older boys grew wilder, Rákoczi Street became impossibly cramped. Náci bought a run-down villa in the Buda hills, which he proposed to redesign himself. It was in a suburb called Rózsadomb, which means Rosemount.

He had grandiose plans for an ordinary-sized villa; a circular driveway, urns on the stone steps spilling geraniums. Inside, he wanted classical doors, and handsome octagonal-patterned ceilings. Heddy was to have pretty garlands on the ceiling of her room.

Kató settled the palm and the clock in the drawing room; for the first time she had a separate dining room. Upstairs, Heddy had her own room with a Juliet balcony. Pali was to share a long, sunny room with the older boys.

Heddy didn't want to leave the apartment house courtyard and the seven stories of iron-clad walkway around it.

'There were always children to play with. I loved the Kiss girls especially. Their father was the son of the famous writer József Kiss, but he was a failure – a card player, always morose, hanging around the flat. His wife was a lovely woman – a Christian. He gave her a hard life. Although their flat was only two rooms and darker than ours, the girls had a complete set of Thonet furniture, all in miniature. I was so jealous! When Kató told me were moving, I cried. But she promised that the Kiss girls could come to visit me at Rózsadomb. And she promised me my own set of furniture, in cream lacquer with flowered upholstery; she said it would be so pretty that I could take it with me when I got married. And that's exactly what happened.'

After Feri bought the Pólya picture, Heddy thought that all the portents were there for a proposal. She began to look at her options seriously.

'I wasn't in love. He wasn't good looking, he wasn't Prince Charming, but he was decent, affectionate, honest. I wasn't full of illusions any more, my dreams had been shattered by life. My youth was taken away from me – those years took everything from me …'

Her voice trembles with a disappointment that she still can't erase. She always refers to the time before she met Feri, the period between fifteen and twenty-one, as a catastrophe – a time which changed her very nature. The war years, full of drama and terror, were as nothing in comparison, simply because they came later. I am puzzled by the magnitude of the feeling, and she cannot put a finger on just what it was – but I suspect that whatever is obsessive, fearful and dark in her comes from the years when her father gambled everything away on the horses.

Some six weeks after Heddy and Feri started going out, Feri came around one afternoon. Only Baba was at home. They chatted for a while, then he plunged in.

'You know, don't you, that I had tuberculosis as a child? I am quite clear of it now though.'

She nodded.

'But just to make doubly sure, I went to see my specialist last week, and he's given me a certificate that says I am fit to have children.' He fumbled for the document and cleared his throat. 'Heddy, I want you to marry me.'

'You know there's no money behind me, no dowry to speak of, only me.'

'I'm only interested in you! Look, this is the ring my father gave me just before he died – for my future wife.'

The ring on her finger, and no one to show it to! She found an excuse to leave the room. Where was Baba?

'In the toilet!' he yelled.

'Open the door, just a *bit*!'

She shoved her hand through the crack. 'Look what's on my finger!' Then she went back to Feri, proper and serious again.

'I want you to come and meet my mother. She's waiting for us.'

For the first time ever he addressed her with the informal 'you'.

Heddy scribbled a note for Kató: 'Mother, I'm engaged!'

'Old Mrs Schwimmer just opened her arms to me as soon as she saw me. She bought me a lovely diamond watch as an engagement present which made János's wife furious. The Schwimmer parents never liked Margit. She came from a Hódmezövásárhely family they didn't approve of ... And then I turned up with my big smile; I was fresh and blooming. Feri and his mother were so happy to find me, and I was so happy to be found!'

Mária Schwimmer called Kató over to afternoon tea.

'My dear Kató,' she said, 'don't bother to buy anything for the trousseau. I have everything prepared for my son. Come and see.'

Over the years, she had collected the coffee and tea sets, the china garnered from her annual watering at Karlsbad, a complete set of monogrammed and embroidered linen and a set of plain linen for the maid.

Normally the trousseau was the responsibility of the bride's parents, but Mária Schwimmer's husband had left her a fortune and no girls. When János got engaged, there was no great dowry forthcoming there either, so she had started to set him up, buying corresponding items for her younger and favourite son, should he ever marry.

In Hungary the bride's dowry was surrounded by strict rituals that remained fixed until the War swept them away. The peasant bridal chest was stuffed with embroidered pillows, feather duvets, elaborate blouses and skirts. The middle class elaborated the practice. A girl was expected to provide a full set of household accoutrements, the furniture for the new apartment, her own extensive trousseau, and if she was well-to-do as well as middle class, a monthly income. There might even be a lump sum negotiated, which enabled the bridegroom to set himself up in his lawyer's or doctor's rooms.

Heddy laughs, a bit guiltily. 'But it made sense, in a way. They were hard times, just after the Recession. Young people just couldn't get a start without that kind of support ... You know, I still have the coffee set that Grandmother Schwimmer prepared as part of that trousseau. I'm thinking of selling it. It's far too elaborate for these times.'

I go home and listen to the tape. Which coffee set? I ring her.

'Show me the coffee set when I come tomorrow.'

She leaps at it.

'You can have it if you like. It's not right for my house, but your house might cope, if you know what I mean.'

I end up with the coffee set, an elaborate Edwardian silver item. I know she is pleased. I am pleased, too, as if we had made some tribally significant exchange.

★

The wedding took place on 21 March 1938, at the large, confident-looking Dohány Street synagogue. In the wedding photos, my mother looks very young in a simple dress. My father looks puritan in small metal spectacles. If you look closely, you can see a false thatch of hair woven in by the photographer to hide Feri's balding pate.

Ten days before my parents married, Hitler's troops marched unopposed into Austria, and Hungary's neighbour 'disappeared' in Anschluss with Germany.

It was a schizophrenic existence over the next few years. They lived a life that was prosperous, happy and settled, and they lived a life of insecurity, fear and foreboding. It was the same life that hundreds of thousands of Jews lived all over Europe. They glimpsed the void and were afraid to look in. They flirted with escape, then escaped into optimism. Things would get better. Governments would change. The impossible was just that, impossible. And such ties at home, to home ...

Chapter Three

Returning from her honeymoon in Italy, Heddy tried to ignore any danger signs for the future. She put aside that morning in the hotel room in Capri when my father had read about the first anti-Jewish law and wept.

'I wanted to live. Life had turned around for me, and things were beautiful and good again. People were looking after me, spoiling me … Yet it wasn't really a trouble-free time. Fear came into my life again, just in a different form.'

The 'first' anti-Jewish law of 1938 was not in fact the first such law; it was just the first preceding the Second World War.

In 1920, following the Communists' downfall, the Hungarian Parliament passed a law known as 'numerus clausus', the first of its kind in Europe. It limited Jewish intake to universities (then thirty per cent) to six per cent, their proportion in the population. Other measures tried to limit the number of Jews in public employment and to curtail their economic power.

During the twenties these measures were implemented patchily, often forgotten. The Jews had the protection of the old aristocrats, although their own power was being eroded by the growing Christian middle class.

Bartok, Lukács and Koestler were gone. Yet the city pursued an intense and sophisticated cultural life. In this 'Silver

Age' of Hungarian literature, novels were still being written about the mutually profitable and enduring friendships between Jewish and non-Jewish young men, although by now they were often in wistful retrospect. The much-loved Catholic writer Babits, in a 1927 novel, *Halál Fiai*, wrote about the 'naivete and optimism' of his two heroes, young Imre and Rosenberg: 'These two descendants of Eastern races, the Jew and the Magyar, grasped each other's hands enthusiastically, professing their devotion to the common culture and their faith in the future with shining eyes.'

And for much of the prosperous middle class, life between the wars went on in a comfortable round of fixed pleasures and duties. Budapest's Jews felt so much part of their city that anti-Semitic measures and incidents were just flurries offstage, distant alarms. The numerus clausus law was a fact of life, to be circumvented wherever possible. The city's Jewish-Christian rivalries and divides were, to them, just part of its flavours, not to be taken too seriously.

When Heddy was growing up, she didn't even know that Pubi and Baba were half-Jewish, half-Christian; the name Hiekisch was never uttered in the house. They were just her handsome, much older brothers – Pubi by ten years and Baba by eight – who were always in trouble. At Rákoczi Street there had been an awful row about Pubi and the pretty Markovics girl on the third floor. Years later, Heddy heard that Náci had provided the money for the abortion. Once Baba transgressed so badly that gentle Náci resolved to thrash him. Heddy watched the scene from a window of the flat, crying with fear, but Náci only gave him a couple of whacks with a tennis racquet, then let him go.

One day, a sour woman who lived alone on the third floor drew Heddy inside.

'Little girl, Pubi and Baba are not your real brothers.

They've got a different father, and a different name. Their father's a Christian called Hiekisch … Now don't you dare tell anyone I told you.'

Heddy was terrified. Náci not the father of the older boys? It was inconceivable. She poured it all out to Pali. But Pali was lofty: 'That? I've known that for ages. It's no big thing.'

For years, this other Hiekisch father was a remote, sinister figure. Heddy found out what she could about him, but she didn't tell her parents that she knew.

One day, when she was already in her late teens, she recognised him on the street. She surprised herself by going up to him.

'Good afternoon sir. Do you know who I am?'

'No, no, I'm sorry …'

'I'm Heddy, Pubi and Baba's sister,' she burst out, and shook his hand.

'Aah, so I see, I see it now. I'm very pleased to meet you. And how is your dear mother?'

He was urbane and mild and held onto her hand until his tram came. She went home elated. She'd accosted him and said hello. It helped cut the family secret down to size.

The Bleier family saw itself as comfortably if irreligiously Jewish, despite the older boys. They mixed with Christians, to a degree, and according to unstated but definite rules. At Heddy's high school some of her friends were Christian, but the line tended to be drawn at the ceremonial birthday 'jours'. Only a few of Heddy's invitees were Christian girls, and it was rare indeed for an invitation to come the other way. To get in with the Christians, you really had to become one, and even then both sides whispered about you for years to come.

Hungarian Jews refer to someone who has changed

religion as a 'turned-out'; it has connotations of both leaving and straying. It was thought contemptible to want to 'turn out', yet a great compliment to be accepted by the Christians, even momentarily. Náci's patrician nose and gentle manner made him much loved, even among the Christians. They took to Kató too, in a different way. She was queenly in her immensity and gusto, and the men addressed her at the beginning of a phrase, as was the custom, as 'handsome Madame'.

The older boys crossed and recrossed between the two worlds easily and carelessly. Once they reached marriageable age, both married often, and to Christian and Jewish women, indiscriminately and almost alternately. But it wasn't till half way through the War that these Jewish-Christian configurations in the family became at all important. Then suddenly they were a piece of luck, a lifeline.

★

I arrive at Mother's house in Bellevue Hill, set up the tape-recorder in the dining room. She wants to get some 'practical' things over with first – she sees herself as the practical one, me as the dreamer – so she talks about a baking dish she's lent me, and do I have any broken jewellery she can take to 'her man' on the North Shore? Then we settle down to talk about Rózsadomb, the villa in the Buda hills.

I enjoy her talking of that time; her images are pure, sunlit – the garden with the fruit trees, Cézár the dog.

'I think it must have been 1927 – I was about eleven – when we got Cézár. He was only a tiny puppy. He was so small he could only roll down the steps; then he learned to walk, then run. He was a wonderful thing in our lives, that dog. The nicest memory of Cézár is with the sled in winter. Our house was on a high point; there was a steep little street in front of it, and beside it an open field. When it snowed, this little field became our sledding ground and we went out every day we could. The arrangement on the sled was Cézár at the head, then Pali, because he was that eighteen months older than me, then me. We'd roar down the slope a hundred times, climb up, down again a hundred times.'

After the dusty little parks and noisy courtyards of Pest, the garden was pure pleasure. The apricot tree bore plump, fragrant fruit every year, and in the languorous summers Heddy would climb up to eat the soft fruit by the hour. The pear tree also bore well and Kató would wrap the pears in newspaper and store them over winter in the mansard rooms of the attic.

When she was thirteen, fourteen, Heddy spent delicious hours in one of the attic rooms, weeping over the novels of Mór Jokai, Hungary's Sir Walter Scott. In the other mansard room, where a wash basin had been installed, lived Mrs Trivál and her daughter Anna. Mrs Trivál had been with them in Rákoczi Street; now she was old, her daughter did the heavy work.

Heddy and Pali addressed Mrs Trivál with the respectful form accorded to the elderly: 'Trivál-néni'. On Sundays, Trivál-néni always went to church, carrying her Bible. Heddy asked her once, 'Why do you take the Bible, Trivál-néni, when you can't read or write?'

'That's exactly why I take it, child,' said the old woman, 'so no one will ever know that I can't.'

At Rákoczi Street, when Trivál-néni used to accompany her every day to school, Heddy had extracted the facts of life from her, bit by bit, the old lady shushing with each morsel, begging her not to tell anyone.

It was taken for granted that Heddy must be still chaperoned to school, so Mr Riffert the chauffeur now drove her over the river to the Gymnasium. Mr Riffert came with

Náci's job as managing director of a large firm that designed
and manufactured insulating materials.

Mr Riffert was everywhere in their new lives. He ferried
them across the Danube to and from school, he took them
on outings and taught them to drive, and he went on errands
for Kató, took Náci back to work after lunch, home again
in the evening, out again if they were going out.

Mr Riffert was a very tall, sweet-natured man. When he
was sent on errands he'd forget what he had to do and come
back for new instructions. But he was always there, and he
loved the family and they him.

Most winter afternoons, Mr Riffert would take Heddy
and Pali skating. Kató would often come with them. In her
own country-town girlhood, there had been no money for
extras; all her musical education had been on scholarships.
Now she threw the lot at Heddy and Pali – French in the
afternoons with Monsieur Pierre, singing, piano, swimming
and skating.

She accompanied them to swimming lessons, too, and at
age forty had herself taught to swim, her huge bulk sus-
pended by a rope above the water. My favorite photo from
that time shows her at Lake Balaton, seated profile to
camera, attired in a massive bathrobe and something resem-
bling a hairnet. She looks like a benevolent sphinx with her
handsome brood of four arranged at her base. All the boys
are skinny; only Heddy looks as if she could go the way of
her mother.

Kató learned to skate, too, at the Városliget, the city park.
She hated sitting on the sidelines with the other mothers.
She edged her bulk around the ring, clinging to the rails,
while Heddy and Pali twirled past her in the twilight.

The park became the centre of Heddy's young social life.
There was a large lake with wooden bridges crossing, and
willows trailing in the water where people rowed in the

summer. In winter it became an artificial skating rink. In a nineteenth-century building next to the lake, Budapest's gilded youth gathered every afternoon to have their skates fixed on by poor women whose living was in the tips they received. After the hour on the ice was over, the teenagers teetered back to have the skates removed. On the ice, two huge megaphones blared the Radetsky march, the invigorating Rákoczi overture and the soft waltzes of Lehár and Strauss.

Heddy's voice grows musical with memory.

'It was a very atmospheric thing; the music playing, the white snow, and we decked out in every colour, red and yellow and blue ... The romances blossomed, and the flirting! Will he come over, won't he? ...'

She was grateful when Enci Friedman came over every afternoon and held her hand while they skated around the ring. Enci was intelligent and nice, but ugly, not a great catch. 'But I was no seductive beauty at that stage either – I was fat from Kató's cooking. My parents believed that children should eat.'

Enci was the son of a lawyer who lived on the best street in Budapest, Stefánia Street, a broad avenue lined with burgher mansions. Young Zsa Zsa Gabor and her family lived nearby, although the two families did not know each other. Zsa Zsa also came skating in the afternoons.

Heddy and Enci were good mates. He'd ask her whether she'd been called up to recite the history homework in front of the class, what had happened in the geography hour, had she got into trouble that day with Mrs Geszti, the saturnine maths teacher.

One afternoon he said to her, 'I'm leaving you early today.'

'Oh, why? What have you got to do?'

'I've noticed that Zsa Zsa goes home at 5.30 on Tuesdays. I want to be there to open the gate for her.'

And he hurried off, leaving Heddy biting her lips. To be left for Zsa Zsa Gabor, even by ugly Enci. And Enci hadn't even been introduced to Zsa Zsa!

'Such was her sex appeal, even then ... I must have been fifteen at most, she thirteen, even though she only admits to sixty-five now, and I'm seventy-three!'

Kató was a strict mother. Most of Heddy's small rebellions came to nothing. She was not allowed out alone, all make-up, even lipstick, was forbidden, and any criticism of either parent was not tolerated. When once Heddy ventured that she found Kató's habit of sucking her teeth irritating, Kató sucked them all the more as rebuke for Heddy's presumption.

Unlike Pubi and Baba, over whom Kató had lost control long ago, Heddy and Pali were 'good' children. Heddy knew that they were supposed to make up for the older boys who had left school early and spent all their time chasing money and girls.

Heddy was enrolled at the Veres Pálné Gymnasium. She was good at history and Hungarian, and sport. She liked school but was never brilliant, like Pali.

The Veres Pálné was named after its founder, a Hungarian gentlewoman of feminist persuasion. It had a liberal reputation; overt anti-Semitism had no place there, especially as thirty to forty per cent of the girls were Jewish. The divisions were mostly subtle, both in school and out. Everyone knew who was old gentry, who middle class, who was 'turned out' Jew, who moneyed Jew, who was scholarship, and they tuned their behaviour accordingly.

Miss Klein, the Jewish scripture teacher, was Heddy's favourite. She was an unexpectedly modern, delightful young woman for whom Heddy learned Hebrew and Jewish history with a will. Then she was replaced by a rabbi, nicknamed Kóbi, a learned man with shabby clothes and a strange smell – Kóbi's smell. All the secularised young ladies were contemptuous of him. No ghetto world of long beards and caftans for them. They were patriotic Hungarians, who happened to be of the Jewish religion.

Heddy, too, drank in the glories of Hungary's pre-Trianon exploits and learned the great Hungarian poets off by heart. She did not want reminders of the 'otherness' of being Jewish. Once old Kóbi took over, she lost interest in Judaism.

Heddy had always known about Náci's gambling, but she had never thought much about it. It never seemed to make a difference to their lifestyle. In the Rákoczi Street days, Kató used to joke that the form guide, always by Náci's bed, was his 'Bible'; she saw it then as a harmless hobby, and an eccentricity in a Jew. Racing was regarded as a curiously Christian sort of profligacy by the Jewish bourgeoisie; an inexplicable waste of good money well earned.

Heddy never understood exactly how the horse racing changed from a harmless hobby into something else. Her parents did not tell her much. They had strict views about what children should know. She was being raised as a 'Pesti úri lány', which is untranslatable in its connotations, but means, roughly, a nice young girl of good parentage, brought up in the Budapest style.

In the autumn of 1932, the fruit trees in the garden of the villa were starting to lose their leaves, the lazy summer holiday by Lake Balaton was over, and the family had just been on the last of the picnics in the country with Mr Riffert at the wheel. Heddy would be sixteen in November.

It was then Náci broke the news that they could no longer afford Rózsadomb.

Heddy would not have cared so much if they could have

taken Cézár the Alsatian with them. Life in the rented flat in Pest was not too different at first. The skating rink was close by, Náci still had his prestigious job, Mr Riffert was still around to chauffeur, the afternoon French lessons continued.

But there was a new bitterness and sourness between her parents; there was no more hiding or ignoring their quarrels. Heddy found herself taking Náci's part, although she knew he continued to gamble. She felt her father's shame on her own skin. She began to be afraid.

Within a few months, they had to move again. Cheaper rent was Kató's only recourse. In the second flat, near the river, where to the stranger's eye all seemed still serene and prosperous, the serious penny pinching began. There was no ready money any more, no money for the sort of clothes the other girls at school had. Anxious to help, Heddy saved on the tram fares to school and walked the forty minutes each way.

A year after they left Rózsadomb, they went to visit Cézár. They had left him at the villa and had promised his new owners time for the dog to get used to them.

'On the exact day the year was up, Mr Riffert drove us to Rózsadomb, all six of us. The dog knew us immediately. The joy! I spent an hour playing with him. We were so happy. When it was time for us to leave, they took him out of the room so he wouldn't see us go. I cried my heart out on the way home, all the way down the Buda hills towards the Danube. We were almost at the Margit Bridge when something – I don't know what – made me turn around. I screamed, 'Look, Cézár!' and there he was, panting behind the car, still trying to keep up. Mr Riffert stopped and we picked him up and took him back. What else could we do? I never saw him again. After that last time with Cézár, the really bad times began.'

In September 1933, when Heddy started her final year of school, Pali was in his first year of architecture at the Technical University. Under the 'numerus clausus' law, he had been one of three Jews admitted in his year. He was withdrawn and unhappy. He hinted at anti-Semitism at the university, but didn't elaborate. His parents told him to grin and bear it; he was lucky to be there.

The early thirties were grim years generally, and unpromising ones for the Jews. The depression had brought down the long-serving and moderate Prime Minister, Bethlen. His successor, Gömbös, a right-wing hero of the White Terror years, was open about his Fascist inclinations. Gömbös saw his enemies as the old aristocracy, foreigners, Social Democrats and Jews. In 1935, after rigged elections, he entrenched himself for another term. He wooed Hitler, and when Hitler proved indifferent, allied himself with Mussolini, earning himself the derisive nickname 'Gombol-ini'. In the new Parliament, the Arrow Cross, the local Nazis, won two seats.

While the family was living in the flat by the Danube, Náci lost his job. Not lost, that was the euphemism. Dismissed. Dismissed from the insulation works where he had been for many years, the last seven as managing director. He had been 'borrowing' money from the firm – Heddy never knew the details – to shore up his betting losses. The firm allowed him to resign, and kept quiet about the reason.

The true extent of the calamity began to dawn on Kató. Her husband was unstoppable. He gambled in secret. She found out. She ranted and threatened; he promised. But her will could no longer overbear his, as it had before in most things. He was strangely confident, when he wasn't remorseful and withdrawn. He'd get another job. He was due for a big win, any day; he pinned his faith on his own ingenious betting scheme. Any day now the whole thing would be a hiccup in the even tenor of their lives.

Neither parent would hear of Heddy leaving school or Pali leaving university. The older boys were not much use, preoccupied with their own lives; Pubi engaged, Baba seriously going with a girl. There was no help from anywhere.

Heddy felt all life's little pleasures leaving, one by one. No one laughed any more, in a family where everyone had loved to laugh, lustily and often. Her parents did not confide in her; they still treated her as a child. She shut the door on their shouting voices and worked like a fiend for her matriculation. It was what they expected.

She was in a panic as the big exam approached. The Hungarian Matriculation was an awesome business along the lines of the French Baccalaureate.

'If it's so awful my darling,' Náci said, always indulgent, 'I don't mind if you don't do it.'

Even then, at seventeen, she still liked to sit in his lap, stroke his silky hair, sniff his cologne. She bathed in his protection, even when it was no longer there.

★

Heddy's face is bleak and pinched once the tape is turned off. I can tell it's not just about the hard teenage years but something about the present. I dread what she's going to say – that pinched look is always a bad sign.

God, I think, she's still brooding over my latest shock to her system. A few months back I announced that after years of rocky heterosexuality, my new love, and finally I hope my true partner, is a woman. But she says no, it's not that: 'I can better understand you being with Anne than why you spent nine long years with Jim.'

She surprises me sometimes, really surprises me.

'Okay then, what is it?' I ask, still dreading.

'Well, when I look back on my life, I've always been struggling to get back to normal after some sort of setback. My whole life is the struggle for normality – to recover after those awful teenage years, then after the wreck the War made of my life, then the strain of emigrating. I'm always just trying to get back to normal, live an ordinary life. Whereas you and your sister, you've had a perfectly normal life, and you spend all your time making it abnormal, trying to get away from normality. You haven't been content to leave things be, just to live. You've gone about making your-self unhappy, making things as complicated as possible ...'

And on and on, in the same bitter vein.

I can't think of anything to say that wouldn't provoke a fight, but inwardly I am bitter, too. Here she goes again with a mad, simplistic misinterpretation of my life. We are again at loggerheads about what it is to be 'normal'.

Yet I must admit, since I have been listening to her stories, that even taking into account the benevolent haze that memory gives, there is something fresh, almost sparkling about that prewar life. There was a kind of innocence in their unembarrassed enthusiasm for the bodily and material pleasures, for the little milestones and achievements – the first skating lessons, the first bedroom suite, the first fur collar on a young girl's coat. I am fascinated by their solid-ity, the ease of their assumptions. I can see why Heddy saw the bad years as a fall from Paradise, the War as an unwar-ranted, unforgivable interruption.

That life she has described to me makes me wistful and suspicious all at once. Its feel, its inner life is so different from what she and Dad had recreated here, or the suburban life I watched around me as I was growing up.

Perhaps I saw the War as some sort of punishment or retribution for that fat, unquestioning existence. Or if not that (because I knew that was irrational) then surely that complacent good life was somehow dangerous for the moral health? But my parents and their generation didn't see it like that. Their priority in Australia was to recreate their lost world in whatever ways they could. Most of them have become more conservative, more sceptical, more right-wing. It has worried me that their sole concerns seemed to be to put their lives back together again and to protect their children. Wasn't there some other lesson to be learned from the nightmare slice of history they had survived? Some different way to be?

Yet, reluctantly, I have begun to be impressed by their determination to recreate everything as near as possible to what it was. It's because of that recreative urge, I now realise, that you'll see my mother and aunt and dozens like them turning up to the Musica Viva concerts, the opera, the symphony concerts, year after year. You'll see them on any night in the foyers; the women are carefully dressed and coiffed, safe, smart, some of them elegant. The men look either rotund and prosperous or faintly scholarly. When they meet for the nth time in the corridors of the Opera House or the Town Hall, they exchange ritual greetings with no diminution of enthusiasm. Watching them over the years, smiling real smiles at each other, I am dazed. This is what they were doing in Budapest before the War interrupted them. They are recreating themselves on distant shores, in other times.

All the essential rhythms have been revived: the well-stocked linen cupboards, the serried rows of skirts and blouses, the silver, the opera, the bridge games, the invitations. They are back to normal.

But in fact things are utterly different, and everyone knows it. What happened between the lost worlds of Budapest or Prague or Vienna and the recreated worlds of Sydney or Buenos Aires or Montreal was too huge and terrible for them to be able to truly recreate the bourgeois solidity that so fascinates me. Its real feel, its kernel, is gone forever.

They tell me I cannot possibly understand the experience, its consequences on lives and personalities. But I was born into it, in 1943, right into it. And I have been embroiled in its consequences ever since.

Mother is right in a sense. I have been trying to get away from her version of normality. Her version of it has never made sense to me. It didn't *feel* normal – it felt troubled, transplanted. I didn't understand the prototype. It wasn't until I smiled at someone in the corridors of the Budapest Opera House and felt what it was, still is like to live there, that some things began to fall into place.

Chapter Four

Heddy matriculated with creditable results. She was out in the world. But what sort of world was it going to be? Náci refused to hear of her going to work. No daughter of his would demean herself in that way.

He had got himself another job, with a rival firm. It was less money, less responsibility – the rumours about his gambling had circulated – but face was saved temporarily, the financial crisis averted.

They decided to send Heddy away for a while. She had long ago given up her dream that after school her parents would send her away to somewhere like Lausanne where she would learn German and French and have a glamorous, properly grown-up life. Instead, Kató scraped together the one-way fare to send her to her aunt in Vienna; Rózsika would look after the rest.

'Don't worry,' Kató said at the bus terminal, 'I'll get the return fare together and send it to you in a couple of weeks.'

Vienna was a curious time, part relief, part hiatus. A time of tranquillity and terror, private woes, public unease.

It was good to be in a family circle where there were few tensions. Heddy knew Rózsika's husband and children well from holidays together at Balaton. She met Rózsika's parents, the Duklers. Old Dukler was a traditional Polish Jew, with a fine head and an impressive beard. He was mildly shocked at having a 'goythe' such as Heddy in their midst, who hardly knew any religion. Every Friday night in the Haydn-Gasse, he led the family in prayers and songs, and coached her in the words.

The Duklers had lived in Poland all their lives. On a trip to Germany in 1933, Nazi youths caught the old man on the street and beat him up so badly that he never walked again. He took refuge in his daughter's Viennese home.

A curious refuge, Vienna, at the end of 1934 when Heddy came to visit. Earlier that year, Chancellor Dolfuss had been murdered by Austrian Nazis. Many Jews tried to ignore the tension, and others, like the Viennese Bleiers, were pinning their hopes on Zionism. Rózsika and Max tried to infect Heddy with their enthusiasm for a homeland for the Jews, but she felt puzzled and alienated. Hungary was her home; she didn't need another.

The weeks went by pleasantly enough, but there was no money. Kató had written, but with no mention of money to keep her going, or of the return fare. There was no money for outings or theatre or presents. And no cakes, in Vienna, the city of cakes! She'd stop outside the cake shop windows to marvel and break her heart. One day, she would return to the lost world in which she could buy any, all, the cakes that she wanted.

'I can laugh at myself now, standing in front of all those cake shop windows, sick with longing. It's only a little thing, but how vividly I remember it! I think that's why, even today, I savour the little pleasures that money can buy. I haven't forgotten.'

A young relative of Rózsika's started to pay court. His shy attentions helped to pass the time. He took her to the opera where they sat together in the gods, struggling with her indifferent German and his worse Hungarian.

'You'll see the Opera House when you stop off in

Vienna,' Heddy says. 'It's worth a look, although it's nowhere near as nice as the Budapest Opera House.'

A rare piece of chauvinism, I note, for things Hungarian.

I stopped off in Vienna on my way to Budapest. I went past the busy Maria Hielfer-Strasse where all the cake shops still stood, and found the Haydn-Gasse where Heddy had lived with my Great Aunt Rózsika. (Rózsika ended up in Brazil. I never met her. She died before I became interested in the past and all the scattered relatives around the globe.) In the Haydn-Gasse I picked out a couple of sombre large-roomed buildings that I thought could have housed Rózsika's flat, but Heddy told me later I had the wrong building. They had lived in one of the two remaining eighteenth-century houses, where Haydn himself had once lived, the ochre-yellow ones with pretty courtyards.

At night we returned to the street, to a beer garden in one of those courtyards. We drank young wine and ate sausage and stared covertly at the amiable locals who stared covertly at us. This was Vienna, charming, tradition-bound Vienna. No Horst Wessel rowdies there. I didn't even know why I was on the lookout for them, except that I knew how many of the city's worthy burghers had welcomed Hitler enthusiastically when he marched into Vienna in March 1938.

Kató didn't write again. No sign of Heddy's fare, no indication of when it might arrive. What was happening at home? Had things got even worse? Was that possible?

There was no way she could tell Rózsika. It was too humiliating. She had never talked about it to anyone, even her best friend Éva Kort.

Now every time she tried to say, 'Rózsika, I have no money to go home,' the words clove to the roof of her mouth.

Nearly three months crept by. Every day she watched for the mailman through the curtains, desperate with hope.

Finally Rózsika spoke.

'Heddy dear, do you want to go home? Is it that your mother can't send the money?'

The next day she was on the bus.

They were moving again, to the inner city, to the cheap end of Damjanich Street.

Number 9 Damjanich Street was a dark and cavernous flat, but no slum. When I saw it in 1990, I was surprised how reasonable it looked. It wasn't so bad even then, Heddy admits. It was what was happening inside the walls that gave 9 Damjanich Street the quality of nightmare almost equal, for her, to the worst days of the War.

Hunger and the pawnshop entered their lives as dreaded familiars. The days were filled with money and food – how to get them, what to do about them. Sometimes there was not enough to eat and Kató panicked. Pali was on his way home from a gruelling day at the university and there was not a loaf of bread for her beloved son.

'She'd send me down to make up some story to the grocer, like, "Mother's not home yet and I don't have any money, but she'll definitely pay you tomorrow, so could I please have a loaf of bread?" That's what I had to do. Can you imagine that situation? With my childhood, my upbringing, and then I was swept into this hellish situation ... And it all had to be kept secret. I withdrew from the circle of girls I had gone to school with. I had to. I couldn't keep up.'

'Didn't other people know? Didn't they talk about it?' I ask.

'Oh yes, people knew, it became so obvious, but no one talked about it.'

Kató was selling off or pawning many of their belongings. She had already sold one of her most treasured possessions, the six oil portraits of the Musical Greats. That had been the ultimate reproach to her husband.

Heddy became the trusted second in the battle, and Kató's envoy to the pawnshop. Heddy loathed and dreaded going there. If it was a piece of silver to go next, she might be able to walk, unnoticed, with the piece hidden under her coat, but if it was a Persian carpet, she would have to struggle onto a tram with the thing rolled up under her arm, and pray that no one she knew would see her. She kept her eyes down and scuttled past people towards the old part of town where the pawnshop was, near the markets and opposite the run-down old building where her grandparents had lived. Her grandfather was still alive, in the Jewish old people's home. Náci had always paid for his upkeep, but when his debts mounted, he had to ask the other brothers to take over. They had not been pleased, found excuses. Heddy knew that this had depressed and embittered her father more than the lack of food on the table.

The pawnshop was a government-run institution, a huge sombre building of red and black brick. It had different sections for glass and silverware and furniture. She'd get a chit from the official at the window to take home to Kató, who kept a pile of chits on a spike, scanning them anxiously for the due date. When she could, Kató scraped together the money and Heddy was sent to bring the china or silver or the carpet home again. Often the due date came and went, and Kató wailed that there'd be nothing left for her daughter's dowry.

Kató knew what Náci wouldn't face; that for the Budapest bourgeoisie a poor girl was anathema, and that Heddy's prospects of any sort of marriage were negligible. She was determined to hang on to whatever she could so that her daughter would have something, a bit of bargaining power.

The trips to the grocer and the pawnshop burnt into Heddy's soul, eroded her sense of self. Who was she now? She wasn't the young lady she'd been brought up to be any more. There was no question of leading the life of other girls of her upbringing; perhaps a little genteel occupation, certainly shopping parties and balls, waiting to get engaged and get married.

She had come home from Vienna determined to begin earning money. But Náci was obdurate. No daughter of his would ever go to work. This was the same man, after all, who some twenty-five years ago had asked Kató to leave the stage for him, so confident of his future, and her love for him.

Heddy wept and begged, but she could not bring herself to blame him.

'I never quarrelled with my father,' she says again. 'Never.'

In the end he agreed to let her do a shorthand and typing course. He seemed to have given in. At the end of the course, he actually wangled her a job with his own firm.

But she had no dress suitable for work. Kató got hold of some cheap blue serge, but the only dressmaker she could afford was Cousin Olga who would do it for less than anyone else. It was a poorly made high-necked dress with long sleeves, but what could be expected from Cousin Olga who charged so little?

Heddy typed all day in the prim serge dress. The sleeves were so tight that the circulation in her wrists was cut off, and they ached and ached. There was no more material, it was no use complaining.

Her salary at Nagybátonyi as a beginner clerk was low and went straight to Kató. Kató continued to scrimp and save, Náci to gamble. Heddy remembers little of this time, except for the constant ache in her wrists from those wretched sleeves.

She'd been working some six months when the secret leaked out. Náci was paying her salary himself, out of his own earnings, and half the staff knew about it. Her 'contribution' was a humiliating joke.

Heddy felt defeated in the face of her father's madness. She went home to help Kató in the daily grind. She found herself going to synagogue every Friday night with her mother, to pray to God for help.

Both older boys had left home and were married well before the worst days of Damjanich Street. Not long after they left Rózsadomb, Pubi married a middle-class Jewish girl; her parents wanted him converted and circumcised before they would consent to the marriage. For the time being, Pubi had joined the Jews.

They were married at the Dohány Street synagogue, the hub for the relatively godless Jews of Budapest. In the wedding photo there are no signs of what is to come. Everyone looks prosperous in formal clothes. Heddy is plump and pretty in a slinky dress, with bridesmaid's flowers.

Baba also married a Jewish girl, first off. His more modest wedding, some eighteen months later, to Ibi Berger, had some fallout for Heddy. Ibi had a brother, Laci, who started coming around to Damjanich Street. He was her first serious suitor. There had been no question of a real boyfriend while she was still at school. There was only one boy she had really liked anyway, but he was keen on Mandi Barna, and there was no competing with her. Mandi was sexy, stylish and fun. Even the girls liked her. She was impoverished gentry, from a family with some sort of title, 'though she didn't use it at the time,' says Heddy. 'I admired Mandi; so did everybody. I was so disillusioned when I heard, much later, that she'd married some German and become a big Nazi!'

She could not keep up with the old crowd from school. Once or twice she went to a dance; Kató organised a dress for her through Cousin Olga. It was presentable, just, but nothing like what the other girls wore, especially Éva Kort, whose mother was outdoing herself now that Éva was out on the social circuit.

Laci Berger must have known about their situation, but he didn't seem to mind. He was a pleasant, slightly colourless youth, who wrote her verses. It was lovely, diverting to be loved. When he asked her to marry him, she said yes. She didn't quite know what else to do. Perhaps if she married reasonably well, she would be able to help her parents from a position of strength.

There was a passivity about Heddy at this time that was never to come again. She says she felt as if all their lives were sliding down a slope without end, and she didn't know what to do to stop the slide. It is around this time too that her memory and sense of chronology slips. Usually she knows exactly what happened when. Here, she is stumbling about with images only, not sure of how things fitted together, but with an overwhelming sense of the dark mood, of being swept along by an inexorable fate.

She did not want to know what was happening to her father. She could not bear to let her vision of him go, and turned away from any knowledge that would have belittled him irreparably. And she needed, still, to believe in the efficacy, if not of Náci, then of Kató.

She went out with Laci, Pali chaperoning at all times. Occasionally he would persuade her to go skiing on the slopes of the Svábhegy, just beyond Buda. Sometimes it was like an approximation of normal life; to have a presentable fiancé, to talk of the future. Sometimes the three of them would forget and fool around and laugh like kids.

There were some months in Damjanich Street when things became utterly desperate. All the rugs were gone, and most of the furniture. Heddy was always at the pawn shop, or begging for credit from the shopkeepers. Kató expected it of her.

Her mother's enormous energy seemed to have drained away. She was starting to lose her rear guard action with the creditors, and the bailiff had been more than once.

One day, without warning Laci called off the engagement. Perhaps he had been frightened off by the situation, perhaps it was pressure from his parents, perhaps he had never really been in love. Heddy didn't care which. She was relieved.

Heddy and Pali didn't talk a lot to each other at this time. When they did, it was to fantasise. 'I would fantasise about the elegant furniture I would have when I got married, that would be quite different from my mother's, more like what I saw at Mrs Kort's place, and Pali would talk about the sort of car he would buy when we had money again.'

Even as things grew worse through 1934 and 1935, Kató expected Pali to stick it out at university. Her favourite son was to become a professional man.

Heddy knew Pali was not happy there. Anti-Semitic remarks, graffiti and demonstrations were increasing. At school, Pali had been popular, good at sport; his Jewishness had seemed genuinely irrelevant. The hysterical anti-Semitism among the student body was something quite new to him. He chose to downplay it, especially as the topic wasn't welcome at home.

At the beginning of his third year he was immersed in preparing a set of plans for a large project. He worked on them day and night for months. When they were finished, he set the plans up carefully in the exhibition hall. The following day he went back to check on them, and found ink and excrement smeared all over them. There were racist scrawls over his name.

He went home and said he was never going back. He would not listen to his parents' pleas. He took a job, first with a plateglass firm, then with a shoe shop chain, and withdrew further into himself.

For the second time, Náci lost his job.

It was time, Kató decided, to take over. First she managed to stop the bailiff auctioning off the entire contents of the flat. Then she met with her creditors, one by one, and laid her cards on the table. She could not meet the level of payments they were demanding. But she could meet a much lower figure on a regular monthly basis. The exact amount would be there on the exact date. They agreed.

'If I can achieve anything with people,' says Heddy, 'I learned it all from Kató. She had such an approach with people. She was outspoken, frank, she could ask ... So she got the impossible done, just as I did, very often, when I had to start again after the War, with you two children.'

Kató kept her word. Heddy was her messenger. Every month, on the dot, she'd deliver the small sums to businesses and lawyers' offices. She'd try to avoid the owners and just make the payments to the secretaries and underlings, more quickly to get the ordeal over.

Náci was on the job market again. By this time he was virtually unemployable. He had old friends at the firm of Helvey who respected his expertise and wanted to help him. They called him in, specifying that Kató was to come with him. They proposed to give him a job, although not much of a job, as long as every penny of the salary went to his wife.

Kató saw her first real chance to get the family back on its feet. Her first move was even cheaper accommodation. In 1937 they moved for the fourth time in as many years, to a crumbling flat in Isabella Street. Kató put Náci on a pittance and no longer cared so much what he did with it.

It was in grimy Isabella Street that things began to get better. Some furniture and carpets came back; the place began to look respectable again. Heddy's spirits lifted, cautiously.

Náci worked hard at Helvey, as he had always done. He went more occasionally to the races, still betting with the piddling sums he could get his hands on. Kató left her husband alone. She was contemptuous of him, and he turned for solace to another woman. Heddy knew about it.

'No, I wasn't really angry with him. He had been so humiliated, wrecked by what had happened. If it helped him in his misery ... He couldn't resist arranging for her to meet me, just once; he was so proud of me. She seemed an ordinary, nice woman. He introduced her as just a good friend, but I knew, really, who she must be.'

She began to feel she could invite people home again. Her cousin Zoli was hanging around now that Laci Berger was gone. It was nice just to have someone to flirt with. There was an older man, too, but he had little to offer.

She still went to the synagogue to pray, and God seemed to be responding, if slowly and mutedly. She began to read more. There was a little lending library around the corner, run by two small and friendly Jews who seemed to sense her predicament and were kind to her.

She was nearly twenty-one. She helped Kató, she tried to mediate the quarrels that still flared occasionally between her parents, and she waited.

Chapter Five

When she married Feri in March of the following year,
Heddy took up her life as a prosperous young matron with
enthusiasm. They settled in Uj Lipótváros near the river, a
newish part of town with a young, predominantly Jewish
population.

While Feri was generous, she was not on an unlimited
budget. Once the anti-Jewish law was passed and a second
mooted, he was determined that they live with a minimum
of ostentation. He refused to buy a car because he thought
it showy. When their first anniversary came around, he was
happy to buy Heddy the black lambskin coat that other
prosperous young wives were getting that year, but he
begged her not to wear it too often.

The Schwimmers had always been conservative; they had
never diversified beyond feathers or thought of foreign bank
accounts. Now Feri bought a small apartment house as a
safeguard against the future. He began, periodically, to bring
home amounts of money from the office and store them in
the safe, just in case.

At the same time, he was happy. He had a young and
beautiful wife who was making him a harmonious home.
And Heddy, never one to strike an unfair bargain, paid for
her life of ease by making the provider of it happy. She
looked after him and protected him – that came easily to
her. She smoothed him out, made him presentable. Within

months, his friends, who had indulged him before as a withdrawn, slightly eccentric bachelor, said to her, 'Heddy, what have you done with Feri? We hardly recognise him.'

She still beams with pride over this. She was making him over.

By 1939, Náci and Kató had settled in a small flat in Tátra Street, close to Heddy. Kató had things in hand but every now and again there was a crisis, as of old. Once, when Heddy had been a married woman for perhaps a year, Kató confided that she was again desperate for cash.

Heddy didn't want to ask Feri for it. She went to the safe in the flat and took some money out 'as a loan'. She said nothing to Feri.

Feri never kept a tally of the money brought home. Yet one evening he asked her to open the safe and count it. What could she say to him if he found out? Her heart beating, she opened the safe and counted. He made no comment.

'Did he know, do you think?' I ask.

'No, he didn't know, I'm sure. So that was that. But I didn't feel myself to be a liar, or unfair. I was being fair to my mother – and the amount didn't count for him. There was still that pride, and the feeling that my parents would be obliged, so I cheated a little. It's not all that important, but I remember the trauma! It might all be taken in the end, so let it go to them. It was a sign of how things were.'

I'm surprised, not so much by this minor ethical slip, but by her telling me about it. She's told me, I think, to show how deeply the bad years had cut with her, how even the new prosperity seemed fragile and uncertain (in that she was prescient) – and how it had made her bend the rules.

I'm pleased she told me. It gives me a glimpse of an uncertainty she rarely shows. It adds a little complexity to what I have seen as her rigid, simplistic moralities.

For her new flat at Number 32 Pozsonyi Road, Heddy bought furniture from Braun, specialists in classically inspired 'style' furniture that was all the rage. She covered the modern picture windows in a sheer beige material with a discreet leaf pattern.

'People passing on the street would look up to admire that curtain, and people would come to see the flat,' she glows, 'just as now they come to see the house here in Sydney.'

Her domestic arrangements were not much different from Kató's. Just like her mother, she had a bunch of keys to the pantry and the linen cupboards and the silver, and opened them for the maid only when need be.

'After a while, if the maid proved trustworthy, you no longer locked everything up, if you were a liberal sort of person. Yes, I know it sounds extraordinary but it was the way things had always been.'

One of the few changes was in the layout of the flat. There was no internal courtyard as in the old apartment blocks. Status could no longer be measured by how many of your rooms faced street light. The new apartments had modern bathrooms with bidets, and smaller kitchens, and the maid's room was no longer a walkway to the kitchen. But there still was a maid's room.

The washerwoman came once a month, as she had always done, to wash the linen in a special room on the top floor. The smaller washes were done by the maid in the kitchen and hung up on a wooden contraption called a fragoli.

Once a month, Mrs Bak, the ironing lady, came.

'In every better house, the linen was beautifully ironed by a Mrs Bak and then folded and wrapped in pink tissue paper and tied with a pink ribbon, and placed in the cupboard, just so. Oh I can laugh at it now, but imagine starting from that. I've had to change a little, no? Back then, it gave me a good feeling when I opened the cupboard and there were Mrs Bak's rows of pink tissue paper and ribbon; the beautifully embroidered linen, the duvet covers, the sheets and pillowslips, all in rows. It fairly overflowed. That's why my poor mother always had linen to send to the pawnbroker once the carpets had gone. In a "better" house, there was plenty to get rid of!'

I think about my parents, and people like them in that prewar middle-European world, clinging to continuity while awaiting upheaval. The washerwoman every month, the tissue paper around the linen, the linen cupboards stacked, all bespoke a longed-for solidity, a going-onness that never came to pass. On the other side were the portables: the money in the safe, the diamonds at the ready, the suppressed fear.

Here in safe Australia, there are versions, still, of that double syndrome. Take Heddy's cleaning ladies. After the first few years of getting on their feet, my mother and women like her employed once-a-week cleaning ladies of Spanish or Portuguese origin. After a few more years they could afford domestic help two, three times a week; not live-in maids as in the old Budapest days – this was Australia after all. Then twenty years down the track, the Hungarians refound each other. From across the wilds of Sydney, from the Blacktown region the peasant women came, to the shores of Bellevue Hill and Vaucluse. No longer quite maids, no longer as poorly paid, a few more liberties allowed, better able to discuss consumer goodies together, they nonetheless refound the Jewish ladies of Budapest. And they get along as well as they ever did (or as badly).

The old clothes are still passed on, the passionate loyalties established both ways. Everyone feels a little more secure in an alien world.

Now I have to confess to having a Hungarian cleaning lady, too, only a couple of years older than I. I try to behave as 'equals' with her, but she won't have a bar of it – except to take a little good-humoured advantage of my foolishness. We speak a mixture of English and Hungarian to each other, but in Hungarian we both use the formal 'you'. We're both conscious of a continuity, weird and transplanted as it is.

The other side of the double syndrome, the fear of impermanence, the readiness to flee, takes the form, among others, of a deep conservatism running through the older generation, as if any change at all could result in their lives being uprooted again. They are over-protective, still prone to buy their children a diamond, something portable, just in case.

And we children feel a pervasive fear that we do not know how to express. Impermanence and insecurity lurk in the shadows behind this all-Australian red-brick solidity.

For our parents it has been a long pendulum swing; living for years in comfort, awaiting horror, then living the horror, longing for the return of warmth and comfort. For us the pendulum is internal. We seek continuity but cannot believe in it. We are free to choose our own hell, and that is what our parents resent most. What will it be; mortified careers, private terrors, misdirected hatreds?

Mother says, without too much regret, 'It's a different world.'

Is it? The Hungarian cleaning lady has just left. Germany has re-united. Many Germans, many in Europe, are growing up with no memories and no guilt. What if it were *really* to happen again? I remind myself that it has already happened again, in many places, in Cambodia and, in obscene mini-ature, in what was once Yugoslavia.

But it's no use; this is my territory of fear – a re-unified Germany, the jackboots, and all the other terrible images, and we Jews to battle for our dignity again. I shift uneasily in my chair. The past is snuffling at my feet, as always.

★

The coming war floated in and out of my parents' reality. Sometimes it impinged peripherally, mildly, then with a sudden savagery. Their own fears ebbed and flowed in the same way.

First there was Rózsika and her husband Max. After the Anschluss they fled Vienna to find refuge in Hungary. Hungary offered no particular welcome; nor did it hand over refugee Jews to the Germans. Max worked illegally for a while until he was reported to the authorities and they had to leave again, quickly. He went to London to investigate possibilities, Rózsika to Trieste. She ended up living out the war in provincial France, separated from her family, making corsets – a skill she had learned in Vienna as a precaution against the future.

The War bit next in September 1939. Feri's brother János was on holiday in Italy with his family when war was declared. He telephoned to say that they were not coming back. They were off to America with just their suitcases of summer clothes.

Feri was left to run the business, although he had no taste for it. He now had the sole care of his ageing mother. Because of her, especially, there was no serious talk of following János out. But they continued to think about leaving, on and off, as did most of their friends. Feri bought books about South America and Australia and read them carefully, pondering his dwindling options.

With their friends, the talk was always, obsessively, about the political situation.

'We talked about the anti-Jewish laws and whose liveli-hood had been affected and to what degree, what this or that politician had said, which of them was more an anti-Semite, which less. We were always looking at the paper, always talking, always in fear ... what will they take away next, how will they curtail our rights? There was such an atmosphere of fear, always. It was a sword of Damocles over our heads. We were always waiting for it to come down on us. But you'll have to ask Daddy for the details, and look up the books. It all melts into one for me. I don't remember history, only the feelings.'

It was a bewildering political world in Hungary, post-1939. It was perfectly possible not to see the wood for the trees, if you didn't want to. The first anti-Jewish law had turned out to be surprisingly mild, curtailing the number of Jews to twenty per cent in the professions. And while Prime Minister Imrédy tried to out-rhetoric the Right, he put the head of the Arrow Cross into prison. The bomb attack on the Dohány Street synagogue in February 1939 had shocked the liberals and Jews. But such things happened, from time to time.

The sophisticates of the city had a good joke at the Prime Minister's expense. This instigator of the second anti-Jewish law of 1939 was discovered by his enemies to have a Jewish great-great-grandmother. The Regent Horthy asked for his resignation.

Teleki, Imrédy's successor, was of the old aristocratic school, a 'civilised' anti-Semite and anglophile. From the time of Gömbös, the country's ruling politicians were all right-wing anti-Semites; power only shifted between the civilised anti-Semites and the crude ones. The Jews set much store by the difference; they fancied that while the civilised ones were in power, their rights might be curtailed but no actual harm would come to them.

Yet it was Teleki, the 'civilised', who promulgated the second anti-Jewish law, which meant serious business. Jews were no longer allowed to acquire Hungarian citizenship by naturalisation, marriage or adoption. They were no longer to hold Government positions, nor to be schoolteachers, editors or editors-in-chief, theatre producers or directors. Their licences to run certain sorts of businesses were to be withdrawn, until their percentage was down to twelve per cent in some cases, six in others. The number of Jewish employees in firms was restricted. An estimated 250 000 Jews were affected, some 65 000 in the capital. Those whose lives were upset or ruined were mostly the salaried and the unskilled. The more prosperous Jews in the professions and commerce often circumvented the law one way or another, and found plenty of Christians to help them.

With their Christian birth certificates, Pubi and Baba were much in demand by Jewish firms needing Christian 'partners' or heads of businesses who could hold trading licences. They were paid large sums for their phantom jobs. For the first and only time in their lives, Kató's older boys were both doing well.

The Government touted the restrictions as the 'solution to the Jewish question', hoping to silence the fanatics. There were Jews who half believed the Government rationale; others whose genuine patriotism did not waver, even then. They petitioned the Government, citing the Jewish heroes of the 1848 war of independence with Austria and World War I. They believed themselves part of the nation; they only had to 'prove' to those in power how much they were so. In reply, the Government exempted Jewish war heroes, university professors and olympic champions.

At the same time, things in Hungary were curiously quiet. The country was not yet at war, might never be. She was officially neutral. Successive governments were being drawn into, then struggling to get out of, Hitler's net. Towards the end of 1940, Hungary acceded to the Tripartite Pact between Germany, Italy and Japan. Then it withdrew from the League of Nations.

Many Jews rejoiced with the rest of the nation when, as a reward, Hitler gave them a large slice of Czechoslovakia, formerly known as the Upper Province, then returned them Northern Transylvania under the Second Vienna Award. At last the injustices of Trianon were being addressed. Hundreds of thousands of 'alien' Jews were also returned to Hungary with these territories, and they were from the beginning without rights. Many in Budapest tried to ignore the massacre of some 11 000 Jews on the border of newly acquired territories at Kamenets-Poldsk, in which the Hungarians were deeply implicated. They hoped it was a freak border incident. The Hungarian Government would never turn against them, the Magyarised integrated Budapest Jews. They were mollified when some time later, one of the 'civilised' Prime Ministers, Kállay, set up an inquiry.

Life in Budapest went on in the way it had always done in that hedonistic city; a round of coffee houses, shops, good food, theatre, opera and comfortable apartments. And this rhythm was not for the bourgeoisie alone. The soul and ethos of Budapest was middle class. The aristocracy, the petty aristocracy, the petty bourgeoisie, the upper echelons of the working class, all had the same notion of the good life and did their damnedest to live it. Even in the grim times of Communism and now in the mess after its fall, I have never seen a city, except perhaps Paris, where so large a percentage of the population devotes itself so seriously to life's small pleasures; good food, good jokes. A Budapestian will put up with much as long as the coffee is up to scratch and he can look forward with relish to the next meal.

One of the great Budapest institutions was the Corso, the

promenade bound on one side by the Pest river bank and on the other by a line of grand hotels. The Ritz and the Hungaria were the most famous; the Prince of Wales had stayed in one of them, everyone who was anyone had stayed in one of them. They were hotels in the old tradition; grills, bars, piano rooms, chanteuses.

Heddy remembers Sunday mornings in May as the most enchanting in the life of the Corso. Months before, in February, Budapest's bourgeois ladies had been planning their spring outfits, running up to Móguc or one of the other couturiers for their fittings. When the first shy spring sun came out, the matrons, young and old, husbands on their arms, strolled up and down the Corso, in their new soft grey flannel suits or tasteful little beige suits, with perhaps a white piqué blouse subtly cut just so, perhaps a small posy of violets in the lapel.

There were those without taste or style or money, who came to look at those with the magic attributes passing in parade. They sat on seats and benches lining the Corso; old women came around collecting seat money. Old men stood at the corners with great bunches of many-coloured balloons and shiny fly-aways for the children to buy. The flower sellers offered spring posies.

Everyone was there, Jew and Gentile alike, except the old aristocracy, who kept themselves to themselves in the castle district on the Buda side of the river. After you'd paraded up and down and eyed the competition off and greeted your friends and acquaintances, you would either stroll across to the busy restaurant in front of the Vigadó, the extravaganza Budapest landmark where concerts were held, or you'd take a fiacre to the famed Gundel, where you could sit out in the gardens and partake of goulash or pörkölt, or indulge in Gundel's own chocolate-covered nut-filled pancakes, perhaps the richest sweet ever conceived.

In the second half of 1940, Heddy was strolling down the Corso on Feri's arm in the lace-up ankle boots that were the give-away of a pregnant woman in Budapest. The cheeky little grey suits were replaced by a dove-grey tent coat. Pregnancy gave her a special sheen.

Jutka was born on 9 February 1941. Heddy woke with the first pains at 1 a.m. She had a small bag packed and ready. She had no intention of waking Feri; he would get too excited and get under her feet. She woke Dora the maid instead and unlocked the pantry door, got out the food for the next couple of days and told her what to cook. She was not to wake Feri before the usual time, 7.30, and tell him the news after his first coffee. Then she rang Kató and ordered a taxi.

The time around my sister's birth, was, in Heddy's memory, one of the best times. She bought all the baby clothes in advance, pink sets, blue sets, little bibs and socks, dresses and aprons. She invited her friends around to see the layette. She was having a good time, half playing dolls, half responsible young matron.

The time was ripe, with the apartment beautifully furnished, she married nearly three years, her appetite for motherhood sharpened by a couple of miscarriages. She was twenty-four and full of optimism, quite unalarmed by the prospect of giving birth in 1941. Not till my conception, in early 1943, did she or Feri question the wisdom of bringing a child into the world.

When the time came, it came with a slow and stately splendour, as if the world was not actually at war, and Hungary on the verge of joining it. The private room in *the* private clinic was booked well in advance. The special linen, made expressly for such state occasions, went with her to the clinic. When visitors came, Kató, sitting in attendance all day long, threw the handsome duvet over her for their better viewing, and Heddy would suffocate in the over-heated February air until they left. Heddy protested but Kató was unfazed.

'You look so splendid with it on, my darling.'

The world changed and revolved around Jutka. Náci dropped in almost every day on his way home and held the baby up to the wide picture windows to show her the world outside. Feri doted and called her Csutka. Heddy shows me a picture of him holding his daughter and says, 'The Adoration of the Magi!'

She threw herself into the pleasures and responsibilities of motherhood. There was to be no nanny. She fed and clothed and bathed the baby. She combed her blonde hair into the most delicious curls. When, in the early weeks, Jutka cried every evening between 5 and 7, Heddy sent Feri on a long walk to the Nyugati Railway Station and back; he was too sensitive to endure it. She would cope.

Summer came, and with it the imperative to give a small child as much fresh air as possible. It was time to go to the country. They rented a villa in the hills outside Budapest, and Jutka was outside all day, in her cot in the balmy garden. Feri came down on the train every night. It was a lovely rhythm. Every morning Heddy would wake to the sound of Jutka chirruping to herself across the room. Mother-hood was good and her first-born was a beautiful and per-fect child.

In April 1941, not long after Jutka's birth, Hungary sent troops into Yugoslavia. On 26 June Hungary joined Ger-many in the invasion of Russia, thereby formally entering the War.

The family's anxieties centred on Pali. He was liable to be called up for forced labour, as a couple of years before he had been called up for military service.

The forced labour camps were first established in 1919 after the fall of the Communist regime. They were a uniquely Hungarian invention. Socialists, Jews and other minority groups were organised into military-style units and put to the building of roads, bridges and public works.

The idea was revived in 1939. Those not to be trusted with the defence of the nation, 'political unreliables' and Jews, were called up, but initially they were to get the same pay and rations as soldiers, and even to wear a military-style uniform. The camps' specifically punitive role for the Jews emerged as successive governments felt increasingly obliged to appease and ape Germany.

But how to deal with the Jews already serving in the Army? The top brass continually debated the question in 1939 and 1940. After Hungary entered the War they decided to strip Jewish officers of their rank, then sacked them. The ordinary Jewish soldiers were weeded out too, and sent to the forced labour camps. This is what happened to Pali.

Pali was worrying his parents. He seemed to be drifting. He showed little interest in the social life of his contemporaries; there were no long-standing liaisons. The job with the plate-glass manufacturers had been replaced by one with a shoe shop chain. Then the military service.

Kató was relieved when, after some pressure from her, he got himself engaged to a suitable girl who was pretty, charming and wealthy. But then he broke off the engagement without explanation. He was withdrawn, often away from home. She found out that there was another woman, had been for some time, a married woman. She was furious. She enlisted Náci in the battle.

In early 1942, Pali received his papers. He was to report to a camp in rural Hungary before being sent to Russia.

Three months later, he came home on leave. On the Sunday he quarrelled violently with his parents. Just before he left for Russia, he wrote his mother a letter.

'Kató kept that letter all her life,' Heddy says.

Her face is drawn and her voice has lost its confidence. 'I found it among her things when she died. I have it in a shoebox upstairs.'

'Does it say when he was sent to Russia?' I ask.

'There's a date on it, but it still hurts me to read it. It's a terrible letter.'

I cajole her to get it out, and read it to me next time. She changes the appointment; she says she can't read it without crying, even now. We make a couple more appointments; there's always a reason to put it off. I put it off too, if we're in a hurry or I see she's tired or upset. She's never really balked at anything else before, so I know it's important.

Finally, one evening before Dad comes home to dinner, she gets out the letter.

'I didn't know about the dreadful row they had about the woman just before he left. I was married then; I wasn't there.'

She reads the letter, crying in parts.

1 July 1942

My Dearest Mother,

I write to you, because I want you to try and understand me, as my mother, and as the woman closest to me, even though we are now so apart from each other.

The events of Sunday have hurt me terribly. I crave your understanding, and only that. I don't want 'rehabilitation' in your eyes. Is it possible that you will understand me?

You remember me as a child; I was a 'good' child,
quiet and obedient, I studied well. I grew within the
strictures of your rigid upbringing, for you were
indeed strict. I was left mostly to myself.

The puberty years were hard. I had no real friends.
You remember Zoli, my 'mate' Zoli? He was no real
friend; he was superficial, jokey; there was nothing
solid there. No other name comes to mind from my
boyhood.

I couldn't be close to you. Perhaps you loved me
too much, in all that strictness, and that took away
the possibility of friendship. You didn't ask me about
my problems. That's just a fact. I became introverted,
closed in; no one knew what was in my heart.

There were a few smaller or bigger romances, but
nothing more came of them. They were no more than
kisses, although there were some successes which
meant little except to fuel my male vanity. Every now
and again there was a prostitute or a sewing girl or a
Fräulein.

I was not interested in the 'well brought up girls' I
was introduced to. I didn't like them much, and I was
not impressed by their big 'jours' and parties.

And then I became a soldier. And within a year of
my return, I, the 'good' boy, who had been supported
in every way by loving parents, became 'heartless',
'degenerate', a 'spendthrift'. How has this happened? I
want to tell you.

Mother, put aside all the anger, and try to
understand me, because I am suffering. I weep as I
write these lines.

After I returned from soldiering, I met someone. We
were both alone. Such a love is different from parental
and filial love. She was simple, frank, good, a total

human being. We established such a friendship; I emphasise at that stage, only friendship. There was total openness and warmth between us; such a thing is rare among human beings. I was happy, can you believe it?

We were both lonely, I for reasons I have already explained, she for reasons I will now tell you about. She was married to a simple musician, a Christian. They had recently come to Hungary, fleeing Hitler. She was here, alone and helpless; her father was in hiding, still is in hiding. Her family had lost all their money in fleeing Fascism. Her mother lives in penury. She was alone. You should understand what it feels like Mother, to be alone. Remember how you wept, those couple of Sunday afternoons when you were left alone, and it was only for a few hours; yet you have your husband, your children around you.

We fell in love. We spent countless evenings talking to each other. We always had something to say. We tell each other everything. And here you are greatly mistaken in thinking that our relationship is based solely on sex. I would not risk the loss of my parents' affection for a sexual attachment.

So this was the cause of my 'degeneracy'. I could only see her at night, when her husband was working. We walked a lot; I took her to the pictures occasionally. That was my 'carousing', my 'night life'.

You know very well that I don't drink or gamble. As for 'spending', you know only too well what life costs today. And now, when life is so uncertain and one does not know the future, it is no time to save. I spent some money on chocolates and flowers, more for myself than her. She gave me back love and affection, which I returned doubly.

Then you found out, and announced, heedless of my feelings, that you didn't like it, it wouldn't do. You disapprove. There is no appeal against you.

You spread propaganda about me through the family. I haven't been able to defend myself. You turned father against me and there were those huge rows that hurt me deeply. You achieved the rift with my woman that you wanted. It's only with the greatest effort that I achieved some sort of reconciliation with her.

And then I was called up.

In striving to achieve your ends and impose your narrow view, you showed no mercy, and you behaved in a style not befitting you, my dear mother.

Came this Sunday. You took over completely; I couldn't even answer you. You drove father to shout those terrible insults. Everyone could hear the two of you.

I have said enough. You have shut the door between us, and on yourselves. You have again succeeded in creating a rift and forcing me to leave her. Everything that has tied me to Hungary and to Budapest is broken. All doors are closed. Tomorrow we leave for the Ukraine.

Pali

We hear the sound of Dad's car. Mother quickly folds up the letter.

'I have been able to accept everything but Pali's death,' she says and weeps again.

The next day, on the phone, I have to ask her to reread part of the letter that I haven't quite understood. She breaks down again and I feel like a cheap voyeur. I tell her it has been important for me too, to hear his voice. That is true.

After a while, she says, 'You have to understand Kató. Pali just didn't compare with the other two boys, who were such rascals as young men ... he was the light of her life.' She pauses then says, 'She lived and died for her children, but in her own way.'

I say nothing. Such echoes.

Part II
Hiding

'A danse macabre had begun'

Chapter Six

Conditions in the Hungarian labour camps worsened dramatically once Hungary entered the War. After April 1942, fifteen per cent of all service units were made up of Jews of reputation or wealth, even if they were above the legal conscription age of forty-two. The initial orderly call-up was scrapped for special notices – Serious, Urgent, Hurry – compiled on the basis of complaints from individuals or 'patriotic groups' (professional, business and trade organisations) who wanted to get rid of the Jews in their midst. In the Ukraine, Jews were stripped of their uniforms because the sight of a Jew in uniform was too offensive to nearby soldiers of the Third Reich. Thousands of Jews sent to the Bor copper mines in Yugoslavia died of ill-treatment and starvation.

In his defence statement after the War, General Szombathelyi, the Army Chief-of-Staff said:

The Jewish question had a catastrophic effect on the armed forces ... a terrible corrupting effect. Every value underwent a re-evaluation. Cruelty became love for the fatherland, atrocities became acts of heroism, corruption was transformed into virtue; under such conditions, we, well-thinking individuals, could not understand events. There emerged two types of discipline. One was applied to the Jews against whom any action was permissible ...

Sometimes the cruelty of the Hungarians shocked even the Germans. A diversion favoured by officers in one unit was '5 o'clock tea', that is, the regular evening beating of the Jews in the guards' quarters. Another was 'lakeside vision' (tóparti látomás), named after a famous Hungarian film; the jollity was in watching Jews do somersaults in the nearby marshes after the day's work, or in forcing them to climb ice-covered trees and crow like roosters that they were 'dirty Jews'. Another amusement was hosing Jews down in winter until they became 'ice statues', or tying them on to tree branches with their hands tied against their backs (kikötés).

As the Russian winter approached, Náci became obsessed with getting food and warm clothes to his son. He knew that food parcels were often intercepted and eaten by the guards and many Jews were selling what clothes they had to ward off starvation. He saw his opportunity when a guard in Pali's unit came to see him. He prepared two identical parcels of food and clothing, one for Pali, one for the guard. He promised him more such parcels if Pali's was delivered intact.

A couple of letters came, long delayed. Pali was in the units supporting the front lines, digging ditches and trenches. Then the letters stopped.

On 12 January 1943, when the Soviet army broke through a Hungarian bridgehead at Voronezh, the tide began to turn for Russia.

Voronezh has become infamous among Hungarians as one of the nation's most shaming episodes. There were huge military losses, mass panic and desertion. Thousands were killed and tens of thousands captured.

The Germans blamed the Hungarians. The Hungarians vented their spleen on the Jews, who were deprived of their rations, thrown out of shelter by the retreating armies, plundered and killed. Many, weakened by hunger and cold, died of typhoid. In one typhoid hospital set up at a place called Doroschich, sick labour servicemen were housed in open barns. The corpses were stacked like firewood by the wall of a nearby stable. On 30 April the authorities decided to stem the disease by setting fire to a barn holding about 600 servicemen. Men in flames, trying to jump out, were mown down by guards with submachine guns.

Less than 7000 of the 50 000 Jewish labour servicemen sent to Russia eventually returned to Hungary.

News arrived in Budapest of the massive defeat at Voronezh. Everyone who had a son in Russia was afraid. But it was to be many years before the family found out exactly what happened to Pali. They hoped that he had been captured by the Russians, perhaps even treated well as a liberated Jew. They were certain he was alive. Anything else was inconceivable.

In January 1943 Heddy was obsessed with life, and the preservation of it. She was pregnant. This time Feri said no, it was no time to have a child. She hesitated, divided between apprehension and a persistent optimism. Here in Hungary they could yet escape the fate of the other Jews of Eastern Europe. The current phrase was 'megússzuk'; roughly, 'We'll make it yet.' Surely time was running out for the Germans. And where else in Europe did a large Jewish population continue to live relatively unharmed? Had not the moderate right always in the end protected the Jews? Weren't things going on much as before, at least for the prosperous middle classes?

In early 1943 Kállay was the Prime Minister. He was a known, familiar quantity; a 'moderate' aristocrat. The Jews knew that, despite his anti-Jewish speeches and concessions to the Germans, the sub-text was that they were relatively safe with him. But if Kállay was to be replaced (and there had been three changes of prime minister since March 1939) they would be that much closer to the abyss.

Heddy went to see the family doctor and Feri's long-time friend, Dáni Kellner.

'Nothing's wrong with me Dáni dear, but I've "swallowed the fly" to use the slang, and Feri wants an abortion because of the political situation, but I really want a second child. I'm ready. Who knows when I'll have another chance? I'm here to ask your advice.'

The doctor eyed her quizzically for a while.

'Keep it.'

'Oh, you agree! I'm glad! You've made me so happy. If we're in so much trouble, there might as well be four of us. Maybe God will help us.'

He stopped her with a gesture.

'Heddy, I said yes because it's quite clear to me that you'll keep it whatever I say.'

As the pregnancy went on, Pest seemed less and less a safe place. The city was in a state of fear; there was no bombing as yet, but there were nightly air-raid warnings. The family pressured Heddy to go to Feri's house in Hódmezövásárhely, where she and Jutka, now more than two years old, would be out of harm's way. The town was 200 kilometres south of Pest, and some distance from a main railway line. Nearby was the large town of Szeged, with a good clinic, the Batisfalvi, where she could give birth.

Heddy took most of the furniture and chattels with her, leaving Feri with a skeleton operation in Budapest. He continued to manage the business. Every ten days he came to visit.

The house in Bercsényi Street was a typical nineteenth-century merchant's house, plain and capacious. The living quarters faced the street, and tall gates at the side of the house opened into a big courtyard. Down one side of the courtyard was a large storage barn running the length of the property. The stables at the back had been turned into an additional storehouse for feathers.

The house was damp and dilapidated. There was no running water; a little man with a hunch back came every morning to pump water from the well. The only person living there was Jancsó, a female cousin of Feri's from the town. Heddy took over two rooms and a verandah, leaving a room for Jancsó, who was staying on to help her with Jutka and the child to come. She stored most of the furniture in one room, fixed up the other, and settled in to await the birth.

A few days beforehand, Kató took Jutka to Lake Balaton, and Heddy went into her private room at the clinic. Feri came to be with her. But as soon as he arrived, a phone call came from Budapest. He was to return at once; his call-up papers for labour service had arrived. It never occurred to him to try to delay the summons because of my impending birth; that was both typical of him and symptomatic of the times.

He spent the whole evening at the clinic. His train was to leave at 7 a.m. the next morning. At 10 p.m. he made to leave.

'He said he hoped all would be well, that I would have a healthy child, and that God would help us through these difficult times. It was a very emotional moment; we both knew we might never see each other again, and that he might never see his second child. He was a very tall man, as you know, and I had to stretch up to hug him. I put my arms around him to kiss him goodbye. With that movement, I felt my waters break. But I said not a word to him, and he went away.

'I called the nurse in and said, "It's started. If the baby is born by 5 a.m., or 5.30 at the latest, telephone Ferenc Schwimmer at the Grand Hotel, and tell him he has a boy or a girl, and to come in."'

It was quite an easy birth. My father arrived at dawn, shaking with emotion, kissed me, then caught the morning train. Yet he was not to enter forced labour for another four months. His papers had to be served on him personally to be effective and, having missed him on 16 October, the bureaucracy did not reorganise itself until February 1944. With a peculiarly Hungarian mixture of formalism and barbarity (which I still sense in Hungarian life), the authorities insisted that what was to be my father's death sentence be legally served.

Heddy stayed on at the clinic until I was a few days old.

'I found out that Batisfalvi, the famous man who ran the clinic, was a rabid anti-Semite, but I was treated well; I was a paying guest.'

The clinic provided an ambulance to transport Heddy and me back in state to Hódmezövásárhely.

This double life, danger and safety co-existing, complacency and threat hand-in-hand, was almost at an end.

This was the world to which I opened my eyes.

Jancsó was delighted with the new baby. She and her watchmaker husband had not been able to have children, and now here were two to watch over and nurture day by day.

My mother often describes Jancsó as a bird; 'a little grey bird', 'a poor little sparrow'. Jancsó's quiet life had been circumscribed by her small home town and it's population of a couple of thousand Jews. Now, for these few months in Hódmezövásárhely, her life was a fulfilled drama.

'She doted on you children. She scavenged and scrounged to provide us with the best available food. She bought fresh chickens and ducks for us from the peasants. We became fast friends, even though she always reeked of sweat, and you know how badly I cope with that! ... Feri came down whenever he could. We lived like country lovers, until new papers were served on him in February. He was to report immediately. We said goodbye to each other on the telephone.'

She was alone but for Jancsó. Once, her father came to see her, although he was unwell with worsening diabetes. They sat on the mean little verandah, the two children nearby. As of old she sat on his lap, sniffing his fine, sweet smelling hair.

'You see my father, how I've borne two children, and here I am, still sitting on your lap.'

'Always my little girl,' he murmured.

Some time in March, the military showed up demanding to see the storehouse at the back. It was part empty; some of the feathers had already been requisitioned. Within days the soldiers moved in perhaps 120 Jews, to be temporarily quartered there until moved on to the Ukraine or labour camps in other parts of the country.

They were all country Jews, mostly from the north. Aladár Patzauer, of a prominent local Jewish family, was in charge of the unit. He had received the highest Hungarian military decoration in World War I, so he was allowed to be an 'officer', and to wear a white armband instead of a yellow one, a privilege awarded to converts as well.

The men in the storehouse were crowded and ill-fed. There were no washing facilities. They would come to the kitchen door, asking Heddy for a pan of warm water. Uniforms were forbidden and their own clothes were already in rags.

Heddy ran errands and sent letters for them.

'Everything was forbidden to them; I did what I could.'

When Mother and I visited the street in 1990, the peasant woman next door remembered the Jewish 'servicemen' vividly.

'I was a child of eight. They would hang over the wall, asking us for water. And they plucked fruit from our trees, those they could reach.'

On 19 March 1944, eight German divisions crossed into Hungary 'at the request of the Hungarian Government'. The SS, the Gestapo and Adolf Eichmann quickly followed.

The Germans arrived in Hódmezövásárhely two days later. Heddy could not resist the temptation to go and look. The Germans marched, impassive and orderly, down the main street. There were so many of them, there seemed no end to them, until she noticed ('you know what an observer I am') the same faces underneath the steel helmets. She realised that they were marching a circuit of the small town, then joining up again with their rear. Then they marched through again, and yet again, to impress and awe the populace with their might.

A nervous excitement gripped Heddy as she watched. This was it. No equivocation now. The fight for survival was on. She found herself dry retching in fear, standing silently on the pavement as the columns went by. That night when she came to feed me, her milk had vanished, dried up.

An edict was issued that as from 5 April each Jew in Hungary was required to wear the yellow star. Heddy had to pick hers up from the police station and sew it over her right breast.

There were other decrees; no employment of non-Jews in Jewish households, the dismissal of Jewish civil servants and lawyers, the exclusion of Jews from press and theatre associations, and the confiscation of Jewish-owned motor vehicles and telephones. Travel was forbidden to all Jews.

This was the beginning of a hail of edicts that isolated and pauperised the Jews. Yet most Budapest Jews clung to the belief that if the authorities were going to the trouble of closing down their businesses, rationing their food, taking their telephones, cars and apartments, then surely they would not bother if they were going to kill them anyway. There were stories filtering through of deportations on the outskirts of Hungary, but they were the unassimilated, un-Magyarised Jews. The Jews of Budapest, so integral to the nation, so woven into the city's artistic, commercial and intellectual life – they might be humiliated, yes, but killed? Impossible.

Yet within days of arriving in Hungary, Eichmann had begun what was to be the largest, best-organised and fastest mass deportation of Jews to the gas chambers in the history of the Third Reich. He divided Hungary into five zones; concentric circles coming in from the outer perimeters. Budapest was Zone Five – with its heavy concentration of Jews, the last and richest prize.

Down in Hódmezövásárhely the restriction on travel affected Heddy most directly. Even before the German occupation, each citizen had to have a registered address, held by the local police station. The police had to be informed of any temporary or permanent changes and the reason therefore. Heddy was registered with the Hódmezövásárhely police as a temporary resident only. Now by law she was required to return to her permanent domicile.

But Náci would not hear of her returning to Budapest. The city had received its first serious bombing raid by the Allies on 2 April, a second on 4 April, setting off a wave of violent anti-Semitism because relatively few Jewish lives had been lost.

But how to stay in Hódmezövásárhely when failure to obey an edict could mean instant arrest? Rumours were flying of people being shot out of hand. She decided to go to the town's chief of police.

He was a fairly young man, square set, with large moustaches. He looked at her impassively.

'And what might you want, handsome Madame?'

'I have a very young baby and a child of three. Budapest is being bombed. We would be so much safer here, in my husband's home town. I would be very grateful if you could give me an extension of time, very grateful.'

Discreetly she slipped him 25 000 pengös, perhaps the equivalent now of 1000 dollars. He signed the documents.

Yet with each day, she became more uneasy with her decision. The presence of the Jewish labour servicemen, crammed into the storehouse across the yard, was an hourly reminder of threat. She was witnessing the traffic in these men; those leaving for unknown destinations always replaced by new ones. The new ones, from the Carpathians in the north-east, had frightening stories to tell of round-ups of their friends and relatives. In the second half of April, many were beside themselves with grief and apprehension over the letters they were receiving from home. The letters told of concentration into camps and thence into wagons. Indeed, according to Eichmann's meticulous plans, 16 April was the date for commencement of his operations in Zone 1, the Carpathians.

Heddy began to think she'd bribed the police chief for her own death warrant. She was alone with two small children, cut off from her parents and brothers. The evidence before her eyes was that they were rounding up the country Jews first, starting with the outer borders of the country and moving in to the centre. Here in a small town not far from the southern border, with only a couple of thousand other

Jews, she was exposed, a rat waiting for the trap to snap shut. And having to wear the yellow star everywhere! There would be nowhere to hide.

In Budapest, she thought, she had a chance. She might melt into the great mass. In Hódmezövásárhely, it was only a question of time.

This time she did not ask anyone's advice. She went into the police station again, to the captain she had bribed two weeks before.

He eyed her coolly, smoothing his moustaches.

'And what do you want this time my handsome woman?'

'Just the opposite.' She looked him in the eye, very calm. 'I have to leave here. I want to be with my family. Give me permission to go.'

He wrote out the authority, signed it, and handed it to her without a word.

'Thank you. I'm very grateful.'

They shook hands.

Heddy says, 'He could have asked me for more money, and I would have given it to him, I was so desperate to leave. But he didn't. You know, at that time, it was a nice thing to do.'

Every instinct told her that the sooner she left the better. And she knew that her father was ill, although they had given her no details. Better to be together, no matter what.

With the help of the storeman who turned the feathers, she cleared space in the back storehouse and packed all the furniture, including that of János in America. She collected some valuables – silver, brocade, linen – and with Jancsó in tow, went out to the peasants on their tiny holdings outside the town. They visited three or four houses, people that Jancsó knew, and in each, Heddy said, 'I am the wife of Ferenc Schwimmer. You know my husband's family.'

The peasants all knew of her; they had sold their feathers to the Schwimmers, as had their forefathers, since the middle of last century.

'Listen to what I propose. Keep these things for me. I am in trouble. I have to leave because I'm Jewish. If I live, you give them back. If I don't return, they're yours.'

She still had some jewellery and gold items that Feri had been buying over the last few years, keeping them in the safe. 'Who knows what our fate will be?' he used to say. Now, by an edict of 6 April, every Jew was to declare, and then deposit with a bank, all jewellery, gold, securities, savings and cheque accounts. They were allowed to withdraw a small fixed amount from one account only. Heddy had handed in all the jewellery that was insured; she did not dare do otherwise. In went her diamond ring and the diamond watch her mother-in-law had given her upon her engagement. The rest she kept back, defying the other part of the decree that forbad Jews to hide, sell or give their jewellery or valuables to Christian friends for safekeeping. The penalties enforced by the local police and gendarmes were harsh. Many Christians who had agreed to take valuables then took fright and reported the transactions to the authorities.

Heddy knew she would need the jewellery if she survived the War. There was nowhere at the house to hide it, with the servicemen and their guards watching her every move. She enlisted the help of a relative, a local doctor. He had a big garden, well back from the street. She put the jewellery in a metal box and in the dead of night she and Jancsó stole over to the doctor's house. They stood shivering in the darkness, watching him dig a hole under a tree to bury the box. It was frightening but funny, too; like an absurd horror movie, not her own life.

Jews were no longer allowed on passenger trains, but she managed to get on a goods train which left Hódmezövásárhely at night. She took me on one arm, Jutka and a small suitcase in the other. At the station, Jancsó wept.

'Jancsó, don't be angry. I have to go, I can't stay with you. The children ... they'll take us from here. I must go.'

'Of course, of course. I understand. You go.'

Jancsó helped her onto the stinking goods train. Peasants huddled on one long wooden bench running down the middle of the wagon, their live produce honking, snorting and shitting around them.

'I hated leaving Jancsó. I felt I was abandoning her to a terrible fate. I said goodbye to her as if I would never see her again. At that time, you never knew if you would see someone ever again. We were hanging in the air, in the very throat of death; fear was everywhere.'

A few weeks later, on 15 June, every single Jew in Hódmezövásárhely was rounded up, concentrated first in a brickyard in Szeged, then deported in wagons.

Chapter Seven

One of the first acts of the SS and Gestapo on entering Hungary was to arrest key anti-German aristocrats and members of the Jewish-Christian financial elite. This intertwined group had been the last bulwark of Jewish safety.

While disposing of the moderates, the Germans, with the help of the Hungarian police, made random arrests of Jews at the railway stations and boat terminals. By 31 March, 3364 Jews had been arrested in these 'individual actions'; by 16 April, 7289.

Heddy had heard rumours of what was happening at the railway stations, but she was desperate to be with her parents again. Kató had let slip that Náci was in hospital; she knew something was seriously wrong.

The journey from Hódmezövásárhely, normally three to four hours, took all night. The train stopped at every hamlet to pick up a peasant with a dozen eggs or three ducks to take to market. The floor was crowded with animals and people, the produce thrown up in wire cages overhead. There was a stench of unwashed bodies and human and animal shit.

The peasants saw Heddy's yellow star and left her alone, out of a silent pity.

The train arrived at 9 o'clock in the morning, on 8 May, in the Victorian cavern of the Keleti Railway Station. Heddy stepped off the train holding Jutka's hand, her other arm cradling the baby over her right breast to hide the yellow star. 'The edicts forbade you to hide your star with a brief-case or your bag, or anything like that but there was no law forbidding you from holding your child to your breast – yet. And it helped that you children were both fair haired and blue eyed. Thank God for that much.'

She glanced fearfully from the corners of her eyes; it didn't do to look around, to look as if you were anticipating any-thing. She saw some uniforms, German and Hungarian, but there was no commotion. No one approached her. Then she saw her mother and thought, God, why has she come? Why has she taken the risk?

Kató came towards her, arms wide, in tears.

'Father is ill, very ill. Only hours to live. Father is finished.'

'That's how she put it,' Heddy says. 'Not "Father is dying", but "Father is finished". I dumped you two children at their flat – and I rushed into the hospital, like a mad-woman. I knew he was sick, but they'd kept from me just how badly. I went in, he recognised me, smiled at me. He couldn't say much any more. I kissed his silky hair, as I always did ... He died the next morning.

'I didn't go in then. I couldn't go in. But I said to myself, at least I've seen him. If I hadn't seen my father, I could not have borne it.'

Náci's worsening diabetes had affected his lungs. A few days before his death, the Gestapo had come to the door. Where was Ignác Bleier? In hospital, already dying. Heddy is not sure why they came; perhaps someone had given his name to the Gestapo out of spite – 'it was enough then if someone simply didn't like you' – or perhaps they were rounding up other professionals as they had already rounded up the Jewish lawyers.

There was the funeral to arrange at the Jewish cemetery, but this simple fact put Heddy in a bizarre dilemma. Did she dare to go to her father's funeral? There were rumours: 'Such terrible rumours people frightened each other with, all the time, one rumour worse than the last. What had happened to Mrs Kálmán's husband, the woman in the next flat taken, someone snatched off the street, and so on and on, yet most of them turned out to be true ... they were rounding people up off the streets – poof, they disappeared. People were disposed of as if they were rags. They were going to the Jewish cemeteries and rounding up the mourners! Anywhere there were groups or crowds, you see.'

Could she go? If she took the two children, we could all be rounded up. But whom could she trust to leave us with? And what if she did not come back; what fate would she leave us to, Judy barely three years of age, I not quite seven months old? Perhaps she should stay away; after all her first responsibility was to the children. But not to go to her father's funeral – that he be buried like a dog, with no one there – was unthinkable.

In the end, she went, leaving us behind in someone's care. Standing at the graveside, she felt nothing, except a crazy gratitude that her father was dead; joy, triumph even, that he had escaped the nightmare in which the living were trapped. God must love him. But why didn't the gravediggers hurry? Why was it taking so long? She could hardly breathe. She was in a frenzy of impatience, turning around, looking from side to side. 'My body was like a piece of wood ... I was not myself, like I had stepped out of myself, looking at what was going on ... just put him in ... just throw the dirt on, hurry ...'

The minute it was over she rushed back to the children.

'Who else was there?' I ask.

'Mother, the older boys. Pali was in Russia.' She laughs

bitterly. 'There was no putting advertisements in the paper, letting people know, sitting "shiva" while friends offered condolences. A terrible cavalcade had started, a danse macabre.'

During Náci's illness, Kató had nursed him with her old devotion and had exercised her iron will. The funeral over, her grief broke free. Heddy sat with her until she fell asleep. Then she fed and bathed the children and put them to bed. The flat was quiet. There was a wail of sirens in the distance. She sat for a long time staring at the kitchen floor.

'The floor's dirty,' she muttered. She let water into a bucket, got down on her hands and knees, and scrubbed and scrubbed.

When the bombing of Budapest began on 2 April, the rabid anti-Semites believed that 'Allied Judaeo-Terrorists' had deliberately spared their 'Jewish fellow gangsters'. They demanded a hundred Jewish lives for every Christian victim of the bombing. The Jewish Council was strong-armed into requisitioning 500 homes for Christians made homeless by the bombing, and 1500 more after the second bomb attack two days later. On failure to meet the deadline, Council members were arrested until the target was reached.

Heddy's flat had been expropriated by the time she reached Budapest. The Schwimmer firm was gone, too, under a decree of 7 April, forcing the closure of all Jewish commercial and industrial establishments. A huge shipment of feather stock was sent to Germany, as part of the Hungarian contribution to the German war effort.

The authorities decided that Budapest would have no ghetto as such, in case the Allies retaliated by bombing other parts of the city. The Jews were to be concentrated in houses where there were already Jewish occupants, and in buildings near factories or railway stations which were likely to be bombed.

Kató's flat was in one of the new Jewish Houses. After the funeral Heddy moved in with her, but she knew that she could not stay there. It became clearer to her with each day that Budapest would soon be no safer than the country. People were hauled off the streets and taken away on any pretext, such as not wearing the right yellow – canary-yellow – star, or for not having it sewn on properly. She watched Jews being herded into the marked houses, the houses subjected to a curfew. What on earth did they think they were doing there? Couldn't they see it was just a waiting game? When the time came, they'd be available, convenient, to be taken to the wagons.

She called Baba and Pubi in for a conference.

'Boys, I'm not waiting here until they come to get me. I'm going away. I'll live illegally. Get me the papers, false birth certificates, whatever's needed, whatever they cost.' She still had ready cash from the money that Feri had stored in the safe. Her brothers were invaluable now, with their Christian birth certificates, still able to move around like free men.

Yet whether Baba was a Jew or a Christian under the law in 1944 is something of a mystery. In 1941, with the third change of law as to who was or wasn't a Jew since 1938, Baba was probably a Jew again. The 1941 law caught more people in its net than the Nuremberg law in Germany. If, like Pubi, you had two out of four Jewish grandparents, but had a Christian birth certificate and a fully Aryan wife, you were not a Jew. But if, like his brother Baba, you had two Jewish grandparents, a Christian birth certificate but a half-Jewish wife, you were a Jew, to be hounded and vilified with all other Jews.

Heddy's memory is unclear as to Baba's status in 1944. If he was still married to half-Jewish Manyi, he was in danger. If, as she suspects, he was already secretly married to his third wife, Aryan Éva (the family did not like her nor she them) he was safe.

Anni, Pubi's wife, offered to have her own birth certificate duplicated for Heddy. It was a generous but risky offer, all the more so because Anni was ten years older; any close perusal of the birth certificate and then of Heddy would give the game away. But then again, it gave her an authentic registered address, which every citizen was required to have.

It remained to have false birth certificates made for us children, as the offspring of Henrick (Pubi) and Anni Hiekisch. There was a flourishing blackmarket in forged and stolen papers. Christians sold their birth certificates, then advertised them as lost. There was also an underground network of dedicated Christians and Jews who forged papers for little or no cost. Among them was an old school friend of Heddy's; together with her Christian lover she saved many lives, manufacturing papers in a below-stairs printing shop.

Heddy waited impatiently for the papers. The heavy bombardment of the city was putting us in double jeopardy. Almost every morning in the dark early hours, the sirens sounded, the sky lit up and the bombs fell. She would put me in a washing basket, grab Jutka and head for the cellars.

Kató, too, had decided not to stay in Budapest and wait. At the encouragement of their sons, her first husband offered to resurrect their marriage on paper. She was to be Katalin Hiekisch again, Christian convert married to an Aryan, and thus safe.

The next question, where to go, was partially solved by a devoted employee in Baba's 'Christianised' firm. The young man arranged a room to rent in his home village of Kisláng, a remote hamlet south-west of Pest. Kató would go to the village with Baba's second wife, the half-Christian Manyi, and their three-year-old son Robi. They would pose as ordinary evacuees escaping the bombing. Old Hiekisch even offered to substantiate the hoax by coming down to the village to visit her, but with Náci only a few weeks in his grave, she could not deal with the idea.

It was too risky for Heddy to go to Kisláng as well. On paper now, she was Kató's daughter-in-law and Pubi's wife, but she and Kató looked too much alike for the daughter-in-law story to wash. Another solution had to be found.

She made preparations to leave, without knowing where. She had to divest herself of as much as possible. The spare children's clothes nagged at her. She had laid them up for us two or three years in advance. She wanted them somewhere safe, ready for us if we came back.

She thought of her friend and neighbour, Józsa. She had become very fond of Józsa. When Jutka was tiny, they used to meet every day in a protected, sunny laneway, nicknamed the Chicheri Corso, where all the young mothers in the neighbourhood gathered to chat while their babies took the air. Józsa was a serene young woman, a Jewess, happily married to a member of the 'gentry' with the distinguished name of Tetétleni. Heddy was sure Józsa would be safe with a name like that. No one would dare touch her.

In Józsa's apartment, everything was normal. The silver shone, the lamplight glowed, as serene as Józsa herself.

'Look,' Heddy said, 'I don't know what will happen to me. I want you to have the children's clothes I've put aside. If I don't come back, use them for your two.'

'Oh, Heddy, of course you'll come back, of course you will. I'll keep them for you till then.'

They kissed at the door.

'Look after yourself my dear.'

'Thanks. Perhaps God will help me.'

As Heddy walked down the stairs, she couldn't help comparing. There was Józsa, tranquil, safe; there was she, with Feri gone, her father dead, her brother in forced labour somewhere in Russia, her home stolen, her possessions scattered, her children in danger, and she not knowing if she would be alive tomorrow.

'Dear God, how lucky Józsa is!' she whispered to herself without rancour.

The first move in disappearing, 'living black' as it was called, was to leave her mother's flat. She feared each day branded in the 'Jewish House'. But it had to be done unobtrusively. On different days, she casually took out two small suitcases and deposited them at Baba's flat. Baba and Éva had said she could stay three days with them, no more. The neighbours would talk; they could be reported to the authorities for harbouring a Jew. Besides, Éva was no Jew lover.

Heddy left the flat one morning. She made no drama of her farewell to Kató. She took just the children and a handbag. Before she walked out the door, she tore off the yellow star. She went straight to Baba's.

As a temporary measure, she had booked a room in a hotel at a small resort an hour's drive from Budapest. There she would be Anni Hiekisch, Aryan matron with two young children, escaping the bombing. Her husband, Henrick/Pubi, would come on weekends to visit her. It seemed simple enough.

But Pubi and his wife Anni were full of foreboding. Taking Jutka with her would be too big a risk they said. There were stories flying around town of Jewish children being picked up by the police and gendarmes, treated kindly, then cajoled into giving their parents away – their new names, where they were hiding. Jutka could talk, and put them all in mortal danger.

All Jutka knew was that her father had gone away to be a 'soldier'.

'I couldn't explain to her that her father was in forced labour, that the rest of us were persecuted and homeless, and that her name was no longer Schwimmer but Hiekisch, that she was from now on to call her uncle "Daddy", and that she must never ever make a mistake. She was three years old!'

Anni made a startling proposition. 'I'll take Jutka with me,' she said. 'It's the usual time of year we go to Lake Balaton, and it's natural that we leave Budapest because of the bombing. She'll be our little godchild or cousin. We'll say we're looking after her while her mother is sick. She'll be safer with us. You can keep Zsuzsi with you. She's safe enough – she can't talk.'

Heddy had to decide, very quickly.

'It was the most terrible decision of my life. My first rule was to protect the children, not to be separated from them. But if I were caught – and that was quite likely – at least Jutka would be safe. Anni and Pubi would bring her up as a Christian, and she could have a normal life. Of course Pubi and Anni could die in a bomb attack, but if that was to happen, well, it would happen. If I kept Jutka with me, the chances were we'd all die.'

But how could she watch Jutka walk out the door, in all probability never see her again? It was impossible. She had to think clearly. No, it was impossible to think clearly. What did her instincts say?

She packed Jutka's clothes into one of the small bags and called the child into the room.

'Sweetheart, you're a lucky girl. Auntie Anni's taking you for a holiday down to the Balaton. Remember, down by that lovely lake, their nice place there? You'll have your own room! It will be lovely and warm down there, and you can go swimmy-swimmmies all day long. And I'll be down soon to see you there. Now you be a good girl for Auntie Anni.'

She kissed her lightly, waved gaily as Anni led the bewildered child out of the room.

She was stunned by the speed and enormity of what she'd done. Would she ever see her again – her beautiful child, her first born? Her life had revolved around Jutka from the minute she was born. And she had let her go, within half an hour.

The next day Pubi took Heddy and the baby up to the hills outside Budapest, to the town of Dobogókö. The police gave them no trouble leaving the city. Pubi stayed at the hotel long enough to establish himself as her husband, then left her in her room, staring at the wall.

For the first time in months, she had time. Such time, time she did not want! She bathed and dressed me, she made up little messes for me to eat on a gas ring in the room. She fed me. She washed my nappies. She stared at the wall.

Lunchtime. She forced herself to go down. The other guests tried to chat; they cooed over the baby. She would smile nervously, refer to her husband who'd be coming up soon, and say as little as possible. What if someone recognised her? Dobogókö was barely an hour from the city. It was filled with Budapestians. She dared not be too friendly, but she dared not miss the lunch hour either. If she did not appear, did not smile, wouldn't that be more suspicious?

She scuttled back to the room. She stared at the wall. She was cut off from everyone. She had not heard from Feri for weeks; she no longer knew where he was. Her mother was gone. Her beloved father was dead, yes dead. This was the first time she could let herself realise it. She had let Jutka go. The child wasn't there. She was afraid even to go out for a walk. She was glad when I dirtied my nappies. Washing them gave her something to do.

The only time she left the hotel was at dusk. There was a wooded area next to the hotel, where she took to walking for a few minutes every evening. The semi-dark, the quiet among the trees calmed her, readied her for the night alone with the baby.

The days dragged. The only relief was when Pubi came up for a few hours one weekend. They spent some more time downstairs letting the guests see the young married couple with the baby. 'How like her father she is! The image!' they said.

Pubi left. She sat in the room. The baby cried; I was crying more than usual. I would not be comforted. I had a rash. No ointment, no powder would ease it. I rocked myself on the bed, trying to scratch myself, howling.

There was no doctor nearby, and Heddy did not dare go further afield looking for one. For a couple of days she sat in the room, listening to the cries that never stopped. She thought she would go mad. On the third day she took a pile of nappies, tore them in two, and sewed them back together again. When she'd finished the pile, she tore another lot of nappies in two and started again.

She had been there for ten days perhaps, and I had been crying for five of them. I had rubbed myself raw, and my howls were of rage as well as pain. She flew from her chair.

'Stop it! Stop it! Stop it!' She hit me hard.

She caught herself, hand raised again. She was shocked, burst into tears.

A couple of days later, a doctor arrived at the resort and gave me something to soothe the inflammation. I subsided.

Rumours swept the hotel of Germans arriving; high-level army officers, not to be seen, but holed up in another private wing of the hotel. The Prime Minister was due, too, to meet them for some important conference. Everyone's papers were to be re-checked as a security measure.

Heddy's fear swelled again. What had possessed her, coming to a well-known resort, so close to the city? She felt herself in the eye of the storm, at the devil's gate.

The security check went by without incident, but she did not sleep that night.

At dusk the next day, she walked again in the little wooded region. She stayed out a little longer than usual, grateful for the scent of the pine needles, the soft shadows. Perhaps she should go, she thought. The isolation, the inactivity, were unbearable. And the Germans now literally next door ... Yet to risk a return to Budapest ...

She rounded a corner in the woods, and her heart stopped. Her breath rasped. This man knew her. She saw from his eyes that he recognised her instantly.

He was a rival feather merchant; they had seen each other at business functions. When the Schwimmer firm had lost their export quota to Christian firms, he had picked up their lost points. He knew exactly who she was and why she was here.

The truth, she decided instantly. She walked towards him and addressed him before he had a chance to speak.

'Good evening, Mr Szekér. Can I speak to you for a minute? I'm not going to pretend that I'm here on a holiday, enjoying myself. We both know that's not true. I'm hiding here under a Christian name, in a desperate attempt to save my own and my child's life. I'm a mother, trying to save my child's life by any means. It will be your judgement – you have a right either way – whether you will help me in this or not.'

They looked at each other for a long moment.

'Tell me, Madame,' he said levelly, 'do you know my wife?'

'No, I have never met her'

'Good. Leave it to me; you can trust me.'

'Thank you, very much.'

They shook hands.

'There were no niceties,' Heddy says. 'It was no time for small talk. The business with his wife – I think he didn't want to share the secret, the responsibility. Perhaps she was an anti-Semite who would give me up.'

She went back to her room, picked up the crying baby and hugged it. What to do now? He seemed decent, but could one trust one's life to anyone at this time? And if his wife found out? And then the Germans, here, in the hotel, the top brass, coming and going. She was nestled right in the heart of the enemy. She spent another sleepless night. The next morning, she telegrammed Baba and Éva.

'Arriving today.'

Chapter Eight

A new fear gripped her as the taxi neared Budapest. There would be a major checkpoint at the city outskirts.

'Whenever I am afraid – and this still happens – my hands become rigid. I can't move them. And that's what happened. They were like blocks of wood – I couldn't move them to get my papers out of my bag. I thought, if they ask for the papers, I'm done for; they'll see my hands.'

Just outside Pest, the car was stopped. A German soldier peered inside. Heddy forced herself to smile, sunnily, winningly, hiding her hands under the baby. The soldier saw me, smiled, waved the car on.

'You were blonde, I smiled. It didn't occur to him we were Jewish.'

She went straight to Baba's. Again, they gave her three days' grace before she had to move on. It was now the middle of June. She had been three weeks at Dobogókö.

In those three weeks, the extermination of the country's Jews had proceeded at a dizzying pace. So efficient was Eichmann that by 7 June he had 'cleaned out' zones 1 and 2, the Carpathians and Transylvania, of every one of their 289 357 Jews. By the middle of June, he had almost finished deporting all Jews from his designated first three zones: a total of 340 162 people according to his own meticulous records. He planned in the next two weeks to deport 41 499 from

Zone Four. His deadline for starting on Budapest, the fifth and final zone, was 7 July.

In the meanwhile, he had hypnotised the frightened and divided Jewish Council of Budapest into a virtual collaboration with him. The Council advised people to be calm, to obey all decrees, to be patient. It helped Eichmann draw up his five zones.

The decrees proliferated. Jewish children were not to wear school uniform; Jews were not to use public baths or swimming pools, or to frequent bars, restaurants, pastry shops or espresso stands. They were to use only certain food-dispensing establishments, and from 4 June, to shop for no more than two specified hours a day. They were forbidden to buy veal or pork, but allowed 100 grams of beef or horsemeat a day.

All books by Jewish authors or Christian authors of a Jewish background had already been removed from school and public libraries; now there was a series of much-publicised book burnings. A major book burning in Budapest on 16 June was presided over by the Government Commissioner of the Press, accompanied by the German Press Attaché. Official reports recorded that works by 120 Hungarian and 130 foreign authors of Jewish background were put to the torch; 447 627 books were destroyed, the equivalent of twenty-two fully-loaded freight cars. The spectacle was filmed for propaganda purposes.

Heddy did not want to stay in Budapest. She wanted somewhere small and anonymous. The idea of Kisláng, the village where Kató had gone, was resurrected. After Dobogókö, she would rather take that risk than be cut off and alone. Besides, no one had a better idea, so Baba's faithful office boy was sent to Kisláng to rent another room at the other end of the village.

She had two days left in Budapest when Pubi burst into Baba's flat with wonderful, fortuitous news. Feri had turned up, on a day's leave from the labour camp. They were in Budapest together, from different places, going different ways, for a single day.

But where to go? Baba's place was only a one-room flat and she was there on sufferance already. Pubi's flat, her registered address, was far too dangerous for an assignation with a Jewish man conspicuous in his ill-fitting labour camp 'uniform'. To ask a friend, even a non-Jewish friend, was to put the friend in danger. She rang Marcsa.

Marcsa was a Christian, married to an engineer cousin of Feri's. She was a strong-minded intelligent woman, with a soft spot for Heddy. The two couples had struck up a friendship.

'Marcsa, Feri is in town for one night only, on leave. We have nowhere to go. Can you take us in for the night?'

'Yes, if you can promise that it's for one night, no more.'

'I promise.'

She met Feri at the flat. It was large and comfortable, and Marcsa gave them a room to themselves. The four of them had dinner together, in a ghostly parody of times past.

Heddy and Feri went to their room. Feri was overjoyed to be with her, overwhelmed at the luck of it. He hadn't seen the baby for four months and was amazed at how I had grown. He learned for the first time where Jutka was. Heddy told him what she planned to do.

As for himself, he knew only that he was to report to the barracks at 8 in the morning to be transported somewhere north towards, perhaps beyond, the border.

Heddy says, 'We lay down together. He made love with me. He had to be up at 6, to get to the barracks on time. We said goodbye. Neither of us knew what would happen to us. He seemed to me as if he was saying goodbye to life. I stood at the window on the third floor, and waved; he walked a little, turned and waved, walked, turned and waved. I saw his figure disappear ... That was terrible.'

'Did you feel that you wouldn't see him again?' I ask.

She pauses.

'I wasn't optimistic about him. Would he have the strength? I had the responsibility of you, I couldn't give up, but he ... he tired more quickly. He was such a sad figure, in that ridiculous labour camp cap, with his clumsy walk.

'Yes, that's how it was, Suzi. There are a few scenes in this life that I can never forget. I can see him, as I lean out the window; he turns and waves, walks, turns and waves, and walks on, until he's gone.'

Forty-six years later, we are in Budapest together and I ask Mother to find the house where she said goodbye to my father on that early morning in June 1944. We stop the taxi on a busy thoroughfare, and she gazes at a series of grimy turn-of-the-century facades above sleazy shopfronts. As usual, once the eye adjusts in Budapest, they are handsome, solid buildings under the accumulated dirt. She is not sure which building now; that one, no, maybe that one; one of the two anyway, but she remembers clearly that she waved from the third floor, and that he walked up the street, to the left.

We get back into the taxi.

A few weeks later, reluctantly preparing to leave the city that has won my reluctant heart, I go to photograph the spot. I take a photo of both houses she pointed to, just in case. The traffic is roaring past, the footpaths are dense, but in my mind's eye it is early morning and the streets are empty. I see his walking figure fade and blur, then disappear.

★

Heddy was obliged to register her arrival in Kisláng with the village clerk. She was afraid; he only had to look at her age on the papers, then at her. But he barely glanced at her and stamped the page.

Kisláng was one straggling dirt road intersected by another; peasant houses, a shop-cum-cafe, a Council House. There were no cars or buses. The nearest railway station was fourteen kilometres away, reachable only by cart. It was ideal.

She took up her rented room with the Farkas family. The house consisted of the best room, which had been vacated for her use, and the back room, which was a kitchen as well. A storeroom or 'kamra' and a little back porch completed the arrangements. It was a typical small peasant house, neat and pretty, geraniums at the windows, embroidered pillows and feather doonas piled high in the front room.

The Farkas family was an idyll of peasant life; a handsome, open-faced couple with a daughter budding prettily into adolescence, a younger tow-haired boy. They were devoted to each other. The four of them slept in the back room, and Heddy noticed that when the children went visiting on a Sunday, the parents took their chance to 'burrow together a little'.

Without Pubi available to play husband, Heddy invented a new story for her landlords. She was a young woman of modest means come to the village to escape the bombing. Her husband had run off with his secretary just weeks after the baby was born; that's why there were no letters from him. They made her welcome, clucked over the baby, and did not pry too much. But there was one thing that intrigued them – her pigskin suitcase on top of the wardrobe. They had never seen anything so fine.

Her days developed an inexorable pattern. She looked after the baby, swept the pressed-earth and plank floor of her room, tidied everything in sight, swept the yard, and waited for the hours to go by. My nappies gave her the most frequent occupation; I was developing an intermittent diarrhoea and starting to lose weight.

Kató was at the other end of the long dirt road, a good twenty minutes walk away. Heddy went over whenever she dared. It was too risky to go every day, but she needed the strength her mother's presence gave her. Anything was better than the hotel in Dobogókö, but life in Kisláng was precarious and hopelessly dull. There was no newspaper or radio and very little real news.

Each day was a long pretence, without knowing when or how it would end. The nights were the longest, unless the Farkases invited her to eat with them. Then they sat together in the warm kitchen, hulling corn companionably and telling stories. But Heddy was always conscious of her part. Her landlords were not Nazi sympathisers, that was clear, but she still played vague, as if lost in grief over her errant husband, nodding, hangdog when Mrs Farkas clucked over the fickleness of men.

The baby was developing all the symptoms of dysentery. Whatever Heddy fed me, I emitted a thin black fluid. She suspected the village water, but boiling it did not help. She spent hours changing and washing the foul nappies. She acquired a small spirit stove and experimented with what to give me; cacao especially sent from Budapest, gruel. Nothing worked.

There was no doctor in the village, so she went to the local dispensary. It was not a proper pharmacy, just the front room of a house.

When she saw the man behind the counter, a little shock of recognition went through her. He was Jewish, she was sure of it. He looked at her too, a brief, half-enquiring glance, but said nothing. A couple of days later, with the baby still sick, she went back. She assessed his every word and gesture. She was sure of him now. Again the exchange of looks. On the third visit, she ventured a hint, and they told each other their stories.

He had owned a pharmacy in smart Váci Street in Budapest. In April he had been stripped of his licence under the edicts. Because of his Christian wife he had not been deported but sent to a remote village; that was Government policy with 'useful' professionals like doctors and chemists.

When there was no one else at the dispensary, they could talk. The chemist and his wife had a radio. Once they trusted her, they told her they listened clandestinely to the BBC. They had real news. From then on she called every day.

She carried a map of Europe in her pocket everywhere she went, fingering it for reassurance. Ten times a day, when she was alone, she got out the map and pored over it. The Russians were creeping up, oh too slowly, from the southeast, pushing the Germans north. She knew every line of the map, every town.

At the other end of the village, where Kató shared a front room with her daughter-in-law Manyi and young Robi, the landlord and his wife had also moved into the back room. Uncle Józsi was a drunkard who cast amiably lustful eyes over Manyi and Heddy.

'I'm pretty sure they knew who we really were, but they never asked questions. Later when I told him the truth, he just winked at me – he was drunk as usual – and said, "Perhaps we always thought as much." '

Kató was in her element in the village. Heddy needed her, Manyi and Robi needed her.

'We'll make it,' she would say over and over, 'you'll see. God will help us. I just know it.'

Her voice would ring with such conviction that Heddy almost believed her.

Kató knew what role to play in Kisláng, and she played it with gusto, enjoyment even. After all, it was a part not far from herself. She had grown up in Transylvania with ribald, commonsense peasant women. She knew what jokes they told, what songs they sang. She coarsened her accent, spread her girth, was jolly. She hadn't had such a good part since her heyday in *Il Trovatore*. The village soon loved her, particularly the local nest of Fascists.

Like most places, Kisláng had its majority of the politically indifferent and its sprinkling of the fanatical. There was a houseful of Arrow Cross supporters a few yards up the road. They stopped to chat to Kató in the street and laughed at her jokes. They invited her to their house, and she sat whole evenings with them as they cursed the Jews. She outcursed them all.

One morning Heddy set off to visit Kató. She knew her mother had gone to the railway station to pick up a parcel sent by Pubi or Baba. She timed the walk to meet her on the way back.

As she neared Kató's lodgings, she saw a cart approaching in the distance. She could just make out a gendarme holding the reins – there was his distinctive, rakishly feathered hat. And beside him – her heart stopped – Kató's unmistakable bulk. Kató was arrested, captured, brought into the village! Next he would take her, the baby, Manyi, Robi. There was no point in running. She just stood and watched the cart coming closer. She could see Kató waving her arms about, as if pleading.

Then she saw the gendarme throw his head back in a hearty laugh. She saw Kató slap him on the back, heard her big laugh floating across the space. They were joking together!

'I felt a stone fall from my heart. Kató was doing her big hearty countrywoman act – she did it so well! As they got closer, I could hear her belting out Hungarian folksongs, beating out the rhythm on his knee. He was lapping it up.'

The gendarme stopped the cart in front of the house, gallantly handed Kató down.

'It's a long, long time,' he said, 'since I have so enjoyed the company of a real Hungarian countrywoman. It was a pleasure, my dear lady. If I can be of service to you again ...'

He tipped his cap courteously to them both, and jiggled the reins.

Kató and Heddy went inside the room and shut the door.

'Katus, I thought it was the end of the world.'

Kató shrugged. 'See, we got through that one, too. We're going to survive this, you mark my words.'

At the end of June 1944, not long after Heddy left Budapest, Eichmann had almost completed the task he had begun only three months before. All known Jews had been cleared from the country areas and deported to the concentration camps. Only Budapest remained.

But on 7 July the Regent Horthy called a halt to the deportations. For months he had been bothered by his conscience, and pressured by appeals from his own son and from abroad. He dismissed his latest Prime Minister, the pro-German Sztojay, and appointed the more independent Lakatos.

For a couple of months, there was a reprieve for the Jews of Budapest. To his astonishment and humiliation, Eichmann was sent home. The Swedish diplomat Raoul Wallenberg, who had arrived in June to save as many Jewish lives as he could, thought his work might be over.

The Germans bided their time with Horthy. They were aware that he had made approaches to the Russians and they prepared to thwart him if he actually tried to change sides. And they never ceased to negotiate with the Hungarians for a speedy resumption of the 'Final Solution'.

Little real news filtered through to the isolated and muddy village. What news did come, Heddy knew, was propaganda, with defeats not admitted to, reverses alluded to weeks after the event. There was no news of Feri, no news of Pali.

The village heard that Rumania had changed sides and joined Russia, then that a combined Rumanian and Russian force had inflicted a huge defeat on the Germans. Heddy exulted in secret. The rest of the village lived in fear. Even the staunchest anti-Nazis feared the Russians – an advancing army, any advancing army, threatened the peasants' livestock, their precious horses, carts and bridles.

Heddy waited for the Russians as for her saviours. Dreaming of their victory, she dreamed of Jutka returned to her, the baby healthy again, and Feri coming home to an orderly and serene flat on Pozsonyi Road. And she fantasised about toilets. As she crept out the back on ever colder nights and sat on the wooden plank in the stink, she said to herself, 'The day will come when I again sit on a toilet that simply flushes when I pull the chain.'

Autumn had arrived and with it, shorter days, and mud. With each day the trek down the two unpaved roads to the pharmacy or to visit Kató became more difficult. The village was dissolving in mud. Some days Heddy could not move from the house, marooned in mud.

The baby was no better. I was losing weight steadily and starting to get the large-headed look of malnutrition. Heddy was afraid to move outside the village to look for a doctor because that would involve papers, questions and the danger of discovery. But she chafed at the enforced passivity. And she chafed at her separation from her first born. She missed Jutka constantly. It would be unwise to move the child; she was still safe at Balaton. But for how much longer, with the battlefront creeping north, ever closer to the Hungarian border?

On 23 September the Russian Army entered Hungary. The village was quiet in anticipation. The Germans were retreating north. The Russians would soon be at their door. Everyone knew that Hungary had again backed the wrong horse, that it might follow Italy and Rumania out of the war.

On 15 October Horthy made an extraordinary broadcast on national radio. He declared an end to the German Alliance. The war was finished.

Heddy dared not show her joy. It could be a hoax, might not last. The village was confused. Was it really all over? Were the Russians still coming?

In Budapest, the Jews crammed into the Jewish Houses were jubilant. Many tore off their yellow stars. But within hours, rumor and apprehension was followed by dread.

The Germans acted swiftly. The morning of the broadcast they captured Horthy's son, Miklós, and dispatched him to Mauthausen concentration camp. Horthy was demoralised, his generals confused. By the late afternoon, the Arrow Cross had captured the radio and were broadcasting German military music. There were many suicides in the Jewish Houses that night.

On the next day, in Kisláng, there was another broadcast, and the rest of the country heard what Budapest already knew. The Regent was deposed. Hungary was back with the Axis. The arch-Fascist, Szálasi, leader of the Arrow Cross, was in power.

The nights of 15 and 16 October set the pattern of terror for the coming months. Hundreds of Jews were taken from their homes by gangs of Arrow Cross youths, tortured, then shot into the Danube from one of the bridges. The favoured method was to tie three people together, then shoot the middle one in the head at close range. The weight of the body dragged the two living people with it into the icy river.

In the country, where there were no Jewish civilians left, Jewish labour gangs were terrorised. In Székesfehérvár, just north of where Heddy was hiding, a whole 'company' of 160 men was slaughtered.

When Heddy heard about the Fascist coup, she knew that from now on there would be no mercy, no exemptions, only blood.

But Pubi's wife, Anni, staying on at the holiday resort at Balaton long after the summer had faded, with a fretful and confused Jutka, was afraid of the Russians. Balaton was in the direct line of the Russian advance. What might they do when they got there? There were tales of plunder and rape. Pubi was mostly in Budapest. She decided to join him there and take Jutka with her.

News of this reached Heddy some time in the second half of October. Her worry about Jutka increased tenfold. Anni was taking the child back into the heart of Budapest where the Germans were entrenched. Jutka would be as safe, possibly safer, in Kisláng. Their terrible five-month separation had to end.

She asked Anni to bring the child to the Kiscséripuszta railway station where Kató would pick her up. Heddy stayed in the village, fearing the risk of a public reunion.

I have often heard her describe that reunion, never without an intense, quivering emotion.

'I waited an hour and a half for them to arrive back on the cart. I can only say that no lover, no beloved husband returning from the war, no one, could be waited for as I waited for my child. The trembling, the beating heart, the fearful joy, the sheer excitement … I was shaking inside. When would she come? How would she be?

'I heard them arrive. I stayed in Kató's room. I didn't dare rush out into the yard for everyone to see my joy. Jutka came in. She looked at me and said, "Mummy, do you love me?"

'She showed no joy at seeing me, just seriously, and straight away, "Mummy, do you love me?"

'My little girl, my darling, but of course I love you, how I love you …

'Then almost as soon as I rushed to hug her, she said, "Ohh, I've got to wee!" The excitement … it was a blessing; it broke the tension – quick the potty! We only had a potty.'

She told the village that Jutka was a little cousin whose parents had been bombed out; the child had once lived with her and had got into the habit of calling her 'Mummy'. To further avoid suspicion, she left Jutka with Kató, and returned to her room at the Farkases with me.

But after a couple of weeks her frustration grew unbearable. The village street was becoming impassable; she could be stuck there for what could be months, almost, in effect, as far from her child as before, alone with a baby who might well be dying.

Better to be together, to face together whatever was coming. She hired a cart to negotiate the mud, said farewell to the Farkas family with real fondness, and took the pigskin suitcase and the almost lifeless baby down the long straggly village street to Kató's lodgings.

There were now six of us in the front room of Uncle Józsi's house: Heddy, Manyi, Kató and the three children. There were two beds, a cot, a stove, the potty.

'Everything happened in that room. What went into us, what went out. The cooking, the washing, the shitting, the kids. We warmed water on the stove in the corner to wash in. By then, we were in such misery, we were quiet ... we just endured. There was no choice but to support each other; at least Kató and I did. Manyi was so afraid and confused; we both had to hold her up.'

Heddy watched the baby obsessively. Thank God, the child had such a healthy start. Before the Germans had entered Hungary, she had sneaked a visit to Budapest and taken me to her old paediatrician.

'A Glasner baby,' he had said, citing a famous commercial for Glasner baby rusks. He held me up by the heels, watching me arch my back and gurgle. 'A perfect child.'

Now the perfect child was a textbook case of malnutrition, with a bulging forehead and distended belly. Heddy began to think that I might really die. Still she feared a journey into Székesfehérvár to find a doctor.

I have often heard the story of my illness. But now for the first time, I get a glimmer that this dying child was not just a prop in the drama, a thing that Heddy had to save, but myself.

This is utterly new to me, astonishing.

Some time in November the retreating Germans passed through the village, followed soon after by the Hungarian Army. Heddy was not much worried; in retreat, the discovery of Jews was not a priority.

The night the Hungarians arrived, the chemist came to the door, in high excitement.

'Heddy, there's a doctor here with the army, an army doctor. Get him to see the baby. It's your only chance.'

Heddy threw on her coat. She found the doctor at his billet and described my condition.

'I'm sorry,' he said, 'I can't treat civilians; army personnel only.'

Heddy stared at him. 'That's just not right. You can't say that.' She was on her high horse now. 'You're a doctor. You have a duty to save life. There are no other doctors around here. My child's life is at stake. You have to come; either that, or I will bring the child to you.'

There was no way around this woman, the doctor decided. He came to see me, and prescribed a medicine available only in Budapest, if anywhere. He said he was about to go to the city on three days leave. If she could organise to get the medicine to him there, he would bring it back to the village.

She flew to the village post office to ring Pubi. 'Move heaven and earth to get this medicine to this address by this time. Zsuzsi is dying.'

Within a few days, the doctor had returned to Kisláng with the stuff. It had to be boiled in with everything I ingested. I seemed to improve, but very slowly, very little. I remained apathetic, unnaturally quiet. My first birthday came and went and I still could not sit up.

Two days after the Fascist coup, Eichmann was back, eager to resume work.

'You see,' he told members of the Jewish Council immediately summoned to him, 'our arm is still long enough to reach you.'

On 20 October, he began with a recruitment drive for 'labour'. On the first day he rounded up all Jewish men between the ages of sixteen and sixty. On the second day he wanted a further 25 000 men and 10 000 women.

They were concentrated on a racecourse and sportsfield, formed into companies and set to digging trenches for the defence of Budapest. Hundreds died of exposure and ill treatment.

On 8 November, Eichmann began the infamous 'death marches' from Budapest to the Austrian border nearly 200 kilometres away. With Germany so weakened, he no longer had his efficient network of trains, so he made the Jews walk. They walked between fifteen and twenty kilometres a day in bitter winter conditions with little food or water. Each day hundreds were left to die on the road. Those who could not keep up were shot. At the border the survivors were loaded onto trains headed for the death camps.

Raoul Wallenberg could not actually stop the marches, but he appeared often on the death route, quite literally a saviour. He brought food, medicine and distributed his life-saving Swedish passports. His assistant Per Anger estimates that on a single day they saved 1500 lives in this way. In a report back to Stockholm, Wallenberg wrote:

The sights that we witnessed moved even the grim-visaged bloodthirsty [Hungarian] gendarmes. More than one remarked that he would prefer being in the firing line ... We saw that in many places the corpses of people who had died or been murdered by the Arrow Cross men covered the roadside. Nobody had thought of burying them.

Chapter Nine

In Kisláng the cold days of late November passed, muffled and miserable. The village reeked foreboding. The official news was scant, but at times a long drrr drrrr of distant fire could be heard. The villagers began a silent busy hoarding. Foodstuffs, implements, whatever could be dug away or hidden in lofts and cellars, disappeared. Food became scarce. The Russians were coming.

There was no doubt they would come through Kisláng on their way to take Székesfehérvár, the last major town before their march on Budapest. As the gunfire drew nearer, Heddy stood at the gate of the house, waiting like a lovesick girl. When? When? Perhaps tomorrow?

She thought it prudent, whatever happened, to buy a pig before all food sources in the village dried up. She paid Uncle Józsi to kill one. He and his wife would 'work it up' into bacon, chops, blood sausage, kolbász, in time-honoured tradition. With a pig, and no need to refrigerate it over the long winter, they could survive no matter what.

When finally the Russians came, in early December, the village was in terror. Every family bundled into the cellar or under hay in the loft.

Heddy made her usual morning pilgrimage to the chemist, oblivious. As he opened the door to her, he said, 'You're mad! The Russians are at the other end of the village! Go home, quick. They're shooting.' She turned back, walking with a springing step down the main street. 'The Russians are here! They're here!' The bullets whistled overhead; she barely noticed them. Her liberators had come.

At the house everyone else was already in the cellar. Uncle Józsi and his wife called, 'For God's sake, get in. Quickly!' And they bolted the cellar door and waited for the worst.

There was sporadic gunfire for a couple of hours, then quiet. People emerged cautiously and stood at the gates of their houses as the great occupying Russian Army entered the village.

'It was morning when the Russians came. There couldn't have been a more miserable sight. It was a heart-aching thing to see, men and women dirty and tired, such tired faces ... sad, worn-out people. Women, too, with the soldiers; the kitchen and catering staff I think. All of them in those grey uniforms, with their carts and bedding and utensils ... an army going by. My heart went out to them. I nearly waved, but there were such rumours of what they would do to you.'

The soldiers camped wherever they could. Every house in the village was invaded. They simply walked into a house and demanded a bed. The first night a soldier came to their door and asked for somewhere to sleep, just for a few hours. He was a middle-aged man, an officer, quiet and courteous. Heddy explained to him with bits of every language that she could muster, that there were no available beds, there was only the kitchen table. He stretched out on the table and was asleep in seconds.

'To this day, it's on my conscience that I did not let him have a bed. I was frightened of what letting him have a bed could lead to. He was so polite, so exhausted. I should have let him sleep on a clean pillow for just a few hours.'

In the morning a fresh battalion arrived in the village. They wanted women. It was no use the village women hiding.

There could be no protest; they had guns, could beat the children to death. The soldiers simply came to Heddy's door, pushed Jutka and Robi into the kitchen and shoved the women into the front room. Kató on one bed, Heddy and Manyi on the other. It was over in minutes. There was no emotion, Heddy says, just revulsion and fear. The soldiers were dirty and smelled of vodka.

When they had gone, Kató said, 'Well, we survived that one too. This all goes with it my dears. Never mind.'

The Russians stayed on for four days, spread over the village, raping and looting, throwing people out of their homes. They tried to evict Heddy and the others, but she stood her ground.

'No,' she said, in a torrent of languages and arms and legs, 'I am Jewish. You are liberating me. I am not going anywhere.' They let her alone.

But the rapes continued. The third night, a strong blond boy, billeted in the back room, knocked all night at the door. He wanted only Heddy and would not go away. He knocked and knocked, and looked at her beseechingly. She feared for the children and finally opened the door to him. There was another soldier who wanted only Manyi. Kató was not quite in such demand. The next day it was a tall, dark Russian after Heddy. 'Devastatingly handsome, a real heart-throb. I even fancied him. And he was strange; he kept wanting me to move over to the house where he was billeted. He seemed to be saying that we would be safer there. But I wouldn't go, and the next day he was gone, along with all the others. They took everything with them they could lay their hands on.'

I am amazed how matter of fact she is about the rapes.

'Oh, I may even smile now, but then, to go through that, with you children in the other room, Manyi and mother being raped at the same time a couple of feet away, I didn't know who I was any more – it was like losing your soul. I just thought, this is the price of survival, it has to be paid. And the soldiers, I felt almost sorry for them. They were like starving, exhausted horses, at the end of their tether. It was hard to be angry with them. They were in an insane situation, poor things; they had been at war for so many years. They had no mercy left in them. They just took what they needed. At least they didn't kill us.'

The Russians left. The village was quiet and bewildered. Within days Heddy's vagina began to itch and give off a smelly discharge. Syphilis or gonorrhea, the Russian legacy. She went to the midwife who gave her a red liquid 'which was as much use as holy water'. A week later, when her period was due, it did not come. She was numb with disbelief. What next?

There were rumours that the front had stopped at Székesfehérvár. The Russians could not break through. The rumble of cannon could be clearly heard. The villagers gathered in knots; what if the Russians were pushed back towards Kisláng again? They kept all their goods and food hidden.

A plan began to ferment in Heddy's mind. To leave. The baby was still sick, alarmingly weak. She needed to get me somewhere quickly where there was a clean water supply and a doctor on hand. Jutka was in a state of terror, particularly after the Russians. She herself was sick and pregnant. But far worse than any of this, the front could roll back towards Kisláng and the Germans could return. And she was now known in the village as a Jew. She had to leave.

Once decided, she was like one possessed. She hired a horse and a sled, but there was not a bridle or harness to be found in the village. The Russians had taken everything. She scavenged until she found bits of telegraph wire that the Germans had left behind, and a piece of rope from a clothesline.

She hired a lad from the village to act as some sort of protection and help with the suitcase. In the suitcase, there were a few badly washed summer clothes and the cured pig.

Manyi wept and vacillated. She was afraid to go with them. They could die on the road, be recaptured by the Germans, raped again by the Russians. Robi cried. He wanted to go with his grandmother and his friend Jutka. His mother stood at the gate, holding him, sullen, in her arms. The villagers gathered in a crowd. The Farkases pleaded. It's January, they said, the greatest cold, you don't have a winter coat, there are roaming hordes out there, dead horses litter the roads, no one knows what will happen. You will be safe here. Stay.

Heddy shook her head. With her mother, the two children and the hired lad, she set off down the snow-laden village street, the same street where a few months ago she had watched with dread the approach of the gendarme with Kató 'captive' at his side.

She had heard that some sort of train had started up again from Székesfehérvár going south as far as Dombóvár. She had no idea how they would proceed from there, but she knew that with every step south and east, she would be nearer safety. The big thing was to get across the Danube somehow; once on the eastern side of the river, there would be no more Germans.

The journey to the railway station, just fourteen kilometres from the village, took two hours. The sled made slow progress through the heavy snow, and they shivered in their lightweight coats.

Heddy clutched me close to her. There was no knowing how much resistance I had left. But sitting in Kisláng watching me die was no alternative.

Everywhere, by the side of the road lay dead horses, their

blood frozen in long untidy red gashes. Human corpses, too, here and there, but nothing living. There was a white weird silence over everything.

A lone Russian soldier rode towards them and gestured for the sled to stop. Where were we going? Heddy had picked up a couple of Russian words.

'Hospital,' she said, and held out the baby to his gaze. He glanced at me, looked into the suitcase, and saw the pig and a few children's clothes.

'Davai,' he said. 'Go, okay.'

'Davai' was one Russian word Hungarians had picked up quickly. It brought joy and relief. 'Davai,' Budapestians said to each other years later in sly parody when they met on the streets. 'Zabra' was another Russian word everyone knew but feared. It meant looting and plunder. The Russians will 'zabra' everything you have, and you, too, the peasants had said to her, you're mad to go.

But this Russian soldier closed the suitcase and waved them on. 'Davai.'

'Did he take the pig?' I ask.

'No. The way we looked in our thin clothes, you in my arms, in the snow; he left us alone.'

They got to the railway station. The man from the village set on back with the cart, the horses and the makeshift bridle.

An hour, then two, passed on that bleak railway station. Heddy began to doubt. The country was at war still, everything in chaos. A handful of people was also waiting, just in case. Maybe a real, running train had been only a rumour. Then, muffled yet definite, the sound of a train.

It was almost empty, derelict. All the seats had been ripped out, leaving the exposed heating pipes which, miraculously, were working. Heddy used the warm pipes to heat my medicine in a small saucepan brought for the purpose.

Squatting on the floor, she fed me the mix and changed my foul nappy.

The train lumbered into Dombovár. I passed through it forty-five years later. I saw only a big, ugly, covered station. But in January 1945, that cover was all important. We spent the night on the floor of the station, the roof giving us shelter from the bitter cold.

There were many others camped there that night. The countryside was adrift with bands of confused and hungry refugees. When the Germans started their flight north, they broadcast incessantly to the populace to follow them. There would be work, food and protection in Germany. If they stayed, they would be tortured and killed by the Russians. Thousands flooded the roads north, but within a couple of weeks they became disillusioned and afraid. Now they were struggling home in misery and chaos.

The next day a train turned up, running further south, as far as Mohács. Mohács was on the Danube. Once across, each mile would bring them closer to safety.

At Mohács, night was falling. By the time they got to the riverbank, there was an impenetrable darkness. It was about 6 o'clock.

'Every time I think of the riverbank at Mohács, I think that was the Cecil B. De Mille scene of my life. Or maybe *Gone With the Wind*, you know, with the sky lit with flames. I can't forget anything about it.

'There was a big crowd standing on the riverbank in the darkness, the refugee exodus I told you about. But there was no transport across the Danube. The bridges were blown up and the Danube was iced over. But the Russian troops were crossing, in barges, detonating the ice before them as they went. They had to get across; they were transporting ammunition to supply the front which had stopped at Székesfehérvár. At the same time their planes were roaring overhead, to ensure the safe passage of the supply barges ... And we civilians were standing on the bank, hopeless, in the dark and cold. People said that there was no way across; the Russians were refusing to take any civilians on the pontoons. But still we stood there, hopeless, waiting.

'I thought it was the end of the earth – we would freeze to death there on the riverbank without shelter. Then Kató went over to one of the pontoons and talked to the man in charge of loading the ammunition. She gestured towards us, and he glanced at us – how we looked! We hadn't washed, and I was going mad from the itch and smell of the syphilis, and you on my arm, crying ceaselessly. He looked at us, and there was humanity in his look. He said, 'Davai!' Again that 'Davai!' like an angel from heaven; could it be true? And with that one movement of his arm, there was a tide of humanity, a sudden surge of perhaps thirty people, all onto the pontoon.

'And then he yelled, "No more, no more, stop!" and the pontoon started.

'It was a miracle, but terrible too, to be on that pontoon. The aeroplanes screamed overhead, the continual bombing of the ice, the pitch blackness, the jam of frightened people. Jutka couldn't understand what was happening, that they weren't bombing us. She howled with terror. There was a man squashed beside me and he said to me quietly, 'Madam, give me the baby.'

'I stared at him, astonished and asked "Why?"

"I'm a deserter," he said. "Give me the child to hold."

He wanted it to look natural, as if he were the father. And that's how we got across the Danube.'

The pontoon juddered safely to the other bank. There were Russian trucks there, loading the ammunition onto the barges. Heddy asked the driver of one where he was going.

'Baja.'

'Take us,' they pleaded, and again a nod, and they scrambled onto the back of the truck. 'The Russians had a human quality, no doubt about it,' says Heddy, 'especially towards children.'

To reach Baja was another wonderful thing. It was on the line to Szeged, and Szeged, where I was born, was not far from Hódmezövásárhely. In this part of the country, there was a good chance of trains running. And indeed the next day there was a train to Szeged, and Heddy began to think the worst was over.

The train was not long out of Baja when it stopped without warning in the open countryside. No one knew when it would start again. Frantic enquiries, rumours all over the train. Several hours passed, with no movement and no news.

Heddy had run out of food for the baby. She was terrified of any further weakening. But if she left the train to seek food for me, it might start without her and there might be no other. The train could start at any moment, or it could be stalled, motionless, for days. Several times she resolved to get off, run somewhere to beg for food, but then she fancied that a wheel squealed or that the train moved forward a fraction.

The atmosphere grew fetid. People were hungry. They got off only to defaecate and urinate at the side of the track. The train would start again at any moment, some said, it had stopped for good, said others. No one dared leave. There was nowhere else to go.

Half a day went by, then more slow hours. Heddy stared out of the window, rocking the baby. I was crying weakly. Darkness was approaching. The train stood motionless on the flat Hungarian plain. Suddenly she pushed me into Kató's arms, darted from the train and ran hard to the nearest farmhouse.

There was a light but no one answered. Everyone was afraid in those days of anything unknown. She knocked loudly and persistently.

'Who is it?' finally, roughly.

'I am desperate for a little food.'

'There isn't any. We have nothing.'

'I only want a few potatoes, boiled, for a very sick child. Nothing else. I'll pay whatever you want. Please.'

They let her in, boiled the potatoes. Heddy gave the woman the small sum she asked for and ran like a madwoman back to the train. She mixed the potatoes with the stuff the army doctor had prescribed and fed me.

After twenty-four hours stationary in the open fields, the train lurched forward again and reached Szeged without further incident.

At Szeged, the bridge across the Tisza had been blown up. But the town had been liberated for some weeks and there were boats for hire. On the other side of the river, the train to Hódmezövásárhely was running as usual; a normal train! It was filled with peasants on their way back from Szeged market, chatting about prices for their pigs and ducks. They stared at the two haggard women clutching the children to them.

'Where are you going? Can we ask your name?' they enquired kindly.

'I am the wife of Ferenc Schwimmer. His family lived in Hódmezövásárhely for a long time. These are his children.'

'Oh, the Schwimmers,' they said, 'yes of course. What can we do for you? How can we help?'

'Nothing, thank you. Just help me get a cart to take me to the Patzauers, if they are still there. They are my friends.'

The Patzauers were an established Jewish family in the town, owners of the brewery. Aladár Patzauer had been captain of the labour camp set up in Heddy's barn. Heddy was relieved they were still alive. There would be someone to welcome her.

She stood at the iron gates of the big complex that was both brewery and dwelling and smiled tremulously at Ilona Patzauer as she came towards her. But Ilona did not smile. She just stared.

'Ilona, don't you recognise me?'

Ilona started.

'Heddy? ... My God! Only from your voice ... What has happened to you? Come in, come in.'

There was a vacant flat where Aladár Patzauer's mother had lived until she was deported to Auschwitz and gassed. While her son had been granted certain exemptions as a war hero, they had not extended to her.

The little flat was beautiful, spotless. There was a toilet that flushed when you pulled the chain. They stripped off their filthy clothes. Hot baths were drawn.

Heddy called in a doctor for me. He had vitamins and prescribed a diet. He told her she had got there just in time; I had one or two days of life left in me.

★

Even as the Russians advanced on Budapest, the authorities continued their zealous pursuit of the Jews. In November there was an edict for the confiscation of all remaining Jewish property, with the exception of wedding rings and two weeks supply of food and fuel. In December, with the Russians at the city outskirts, the Minister for the Interior ordered all street names bearing the names of Jews or persons connected to Jews be changed immediately.

A decision had been made, finally, to create a ghetto in Budapest. It was to be the shortest lived ghetto in Europe, but it was nonetheless terrible.

An area half a kilometre in size was walled off and the gates guarded by Arrow Cross and police. There were 70 000 people – mostly women, children and the old – crowded fourteen to a room. Many died. There was nowhere to bury the bodies. Some were buried in the park or under the flagstones of Klauzál Square, the ghetto's heart. Others were piled in the courtyard of the synagogue, others in empty warehouses and at the ritual baths. When the ghetto was liberated, 3000 bodies were stacked up awaiting burial.

Apart from the 'official' ghetto, there was also Raoul Wallenberg's 'international' ghetto on Pozsonyi Road where thousands were crowded into a few Protected Houses. The crowding became so critical and Arrow Cross raids such a regular event, that Wallenberg was forced to move some of 'his' Jews out into the official ghetto.

The winter of 1944 was unusually cold. Food and fuel supplies were low. The Russians encircled Budapest on Christmas Eve. Their fighter bombers set the city alight. The seige that followed saw some of the worst fighting of the war. Russians and Germans fought each other hand to hand, street to street, house to house.

In the last weeks of the seige, the Arrow Cross behaved as if they were oblivious to their own imminent end, or as if that knowledge gave an extra edge to their ferocity. Gangs roamed the streets of Pest, averaging fifty to sixty murders a night. In December and January, they raided three Jewish hospitals and tortured and massacred the patients. The last such raid was on 14 January. The Pest side of the river was liberated on 18 January. The Jews, who had been forced to pay for and erect the ghetto wall themselves, tore it down with their hands.

Today the taxi drivers point to three or four ordinary inner city streets, a square, the synagogue on the outer perimeter, and say casually, 'That was the Jewish district once. It was a ghetto during the War.'

While the citizens of Pest were free by mid-January, it was another month before Buda was liberated. The city was devastated; her suffering was equalled by only two other European cities: Warsaw and Berlin. People crawled out from their cellars to extraordinary scenes. Every one of the seven great bridges over the Danube had been destroyed. The great hotels of the Danube Corso were in ruins, as was Buda castle. Many fine buildings were gone and nearly every window in Budapest was broken. The streets were strewn with rubble, burnt-out vehicles, coils of wire, and bodies. There was no electricity, gas or telephone.

The Russians counted 124 000 Jews alive on the liberation of Pest, including a few thousand who had been hidden by Christians or who had lived on false passports. Budapest had lost half its Jewish population. Nonetheless, it was the biggest surviving community in Europe, if you didn't count the USSR.

In rural Hungary the extermination was almost total. Within the expanded borders existing during the War, there were 501 507 Jewish dead. The overwhelming majority of these had been deported to Auschwitz and died in the gas ovens there.

Heddy was the first Jewish woman to return to Hódmezö-vásárhely. A handful of men trickled home, mostly escapees from the labour camps, but she knew in her heart that Feri would not be one of them. She dared not even think about his chances of staying alive.

Other people had moved into the Bercsényi Street house, on the assumption that few if any Jews would make it home. Heddy appealed to the Council, which was suddenly willing to help anyone Jewish. Within a week the house was hers again.

She had it whitewashed quickly. She went to the peasants on their smallholdings. Most of them returned her valuables promptly. She ransacked the boxes in storage and pulled out bits of brocade. She found the very best bed linen, the set last used when Jutka was born, and made up the beds with it. She got out the best dinner service, the finest silver, and laid the table for two on a white damask cloth, with candles in silver holders.

She sat Kató down and the two of them dined alone, in state. They laughed and cried, in equal measure, throughout the meal. They congratulated each other – they'd made it!

Each treated the other as her most honoured guest. They felt themselves free again, human and civilised, eating from their own things at their own table. They were happy.

Chapter Ten

To the few Jewish men who returned, Heddy's mere presence gave hope that their women and children might also
come back. They crowded around her, offering help of any
sort. One poor fellow hung around all the time in his lone-
liness and fear, almost in love with her, she thought, except
that love was not the appropriate emotion at the time.

Some years later, Heddy heard from the Farkases, her
landlords, what had happened in Kisláng. She invited them
to Budapest to thank them for their kindness. They sat very
straight in their chairs and did not talk much, but from the
way they beamed at her and the few shy things they said,
she knew they were proud of their role in her salvation. But
she did not ask how conscious that role had been, and they
said nothing either.

They told her that a week after she had fled, the Russians
had come back and turned the villagers out of their homes.
The Germans pursued the Russians. Kisláng was turned into
a battlefield. Then the front was pushed back north, this
time irrevocably.

With the baby starting to recover and Jutka and Kató settled
in the house, Heddy turned to the next urgent items on her
agenda – the syphilis and pregnancy. She went to the Batisfalvi clinic, where I had been born; free abortions were being
offered to women raped by the Russians. The Fascist head

of the clinic, the eponymous Batisfalvi, had fled. In his place – how quickly times change – was the distinguished Jewish Doctor Polgár.

He gave her antibiotics and warned her the abortion would be dangerous because of the syphilis. After the operation he dropped in to see how she was, often. He was handsome, courteous and kind, and he looked at her in a special way.

'Nothing was ever said. There was just something beautiful between us. I was starved, not for sex so much, but for someone – and he was such a refined, wonderful man – to look at me that way ... But nothing ever happened. In the end we became friends. Funnily enough, being in that hospital with syphilis and pregnant from rape, was one of the more memorable times of my life. But a love affair just wasn't possible; it wouldn't have been moral. He had a woman he was living with, and I did not even know what had happened to your father.'

No one had news of my father. Nothing was heard from besieged Budapest. Pubi had one card from him six months before. No news of Pali either, for more than eighteen months. About those who had disappeared, there was a silence, broken by rumours, terrible snippets of revelation.

I have no evidence of my father's movements after he parted from my mother on that June morning in Budapest. All I have from that time is a small photograph, probably taken at a labour camp and sent to my mother. He has on a ludicrous army-style cap, making his full face even fuller. His neck is crammed into an ill-fitting uniform collar. He looks straight at the camera, solemn. His eyes are not so much frightened as baffled. They make me feel sorry for him, but angry too. Bafflement might have been the human, the intelligent response, but not the right one. Fear would have been better, a better weapon.

I went looking in the library for accounts of Fertörákos labour camp. I found the testimony of some men who had survived, first Fertörákos, then Mauthausen and Gunskirchen. In July 1945 one Sándor Hermann, clerk, gave his account of the camp to the National Committee for the Care of Deportees; in August an I. Ban, electrician, gave his testimony. They are distressingly similar, and from them I can get a picture of my father's last days.

On the way to Fertörákos, the men were deprived of any good winter clothing they still had. They were beaten by their Arrow Cross guards and put on starvation rations. On arrival they were housed in open barns. They would wake to find themselves covered in thick layers of snow; frozen limbs were commonplace. Young SA and SS guards beat them and played target practice with any Jew they disliked particularly.

At least 400 men died of cold and exhaustion. The dead were not recorded and their bodies were thrown into a common pit dug by other Jews. The survivors were taken on foot to Mauthausen; many were shot along the route.

There is no surprise in such accounts, but instead of vague and terrible imaginings I now have concrete images. I see why my father turned his face to the wall and died. I begin to sense him, to flesh him out. At the hour of his death he is coming alive for me.

It occurs to me, too, that maybe I am not just searching for him, but also for a small child who didn't die. I am beginning to wonder about her, that child who drank in anxiety and terror with her mother's milk and who hovered apathetic between life and death for months. Until now she has been no more than an object. Heddy's baby, not me.

I inch a little closer to her. She may be nearer than I know, deep within me, still alive. Waiting.

In January 1945 the baby – I – was beginning to put on

weight. In February, when I was sixteen months old, I sat up for the first time.

When Heddy heard that Budapest had fallen to the Russians, she decided to go there as soon as she could. Telephone lines were cut. There was no other way of getting news, of Feri and others.

'And I needed clothes. I didn't have a coat. There was nothing like that to be had in Hódmezövásárhely. On the other hand we heard that Budapest was starving, while our town was full of produce, floating in its own fat.'

She packed a suitcase full of lard, pork, ducks, flour, and fought her way onto a train. Everyone wanted to go to the capital. There was room only on top of the locomotive, where she sat clutching the suitcase for two days and nights.

Budapest was a wasteland. There was not a building unscarred, many done for, with wounds, holes, shattered windows, walls and staircases missing. Even today, it is a messy city, with plaster missing, metal exposed. 'The War,' people say matter-of-factly, when you point in amazement to a balcony hanging by a bit of formwork, or to huge holes in the plasterwork. They talk as if 'The War' was five years ago. 'Oh, and the Revolution didn't help. There was so much to do, there was never any money. And there wasn't the will. We've got used to it.'

Heddy sold her foodstuffs as soon as she was off the train. Then she went looking for people. She tracked down Pubi and Anni, Baba and Éva. All safe. They had no news of Feri, or Pali.

What about Éva, her best friend since Veres Pálné gymnasium days? No sign of her at her flat. She looked for Éva's mother, Mrs Kort, the fabled beauty whose elegance and style she had so admired as a girl. The apartment building in Akácfa Street had been severely bombed. Only half of the flat remained. The bedroom wall was gone, and the room hung out onto the street. In the remaining room where the family lived, Heddy found Éva's mother, sitting at her improvised boudoir to catch the light from the one unshattered window, her little pots of creams and unguents neatly marshalled. Yes, she said, barely looking up from rouging her cheeks, Éva was safe.

Who was alive? Who was dead? It was like a crazy roulette game in which the wheel had only just begun to turn, the counting not yet begun. The Germans were gone from Budapest but were still on Hungarian soil. It wasn't quite over.

She went to Pozsonyi Road to see what had happened to the flat. There were people living in it, Jews from Buda whose home had been destroyed in the siege. It was their home now, they told her flatly, they were not interested in who had owned it before. The authorities were vague. She retreated to Hódmezövásárhely.

On 4 April 1945 the last Wehrmacht unit left the country. On the same date most of the Jews in labour camps were freed. The Russians were now in occupation, although they seemed to keep their political distance in those early days. 'Rebuild your country,' they told the Hungarians.

Heddy was restless in Hódmezövásárhely. She wanted to return to Budapest to look for Feri, get her flat back, resume some sort of life. She was getting worried about money, too. Not long after her return she had gone to the garden where she had buried the jewellery and gold pieces. She dug in the place near the tree, thinking about that absurd night with Jancsó at her side. Where was Jancsó now? Dead, in all probability, along with all the other Jews who had not returned to Hódmezövásárhely.

The metal box was not there. She was in a panic. Without this 'safety net' there was no money. She couldn't borrow for much longer on the strength of being Mrs Ferenc Schwimmer, wife? widow? of a once wealthy man.

But then the owner of the house returned, freed from labour camp. He remembered a different tree. She lived for the next year by selling off the cache piece by piece.

She took the train to Budapest again. She went to the Schwimmer office. It was deserted, the windows shattered, the furniture upturned and piled in heaps, files trampled on the floor. Next she went to Pubi's flat in Révai Street. At the gate she almost ran into the caretaker of the small block of flats that Feri had bought as a precautionary measure before Hungary entered the war.

They recognised each other immediately, but the caretaker seemed flustered, embarrassed.

'What are you doing here?' she asked.

'I … I have to see Mr. Hiekisch.'

Something terrible, she thought.

'Tell me, you can tell me if anything is wrong.'

But he stammered, raced ahead of her up the stairs. He would not look at her but kept his gaze fixed on Pubi.

A gentleman had come to the building, he said, a gentleman who had lain next to Mr Schwimmer at the labour camp. One morning Mr Schwimmer had asked him, if he survived, to deliver a message to a certain address in Budapest. The message was for his wife. It was that he loved her and the children very much but that he was going to die. That was all. He died that same day.

The caretaker cast down his eyes and gripped his hat.

'I had half-known, half-expected it for months.' Heddy is crying a little. 'But to actually know … Your father had thought about where to send that message so carefully. Anywhere else might have been dangerous, or mightn't have got to me, but he knew that the Christian caretaker of the flats would probably stay alive, and sooner or later, I would go there.'

'I got in touch with the man who had delivered the message and asked him what had happened. He told me Feri endured what was happening for a while, then couldn't bear it any longer. He didn't have the strength to fight it. He couldn't bear the humiliation. And he was weak physically; he was never a strong man like Pali. They were starved, too, and worked so hard. Hundreds died. It was almost like a concentration camp, except that it was in Hungary, and not in the shadow of the gas ovens.'

I ask her how long he lasted, but she is not sure.

'I might be able to find out ... I heard at the end of April, or the beginning of May, 1945. Perhaps it can be found out from the books when those in Fertörákos died. It was such an everyday tragedy then, who died when ... the man I talked to, he said his heart was breaking for Feri, watching him get weaker every day. He just gave up – giving up meant that you just didn't get up one day.

'I didn't find out all the details. I think I didn't want to know. I didn't want to torture myself further. It sounds callous but everyone was dead, thousands of people had died. If you ran into someone on the street that you knew, you said, "Oh, Oh, you're alive, you made it!".

'About Pali, there was silence. The vast Russian snow-fields had swallowed him up ...

'Till I learned of Feri's death, I had hoped that I'd be reunited with the father of my children, that somehow we'd get on with things again together. Now everything was changed. I had to do it all alone. There was so much to do.'

The first move in rebuilding her life was to regain the Pozsonyi Road flat. The authorities returned two rooms to her but the third and the maid's room remained with the Buda refugees, with the kitchen and bathroom shared.

In Hódmezővásárhely she loaded her furniture onto an

ancient truck, thence onto a pontoon, which sank in the middle of the Tisza. Eventually she got it all to Budapest. Jutka, Kató and I followed.

'What was Budapest like in the first few months after liberation?' I ask.

'Everything was a struggle. There was tremendous poverty, shortages, hunger. But at the same time there was a boom. Buildings and materials were needed, goods started to come into the country, the peasants grew grain and harvested their grapes again. And the Russians let it all happen. Only when everything was going again, did they put their hands on it all.'

The liberating Russians only added to the city's miseries; they looted, burned and raped. The housing shortage was so acute that two, three families were crammed into a flat, even in the damaged flats. People turned to the famous pleasure baths of the city, those that survived, as the only way of keeping clean.

Food was scarce. Inflation was out of control. A sum that bought a loaf of bread in the mornings would no longer be enough in the evenings. The pengö rose to such incalculable amounts that the peasants traded by colour: 'One red and three blues for my chicken!' 'Only six blues for a kilo of carrots!'

Heddy thought of the spare children's clothes she had left with her friend and neighbour Józsa Tetétleni. She remembered Józsa standing at the door, kissing her, saying, 'Of course you'll come back, just come back.' How desperate she had been that day, about to flee Budapest, her future hanging in the void. Yet she had thought of the children's clothes! They would really come in handy now.

There was no reply when she rang the Tetetléni's bell. The caretaker came to the door.

'Who are you looking for?'

'The Tetetlénis.'

He stared at her. 'Haven't you heard? The Arrow Cross came for them during the seige. They're all dead.'

He told her they had arrested Józsa for safeguarding her sister's jewellery – it was called 'harbouring Jewish jewels'. The Arrow Cross took Józsa, who was six months pregnant, her husband and their two children to the riverbank and shot them into the Danube.

'I went away stunned. I thought how hardly more than a year ago I had envied Józsa, just for a moment. She had seemed so safe, protected. Now I was alive and she was dead. I felt ashamed.'

In the second half of 1945, the enormous business of sorting out who was dead or alive, and where, was in train. Every day, long queues formed outside the Red Cross and other agencies. Gusts of rumour or news ran through the queue; today there would be a list of those in Mauthausen, tomorrow Auschwitz.

Heddy haunted the lists for Pali's name, but Kató could not bear to go. She busied herself and waited for her son's return.

One afternoon Heddy was walking down the stairs from Kató's flat when she saw a small grey figure toiling up towards her.

'It was Jancsó, Jancsó from Hódmezövásárhely! I couldn't believe it. I was sure she had died with everyone else. The funny thing was I didn't rush forward to hug her. My legs gave way and I just sat down in the middle of the steps and sobbed, 'Jancsó, you're here, you're alive.' "Yes, I'm here," she said, and she gave that wry little smile of hers. "You don't believe it? Neither do I, not really." Then she sat down next to me on the step and we cried our hearts out together. She and her husband had been lucky. They were sent to

Theresienstadt, Hitler's "model" concentration camp, where there were no gas ovens, and the War finished before they could be moved on. As soon as she got back home, she came looking for me.'

I met Jancsó when I was in my twenties, on my first short trip to Budapest. She was elderly then and widowed, living on a small Government pension. We sat in her mean one-room flat and ate the goose livers that she had spent days tracking down because my mother loved them. She watched everything we did with a gentle adoring avidity. She stroked my hand. I asked her very few questions. I was not yet ready to face the past she had in her. She died long before I was ready.

Jancsó wrote to us when we went to Australia. She sent us Hungarian peasant clocks, bought from the peasants she and her watchmaker husband knew in Hódmezövásárhely. My mother was incensed when I let one go in a break-up with a boyfriend. I'd forgotten how it came to us.

★

In the Pozsonyi Road flat Heddy lived for some months in a state of war with the intruders from Buda.

'The wife was a real bitch. She had long red fingernails and very high heels, but when she was at home she wore a filthy dressing gown, did nothing all day and worked her poor old mother to death. You know the type.'

In the end, she paid them off. She set about getting the flat organised with a ferocious concentration. Within months, in a Budapest of shortages and misery, the flat became a willed oasis of order. Visitors gasped when they saw it; it was almost as if the War hadn't happened.

She had virtually no clothes, but they were not a priority. 'My home has always been my weakness. Having lost it so recently I wanted it again all the more. I've always felt that if I had my home, I could do anything.' Heddy warms to her theme. 'When we came to Australia and we finally got the Chatswood house, and then the furniture arrived, my whole attitude to being a migrant changed. When I was walking down Pitt Street I was just a "bloody reffo" who couldn't speak English properly, but when I got home, I felt myself. When I could lay my own table again, I was me ...'

'I can understand it,' I murmur, although I am not sure I can.

I am ambivalent, confused about her attitude to her surroundings. Whenever I hear the story of the return to Hódmezövásárhely and the way she and Kató sat down in a near-empty house to that celebratory meal, I am delighted, intrigued, and horrified. Barely had she had time to recover a little from the terrible months that had gone before, than she is getting out the silver and the damask; re-establishing her old patterns, reasserting what is important to her. Things, always things.

I wouldn't call Heddy a greedy woman, but objects have always signified enormously to her. They carry such full symbolism, signs of well-being and happiness, or the reverse. I have little pictures of the milestones: the fur collar of happiness, the too tight sleeves of misery. The piano, always there, in times of happiness and misfortune. The black-and-gold clock. And carpets. Carpets have always figured large in her story. Taking the Persians rolled up to the pawnshop in the bad times. Bringing some back on the tram when the worst was over. Acquiring them again, even better ones, when ease returned in the shape of Feri. Packing them to go down to Hódmezövásárhely before the birth of the baby, Distributing one here, one there, amongst the peasants before she flees.

I can see her, when she gets back to Hódmezövásárhely;

thin, badly shaken, her husband's whereabouts unknown, her future still a void, she sets about regaining her sense of order – through her things. In the two empty rooms of the habitable part of the house, she puts down the carpets, sets up a table and chairs, finds someone to cook, and lays out the dinner service for two. All as for the grandest dinner party.

She always tells me that story as if the act was a triumph over barbarism, the ultimate symbol of survival, but more than anything, as something she felt compelled to do. My reactions are mixed. To make possessions so important to her spiritual life – what can it mean? Setting that table was virtually a political act, for God's sake. Other people might paint, find causes, join movements; she makes statements through her things.

But I am not unsympathetic either. I notice that my house is starting to fill up with things, too. My pleasure in the look and feel and connotation of objects gets more intense and embracing as I get older. The mad black-and-gold clock, now thoroughly at home in my house, *is* my grandmother. The elaborate coffee set always brings me my unknown Grandmother Schwimmer.

But there's another dimension for Heddy. Her creativity has always been through her possessions. They express her beliefs, not just her taste or style. Getting back the silver and the linen in Hódmezövásárhely was getting herself back. When she is dispossessed, she feels humiliated, stripped of her essence, and she fights like hell.

★

She turned next to the office. She cleaned it up, then opened the doors. She went out to the warehouses to look for the stock. Most of it was gone. At one storehouse in a poor part of the city, an informant told her that the tenants of a nearby apartment building had looted the feathers: 'You'll find what you're looking for under their beds.'

She hired a truck, and with a policeman in tow, went to the building – a warren of one-room flats with kitchen attached. She could smell the peculiar stench of the feathers in the hallway. People were frightened at the sight of the policeman, and the big dirty bales were produced from under beds, behind doors and inside cupboards.

'We hauled the bales onto the truck. This went on for two, maybe three days. It made me feel sick to do it; my stomach churned. Imagine it. But it had to be done. I had to have the stock back. Feri wasn't coming home. Everything was on me.'

She found an old employee of the firm and took him on again. She recovered some more stock – a little from Hód-mezövásárhely, a small amount from another warehouse – and business began. She became the managing director, and went into the office every day. Kató looked after the children.

János in America demanded that she begin exporting as soon as possible. She barely knew what she was doing; she knew little about business and less about feathers. When she had gotten together enough for a shipment, János instructed her to make a customs declaration that a shipment of down was only feathers. The surplus payment for the superior down would go undeclared and be kept in America, her share put aside.

She was willing to risk it. She wanted to have money out of the country. She already knew that nothing would make her stay in Hungary, but she just did not know, yet, how she would leave.

She found a shonky expediteur willing to help. But as she stood on Nyugati station waiting for the customs inspection, she wondered at herself. The inspector passed the goods.

In early 1949, when she got to America, the money was waiting for her. That money, along with the proceeds from the sale of the diamonds smuggled out in 1938, went towards the deposit on our first house in Australia.

Regular exports to America began. She was starting to get the hang of the business; there were even parts she enjoyed.

'I liked dealing with the Ministries and big bureaucracies. I could always get what I wanted done; I liked achieving the impossible. It's something I inherited from Kató, dealing with people. Don't ask me how I did it. I was never pushy. "You'll find a way around this, I'm sure", "I would be so grateful", "I know that you will help me" ... I had them eating out of my hand. And I was younger and prettier then, with a smiling face, not an old woman like now; though even now, I have the knack. Not that I flirted with them, of course ...'

'Your Mother,' my stepfather always says delightedly, 'is the biggest flirt in the world. Watch her eyes. Watch her in action!'

★

When the Gestapo had come for Náci in early 1944, the caretaker of their block of flats had pretended not to know which hospital he was in. He was fond of Kató and the family.

Now, some time in 1946, he burst into Heddy's office, distraught.

'Madam, come at once, at once! Your dear mother is beside herself. She is out of her mind! She has news of her son.'

Heddy knew that Pali was dead.

Even then, Kató could not make herself believe her son

was gone. Some time later, in 1947, she tracked down a man who had been with Pali in the Ukraine. She wrote to him, enclosing a photo. She kept this man's letters until her death, along with the one Pali had written her before he was sent to Russia.

Heddy finds the letters in a little shoebox of Kató's things, and reads them to me. I translate freely. They have a strange formality, partly intrinsic to the Hungarian style, and partly, I suspect, because the poor man who wrote them felt his burden keenly.

My Dear Madam,

I beg your forgiveness that I write in reply to your esteemed letter only today, but after a short rest, fate forced me to travel to the country, and they sent your letter on to me there. It is with great pain that I read it and to reply is indeed a thankless task, but Madam, please be strong and trust in the Almighty.

Unhappily your son Pali will not return. It grieves me terribly to sadden your heart, but perhaps the passing of nearly five years may have healed the wounds a little. Your news is correct. Your son died in the first half of March, 1943. Despite his strong constitution, typhoid carried him away.

Dear Madam, forgive me for being the bearer of such news, but after such a time, I feel I must tell you only the truth. In November, I will be coming to Budapest, and I will be in every way at your service.

In the meanwhile, I remember Pali very well, without the aid of a photograph. He was my good friend, and we were together from the beginning to the end. The 'postman', Patek, was in contact with him to the last minute . ['Patek was the man father paid to take him food parcels,' Heddy says.]

Once more I ask you to forgive me occasioning you sorrow, and I remain, in every way, your devoted servant,

Hugó Zipser
Fehérgyarmat, October 10, 1947

Photo enclosed.

My Dear Madam,
... I understand, in fullest measure, your boundless grief ... At your request, I will try to recall all that I know about your son Pali. In the last months of 1942, we were stationed at a place called Alexsayevska, at an army munitions store where we were worked very hard. Towards the end of the year, that corporal Patek, the 'postman', was in contact with Pali a lot, which improved his situation considerably. Even in the last weeks, he received parcels from home, which at the time was a big thing. Because of this he had enough to eat.

On January 18, we were captured by the Russians in our quarters; we were not trying to escape. After a couple of weeks of a forced march, during which we suffered much hunger, we arrived at a temporary lager called Hoboda, where the most primitive conditions prevailed. Typhoid claimed fresh victims every day. Ninety per cent of the lager perished in this way. We were all carriers of the disease, but we were not really aware when poor Pali lay down one night, without the slightest sign of pain or sickness ... yet the next morning when we tried to wake him, it was in vain.

I do not remember the exact date, but it must have been in the first half of March. He is buried at the lager in an enormous mass grave.

After this we lived through more difficult and

*terrible times, until, after a long while, the situation
began to normalise. We often thought it would be better
to remain where we were and to suffer no longer.*

*These in general, dear Madam, are the replies to your
questions. Of course, there is much more to say or write,
and when I come to Budapest, I will take advantage of
your kindly invitation to visit you and will pay my
respects personally. Till then, I remain in every possible
way, willingly at your service. I kiss your hand, my dear
Madam.*

Hugó Zipser
December 3, 1947

'For a long time,' Heddy says, 'we had lived in hope. People
were held in Russia for years and finally found their way
home. . . Mother clung to any tiny hope. Then came these
letters.'

I notice, and not for the first time, that the real loss for
Heddy of this War was not her husband, but her brother.
He was her lifetime icon; Feri a passing fondness, a regret.
My father was, for her, a half-expected casualty of terrible
times. Pali's wasted life was never forgotten, or forgiven.

Chapter Eleven

'A young woman like you, so pretty too, the sooner you get married again the better.'

The matchmakers were urging Heddy to remarry. But she worried that if she did marry again, she could get stuck in Hungary forever. She didn't want to stay in a place where so many of her fellow citizens had wanted to humiliate and kill her.

One of the Rónai brothers was a possibility. Before the War the Rónais and the Schwimmers had been the two most prominent Jewish families in the feather business. Now Heddy persuaded them to join her in sueing for compensation for all the feather stock stolen during the War. Not that the compensation offered amounted to a hundredth of the real value – it was the principle.

A Rónai would be a match made in heaven for the matchmakers; two reduced family fortunes pooled, a new dynasty created. But Heddy wasn't interested in the brother on offer – a dull stick. She did like his brother, but he already had a woman. He was a small, rather ugly man, magnetically attractive. She watched for a glimpse of him in the street.

'He came up to see me a couple of times, but I didn't go to bed with him. My instinct was to stay out of anything complicated. I had too much riding on me; you kids, mother, the business. I couldn't afford a complicated love life. But I did like him, a lot.'

It was different with the Russian army officer. She met him when he was billeted with Pubi and Anni. Russian soldiers were all over Budapest, overseeing the changeover.

The Russian officer was quiet and courteous. He began to pay court to her; 'Don't even ask me in what language, but we understood each other.' It was a quiet and private affair. She visited him when she could, perhaps once a week, less often when things were busy. She knew about the wife and child in Russia.

After about six months, he was called home. Heddy, Pubi, Anni and a few friends stood waving on the street as a big army truck took him away. They had all liked him. Heddy was a little sad; her Russian had been gentle and romantic, and he was wistful about leaving her, perhaps sadder than she.

People were in a kind of frenzy, to start again, to console each other. The men who came back to find their families wiped out, were dazed, looked about them, saw women and children with husbands gone.

'People were returning from Russia, from Germany, Austria. It was like a volcano had erupted, and people landed just anywhere in the aftermath. Some people came back [from the camps] but their children did not. That was the worst. And the other way too; the children came back but their parents had perished. Everyone was desperately trying to get back some sort of life. Everyone had a story. There were stories of luck, and terrible misfortune. How in the camps the Germans had ordered one to step right, the other left. Life depended on a step.'

By mid-1946, we were thoroughly back in our middle-class routines. We were among the best-dressed children in Budapest, even if most of our clothes were hand-me-downs from

America, creditably remodelled by a children's dressmaker. There are studio photos from this time in cute poses, and pictures of us at kindergarten, climbing ladders and looking at story books.

In September 1946 we were invited to cousin Ibi's wedding. Heddy and Kató did not want to go. Ibi's first husband, a Reform Rabbi, had died in Auschwitz. Now here was Ibi, less than two years later, planning a big wedding, with lots of guests and a large reception. People gossiped that it was not in good taste, but they came anyway. Heddy persuaded Kató that they should at least show their faces for an hour or so.

We were impressively turned out for the wedding, we children in snowy piqué, Heddy in a smart tailored outfit made from an old suit of Feri's, the soft silk shirt cut from one of his. She noticed a man staring at us almost hungrily. He smiled when he caught her eye, as if in appreciation of the picture we made.

In the high-ceilinged apartment of the groom's parents, Heddy watched the guests rush the buffet. So much good food was still a rarity in postwar Budapest, and people were greedy.

'Let's stay here,' she said to Kató, taking up a post by the windows overlooking the street. 'If there's anything left later, well and good. Look at that round-faced fellow across the room, the way he's staring at us.'

The round-faced fellow had not wanted to come to the wedding either. He did not like people who flaunted their second marriages in the face of recent terrible events. But a friend from Gunskirchen concentration camp was also invited. And he had met his friend's wife at Mauthausen. There was a bond between the three of them; they went almost everywhere together.

'Come to the wedding,' they urged, 'for a little while. At least there'll be lots to eat.'

When the stampede to the tables came, he hung back. Over by the long windows of the old apartment, he watched a dark woman with two blonde children. How lovely they looked, as if nothing bad had ever happened to them. He feasted his eyes on them.

A couple of weeks later Heddy was walking along Rákoczi Street when she saw the man from the wedding, in a tram going in the opposite direction. Strange, there he is again, she thought. A week later again, she ran straight into him in the revolving doors of the Stock Exchange. They exchanged a glance of recognition, excused themselves and hurried on.

The next day, on her daily visit to the Exchange (money had to be changed almost every day to retain any value), her stockbroker said to her, 'Heddy, that man you ran into yesterday, I know him well. Gyula Weiss. He really wants to meet you.'

Why not, she thought, what's to lose? A meeting was arranged at the Cafe de la Paix.

After Gyula (Gyuszi) Weiss saw the woman with the two blonde children at the wedding, he enquired from the bride's mother, Bözsi Bleier, who she was. He knew Bözsi through one of his businesses as a grain merchant. She was a keen businesswoman, so much so that Gyuszi had a bet with his friends that she'd corner him on her daughter's wedding day and pressure him to sell her some grain.

Sure enough she took him aside, and said, 'Now, my Weiss, now relative (for they were very distantly related), when can I have some grain?'

'Bözsi, my dear, forget business today. Kick up your heels at your daughter's wedding, and call around to see me tomorrow.'

When she called the next day he asked her about Heddy.

'Oh, she's a Bleier girl. You know the Bleier brothers, all from Paks, your home town. But she's too grand for you, she wouldn't have a bar of you. Besides, she's not staying here. She'll go to America.'

Later, when she'd got her grain, Bözsi softened, and asked whether he wanted an introduction. No thank you, said Gyuzsi.

But he asked Paula, his stockbroker's sister, about her. Her face lit up; she was eager to marry him off.

'Oh, I'll arrange it. She'd be perfect for you.'

Gyuszi was appalled when the woman he had so admired at the wedding walked into the Cafe de la Paix. She looked tired, her clothes were carelessly thrown together and her maroon shoes, which did not match anything else, were distinctly down at heel.

They chatted over coffee, and afterwards, he asked her as a matter of politeness merely, when he would see her again. Her reply scared him witless.

'Well, you could come up to my flat Friday night, and we might go somewhere from there.'

Go up to her flat!

'I prefer walking,' he said hastily. 'I'll just meet you somewhere and we'll walk.'

'All right, but come up to the flat to pick me up. I'll need time to get the children ready for bed.'

As soon as she opened the door to him on Friday night, Heddy saw his eyes widen.

'I had on a white blouse and a black skirt, and maybe I'd had those shoes fixed by then. Anyway, I looked good. And the flat looked marvelous, so peaceful, everything in its place. Hardly anyone had a home like mine in 1946. And you two children came towards him, all rosy and ready for bed. I could tell he was terribly impressed.'

'All right, I'm ready to go walking.'

But he stammered, 'Oh, it's so nice here. Why don't we just stay here and talk?'

He told her all about himself; about his small-town upbringing in an Orthodox household, with a strict but loving father and a soft-hearted mother. How he had started in the grain business when he was only fourteen, done well, married a girl from Budafok and had two beautiful sons by her. His young wife and the boys, aged six and eight, had died in the Holocaust. He had survived labour and concentration camps. He was trying to piece his life back together again.

He stayed talking until 2 in the morning.

'Be careful,' Kató said the next day, 'or that small-town Jew from Paks will stick!'

'From that night on he set such a tempo, he warmed up so quickly. Before long he asked if Jóska could come up to the flat and meet me.'

Of Gyuszi's five brothers and sisters, only two had survived the War: Jóska and a sister. The two brothers had no one else left. Both had lost their wives and their two children in Auschwitz. Their parents also died there, as had most of the extended family.

Heddy understood then, what the introduction to Jóska meant.

Jóska was a rougher, handsomer edition of his brother. Both were rotund men of middle height with large, open faces. Jóska was brusque and witty, while Gyuzsi was more diplomatic. He won people around. Jóska did not need to; he had devastating charm.

When Jóska came to the flat, he sat himself in the most comfortable armchair, lit his pipe, and looked around, well pleased. The children gravitated to him. Everything was comfortable straight away.

'And how old are you?' he asked, sitting me on his knee.

'Thwee and a quarter,' I piped, and went into family legend.

Heddy liked Gyuszi Weiss. He was uncomplicated, kind, attentive. He took an immediate interest in the children. He seemed to have pulled himself together quite quickly after the War, and was making money with various ventures. It was obvious to her that he was looking for a home again, a wife and children. He was that kind of man.

One night he came to take her out to dinner. He had come straight from the Stock Exchange, where if one waited till the end of the day to change money, a couple of dollars would buy a magnificent dinner the same evening. Heddy was not long home from the office and went to change. As she left the room, I was climbing into his lap. When she came back, shy Jutka was sitting on the other knee. Heddy took in the tableau but said nothing.

They had been going out a few weeks when Gyuszi asked her to meet him at the Cafe de la Paix, scene of their first rendezvous. He made sure they had the same table. Then he proposed.

He wanted them to start a new life together, he said. It made sense; she had her tragedy, he had his, and the fact that there were two children – and he had once had two children – meant a lot to him. They would make a family again.

'That all sounds fine,' she said, taken aback. 'I'm not against the idea, but it's all too fast. I hardly know you.'

'We could go out for years and still not know each other. When we go out, I shower, put on a good suit. I'm on my best behaviour.'

'I haven't decided, I can't decide yet.'

'Then there are three possibilities ...'

She was beginning to learn that he was quite a tactician.

'You can say "yes", you can say "no", or "let's wait". But if you choose the third, it's up to you to bring it up again.'

'Let's wait then.'

'The cafe was near the law courts,' Heddy says. 'There was a dark laneway nearby. As he was walking me home, we stopped in the laneway and he kissed me and I really began to kiss him back. I thought let's find out what this is made of! I really turned his head. He hardly knew how to pick himself up after that!'

We giggle a female conspiratorial giggle, then she becomes serious.

'You know I'm going to tell you an interesting thing, that just shows you what a child he was, how romantic, even idealistic. He asked me to save myself till and if we got married. Even though we'd both been married before; it was for the illusion. To wait till I became his wife.'

'Cute,' I remark indulgently. 'Were you impressed?'

'Yes. Yes, I was touched. So after that, there were a few fiery moments, but we always held back. It took some discipline, but it was only for a few weeks; it was hardly a question of months or years.'

Gyuszi bided his time, took the pressure off her for a while. He made a point of never bringing the children sweets or presents, but he made himself familiar to them, and to Kató.

Kató was coming around. This small-town Jew might know nothing of opera but he had plenty of nous, and from everything she saw of him, a big heart. She smiled whenever she saw him, and Gyuszi teased and flattered her.

In Hungary, as in other parts of Europe, there is an autumn festival, when a pig is killed in readiness for the cold months. It is made into csabai, blood sausage, smoked meat, and then there is a feast with lots of guests. Gyuszi was invited to such a disznótoros by his business partners in Budafok.

'We can't go out this Friday,' he said to her. 'I'm obliged to my partners to go.'

She was a bit miffed. 'You could take me.'

'Better not. It would look to everyone there as if we'd made a commitment. The news would be out in no time, especially to Bözsi Bleier!'

He looked at her slyly. She pretended indifference.

'I don't care. Let's go together.'

At the end of the huge meal, their hosts presented them with a big parcel of sausages and meat.

'Let's take it home to Kató,' said Gyuszi.

'Yes, let's.'

'And do you think,' he said gently, 'now that you're compromised like this, that we could go home and tell your mother that we've decided?'

'He was pushing me by then ... deep down I knew it would be all right. He was a good man. He was so warm hearted, the way he looked at you kids and you at him. And although I was managing quite well financially by myself, I could see how well he operated. He was earning a lot of money by then. I didn't want to marry a pauper either, with two children to bring up. And Kató had changed her mind about "that small-town Jew from Paks", not that she said anything.'

Gyuszi had a standing joke with Kató about how she had looked down on him when he first started to pay court. Now she sniffed, 'And what shall I tell people my new son-in-law does for a living?'

'Tell them,' he said grinning at her, 'that he's the owner of half a horse.'

Kató laughed. One of his ventures involved delivering grain by cart, for which purpose he and his partner had bought a horse.

Chapter Twelve

In July 1945 when Gyuszi returned from Gunskirchen concentration camp, he went back to his house in Budafok to
find that his wife and children had been taken from there
to Auschwitz. He could not bear to live there again. Nearly
eighteen months later, when he met Heddy, he was living in
a rooming house in Budapest.

A few days before the wedding, she told him he could
move his belongings over. He arrived with a few suits, some
coathangers and a soda water siphon.

The wedding was delayed a couple of weeks because
János was home on a business trip from America. Heddy
did not feel right getting married again with János still in
the country. She had always been afraid of his overbearing
style. Feri had deferred to him, but she was relieved to see
that Gyuszi handled him with ease.

There were no announcements or invitations. They
arrived alone at the Dohány Street synagogue on a Sunday
morning. They didn't even have the two witnesses needed,
so Gyuszi asked the shammes or beadle, and a man on the
street who was waiting for the next wedding.

It was over in minutes. The big synagogue was soundless,
yet as they turned away from the huppe, they saw that it
had filled with people.

'The guests for the next wedding had seen us there and
they crept in on tiptoe. As we walked down the centre aisle

everyone looked at us, but without a word. They didn't know us, yet they gazed at us with such well-wishing in their eyes. They saw what a private thing it was, and their Jewish hearts spoke to us.'

At the Pozsonyi Road flat, Kató had prepared lunch. Gyuszi's brother Jóska and his new wife Klári were there, and the children.

On previous occasions, Heddy had always sat at the head of the table, but when they came home from the synagogue, she ceded her place to him.

They were to catch the afternoon train for their honeymoon in the southern town of Pécs. In the flurry of farewells at the door Gyuszi turned to her and asked, 'Have you left any money for Kató and the children?'

'Dear God, in all the excitement I forgot!'

He reached in his pocket, and gave some money to his new mother-in-law. Heddy is quite misty at the memory.

'That was to be typical of our whole life together, Suzi.'

Gyuszi and Heddy have often told me that neither was in love. Both were wary. After the War years, talk of love, even love itself, seemed out of place. Both knew they had a bargain to fulfil – to walk into the gap in each other's life and ease the pain of the past. In that, it was probably a typical postwar match.

While Gyuszi was more heavily burdened by memory, and so perhaps more needy, he was also the more cagey. He wanted an assurance of an easy divorce if things did not work. He said he had suffered enough from the loss of his first wife, with whom he had been content. But he would do everything he could to make her and the children happy. It was not a romantic approach, but she liked it.

It is a family joke that Gyuszi fell in love with us children, rather than with his future wife. He has told us, over and over, that the sight of two cute little girls in golden curls and white piqué at that wedding made more of an impression than the handsome woman hovering over them. The story is only part joke. I suspect that he made a quite conscious decision that one way of coping with the loss of his sons was to acquire other, fatherless children. We were a gift, if not from God, then a gift of healing nonetheless.

He is such a pragmatist.

And how did we children react? I cannot really remember, but it seemed the most seamless transition. He has always felt like having a perpetual Father Christmas around; as if we got all the benevolence and none of the discipline. I think mother was so grateful that he loved us so quickly that she took on all the hard parts, the moral, spiritual and practical upbringing, and left him the pleasures of being fond and indulgent.

He has been simultaneously the best of all possible fathers and yet no father at all; not much different, perhaps, from other male parents of his time.

It seems we were never asked to call him anything. Mother told us the War had taken our father from us, but God made sure good children got a second father. We accepted this. In the books in kindergarten, all children had fathers. We knew we needed one, and here he was. After only a little while, of our own accord, we started to call him 'Daddy'.

It is only since I started this book that I have thought a great deal about my real father. I have pieced him together from bits of information, from gazing at his photos, particularly one of him as a child, and from some empathy I feel for him that itself may well be imagined or artificial. I have allowed myself, for the first time, to grieve for him.

Yet I have felt a bit disloyal to Dad, the one who has been around since I was three and a quarter, before my conscious memories begin. He stepped in, didn't he? He's been with us ever since. I know that for the sake of clarity I should henceforth call him my stepfather, but I can't do it. The connotation is wrong. He is Gyuszi, or Dad.

I ask Dad if he will do a few hours on tape with me. I tell him Mother is centre stage, but I need some more information on him.

He is by far the more difficult to interview; partly because Heddy sees her life, or the Hungarian years of it at least, as a panorama; a worked-out, worked-over drama into which she can dip at will, whereas his account is more in quirky incidents, moral tales, jokes and stories in which he is the leading light. He has a need to be confident of himself, and to squeeze as many good things out of life as he can.

About the Holocaust, he is closed, perhaps because he was closer to its vortex. When Mother can't remember some historical fact, she says, 'Ask your Father, he'll remember.' In fact he is far hazier than she on dates and places. I get glimpses of abysmal suffering and moments of heroism. It is all in little cameos; of his luck, his helping others, moments when things were funny, moments when things were beyond bearing. I get a strong feeling that I must respect the silences and the gaps.

From 1939 on, Gyuszi was called up for three or four months each year to do a stint in a labour camp. The first three years were unremarkable. He usually managed to get himself a desk job, didn't have to work too hard and got on well with the officers. He made himself and his accounting skills indispensable, so that he could often mediate for the other men, saving them beatings, getting them extra leave.

In 1943 his company was sent into a remote region of

Transylvania, and for the first time conditions were desperate. The men were cold and hungry and morale was low. Rumours swept the camp that due to the intervention of the Bishops in Budapest, all those who converted to Christianity would not be sent to the front. Only Gyuszi and a few others held out.

'But you know when Rosh Hashanah and Yom Kippur came around – I helped conduct the service – most of the new "converts" snuck into the room and joined in.'

In early 1944 they were sent on a forced march to a camp in Poland. They walked through the day and night, then dropped where they stood, waking to find themselves lying on fields of fresh cow dung.

In June, Gyuszi wangled himself leave and went home to Budafok, just outside Budapest. He remembers his eight-year-old son, Gyuri, running towards him on bow legs, arms wide.

His wife and sons were crowded into one room of their house, which had been converted into a Jewish House, but they were well. A Christian friend regularly brought them food – the friend who had bought Gyuszi's business in 1939 when the anti-Jewish laws began to bite.

Gyuszi returned to the labour camp. At the end of June, around Gyuri's ninth birthday, all the Jews in the town were taken to Auschwitz. On 7 July, Eichmann was recalled to Germany. The deportations ceased.

For Gyuszi, as for most Hungarian Jews, the second half of 1944 and the beginning of 1945 was the critical time, the time of jousting with death.

After a few months in Poland, his 'company' was sent back to Kassa in northeastern Hungary. They were used to such sudden uprootings and shifts without explanation. But then they were moved from Kassa in wagons; there had never been wagons before. They were transported to Nagy-cenk, one of the towns on the Austrian border used as staging posts for the concentration camps. Feri's camp, Fer-törákos, was not far away.

At Nagycenk the SS were in command, although the immediate guards were baby-faced Hungarian conscripts. Eight hundred men were crammed into the barn where Gyuszi slept. There was one open pit latrine. Typhoid carried off dozens each day, and a drop-sided peasant cart did the rounds, picking up the dead. Gyuszi came down with the disease but was saved, he thinks, by the advice of a doctor friend to have himself carried into the fresh air every day, and by the extra portions of soup that a friendly woman in the kitchens smuggled out to him.

At the end of 1944, they were moved to Mauthausen, Hitler's 'show' concentration camp. It had a magnificent entrance, like a sports palace. Behind the camp, in a kind of valley, was an extra compound filled with tents, surrounded by barbed wire and high watch towers. The guards no longer entered the compound for fear of the typhoid and dysentery sweeping the camp. Food was brought in on bil-lycarts; each man received half a loaf of bread a week and, twice a day, a thin turnip soup. There were constant fights over food. The Germans stayed in the towers and shot any starving man who went near the barbed wire to eat grass. There was no work. All pretence of running an efficient concentration camp was gone. Everyone was waiting.

Early in 1945 transports moved constantly out of Mau-thausen. Some of the remaining inmates were moved to Gunskirchen, perhaps some sixty kilometres away. On the march they ate grass and raw potatoes from the fields. Anyone too exhausted to go on, or who strayed from the line, was shot.

'I had an inspiration during that march,' Gyuszi tells me.

'My German has always been good because we had a Fräulein as kids, and it got better at Mauthausen. The Nazis were always impressed by someone who could speak German well. I was chatting to this guard; he seemed quite amiable. Suddenly I said, "Look, we both know you've lost the war. It's only a matter of time. Give me your name and address and I'll give you mine. If you don't shoot anyone who steps out of line, I'll vouch for you after the war." He looked at me, and said, "It's a deal." And there were no more shootings.'

Gunskirchen concentration camp had once been a munitions factory. It was in the middle of the forest and well camouflaged.

At Gunskirchen it was a waiting game; who could last another day, then another, until liberation. Many died every day. The survivors tried to stay in the open air, and to avoid any expenditure of crucial energy.

A young French political prisoner had a clandestine radio, so they knew just how close the Allies were. By the end of April they could hear gunfire in the distance.

But the brutalities of the SS did not abate. One officer in charge of doling out food saw a Jewish lad drink his soup in two starving gulps, then asked, 'Would you like some more?'

'Yes sir, I could do with some more.'

'Open your mouth then, I'll give you more.'

He shoved his gun into the boy's mouth and shot him dead.

Gyuszi tells another story, not without a little pride, of the day he saw a youth tied to a tree. An SS guard stood before him, his revolver drawn. Gyuszi didn't know him; he was new to the camp. The boy was trembling in terror.

'What happened?' Gyuszi asked quickly in Hungarian.

'I stole bread,' the boy gasped.

Gyuszi marched up to the SS officer and clicked his heels. 'Sir,' he said in his most officious-sounding German, 'before you take action, I have something I wish to report, sir. In another camp, sir, this boy was in my company, and he was an excellent worker at all times. Completely honest and reliable. He has typhoid; it has affected his brain. There can be no other reason for his stealing bread, sir.'

The German's eyes pierced through him. 'Is this true?' he barked.

'Jahwohl!' Gyuszi barked back.

The officer handed him his baton.

'I won't shoot him if you give him twenty-five of the best, here and now.'

'Yes sir!'

Gyuszi, who had never hit anyone in his life, laid into the boy with all his strength.

'Not that I had any strength left. I don't think I hurt him much. The next day I was making my way to the latrines in the knee-deep mud when suddenly the boy throws himself in front of me, clutching my ankles, trying to kiss my feet. He was just a Jewish kid from Munkács. An orthodox Jew with a long beard said to me, "You're made for life now Weiss, for it says in the Torah, He who saves a single life creates the world."'

One morning the camp woke to find that the Germans had put on the civilian clothes they had long had hidden in their rucksacks, and fled.

Some who were strong enough left the camp then, others stayed on, waiting for the Americans to arrive. Gyuszi did not go. His wife's cousin, a young man of twenty, was on the point of death, and he did not want to leave him.

A Jewish peasant named Fleischner raided the deserted German store and found a horse's thigh. He cooked it and made soup from the bones, and they lived on that until the Americans arrived.

The Americans drove their jeeps into the camp on Friday 4 May 1945. Gyuszi's young relative had died that morning.

A soldier jumped from his jeep and came towards them.

'You're free men. You can go.'

'Where will we go?'

They stared at him. Weak and starving, the words 'free men' meant nothing to them.

Gyuszi explained, through the interpreter, about his wife's cousin.

'Have you buried him?'

'Not yet. We're waiting for the body to cool.'

'I'd like to see him.'

They uncovered the body. The boy was good looking, with a fine forehead and wavy black hair. He weighed perhaps thirty kilos.

The American soldier wept.

The Americans had no rescue plans for the surviving Jews in the camp. But they did direct them to a warehouse full of food two or three kilometres away, and told them they had access to it till 4 o'clock, when it would be open to the public. They stopped frequently on the road because of extreme weakness. At the warehouse, they were too feeble to open the sacks of flour and sugar and take what they needed. They lay on the floor, slit the sacks and fed like pigs from what dribbled into their mouths.

When the local populace began to arrive, Gyuszi said to his little group, 'Look for the farmer with the best horses. We'll billet ourselves there.'

The farmer with two beautiful draft horses was more than willing to put them up in his barn. He thought it would be a mark in his favour with the conquering Americans.

'The Austrians didn't know yet,' said Gyuszi, 'that the Americans didn't really give a damn about us Jews. Why, it's known that Mrs Roosevelt begged the President to bomb Auschwitz to put a stop to it, but he wouldn't do it.'

The sixteen men in the barn lying on clean straw thought they were in paradise. They followed the advice of a local doctor to eat nothing but bread, milk and soup for the first few days. The doctor turned out to be a Nazi in hiding, but he saved their lives. Of the 4000 to 5000 people liberated from Gunskirchen, some 800 died on regaining their freedom. They couldn't stop eating.

It was another three months before they limped home to Budapest. Gyuszi went home to Budafok and learned what had happened to his wife and children. Then he went to Paks, his home town, to find everyone gone. Before being taken to Auschwitz, his father and mother had been put into a Jewish House – the old people's home which Samuel Weiss had founded and funded.

Gyuszi took a room in a boarding house in Budapest. For six months he sat in his room and did nothing. For the first and only time in his life, he lost the will to act. He felt nothing; just gratitude for a clean bed and for food. He barely knew that what he was feeling was grief, deep and intense. He ceased practising as an orthodox Jew.

Gradually Jóska got him interested in a couple of business ventures. They became partners, and by the end of 1946 they were making money hand over fist, with interests in grain, a distillery, a brick factory, the Stock Exchange and Government concessions. One of Gyuszi's partners was the Christian friend who had helped his family in Budafok.

There were women galore in Budapest, eager to remarry. Gyuszi had his pick, but they bored him after a while. There was one woman with two little girls that he wanted to marry, but she said no.

In September 1946, he went with his friends to a wedding, and saw Heddy, Jutka and me standing by the tall windows.

★

In 1966, I visited Hungary with Mother and Dad. It was my first trip back. I hadn't been keen to go. I didn't want to know a great deal about the past, in case it swallowed me up.

One day we hired a car, and my sister and I and Dad (we left Mother behind for some reason) went to Paks, the town where he was born. We did a lot of things on that warm somnolent European day. We ate Dad's favourite fish in a roadside cafe where the proprietor still remembered him, we saw the house where he grew up, we visited the one remaining Jew (everyone else was either exterminated or had left). We tasted wine in the underground cellars in the hills behind the town. We saw the deserted synagogue, whose new stained glass windows had been paid for by my Uncle Jóska while he cursed God and religion forever more.

By mid-afternoon, when the sun was at its hottest, the real reason for our visit couldn't be put off any more. We headed for the Jewish cemetery. It was on a little-used track, a short way out of town. Near the gates was a small house. A peasant came towards us offering Dad water for his ablutions. His wife was hanging out the washing. She assured the respected Mr Weiss that the graves were being looked after, they were kept neat. The couple took care of graves whose upkeep was paid for from faraway places all over the world. Dad sent regular money through channels from Australia.

We waded through the stillness and the waist-high pas-palum and weeds. My sister and I looked blankly at the Hebrew we couldn't read, and burrs stuck to our bare sticky legs. The heat, the paspalum, the silence. Like Australia in a dream with Hebrew letters.

Dad wandered from grave to grave, muttering the names and genealogies and fates of people we'd never known. We were dazed, bored, overawed, hot. Dad was in a trance, plodding on and on, looking for his kin.

When he found the single grave he was looking for, we didn't need Hebrew to know that the names of his wife and two children and his parents were on it, and those of his brothers and sisters. He put one hand on the high headstone, and stood, minute after slow minute, with his back to us, shoulders and head bent forward. I didn't try to look at his face. Then he began to gather stones to put on the grave, and desultorily, we helped him. Then we gathered stones for the grave of Jóska's wife and children.

But it didn't end there. There were debts to pay, to the living and dead, those who would expect him to put stones on the graves of their kin. We spent hours looking for the right graves, looking for stones among the weeds. As we laid the stones on the graves, he slowly recovered himself a little, and told us of family trees, friends, children from his lost world.

We struggled out of the cemetery. There were negotia-tions with and promises from the couple at the gate who were patently not doing their job. We drove back to Buda-pest, worn out.

The window on Dad's pain had been forced open for a little while, and I had seen inside. At that time I couldn't look for very long; I was still scared that the pain he had learned to bear would crush me.

Part III
Sydney

'Crushed jacaranda flowers on hot asphalt'

Chapter Thirteen

When I was in fifth class at Artarmon Primary School, we had to write a novel for our term project. Mine, called *Seven Arrive*, told the story of my new extended family; how we left Hungary to escape the wicked Communists and after some bumpy adventures settled down in Australia, land of freedom and opportunity.

CHAPTER ONE
AUSTRALIA – TO BE OR NOT TO BE?

It was a full moon that night. Its soft light shone on the bomb devastated city of Budapest, showing the terrible destruction that War had caused. Under a ruined building a homeless family huddled together unable to sleep from the intense cold. All was quiet in the surrounding streets, all except a dim light that glowed in one of the wide windows of a flat-house. A sleepy child, snug in bed, might have looked out of the window and have wondered what was going on behind the yellow curtains.

In the room behind the yellow curtains four people were sitting with tense faces and anxious eyes. It was the adults of the Verö family. It was plain that they were going to discuss something important that night – something that must be done ...

The grandfather clock in the silent eerie hall boomed out a ghostly twelve.

'Are you awake dear?' Mr Verö whispered.

'Yes.'

'I thought you might be. Worrying I suppose. Get up and put on your dressing gown. I want to show you something.' Mystified, Mrs Verö got up and put on her dressing gown.

'Come with me.'

He went down the hall, opened the door of the children's room and drew her in. 'Look,' he said, pointing to the two bright heads on the pillows. 'Do you want them to lead a life of misery, fear and oppression, or one of freedom and happiness? The first they, I am certain, will lead in Hungary, the latter in Australia.' Mrs Verö did not answer but gazed with her heart in her eyes at the two children who she loved so dearly. Seeing the look on her face Mr Verö said nothing but after a few minutes gently suggested getting back to bed.

I illustrated the frontispiece of *Seven Arrive* with a picture showing Budapest on one side of the ocean, Sydney on the other. Budapest is being bombed. A big building is prominently labelled Communist Headquarters. On the Sydney side I draw a nice suburb with a park, Artarmon Public School, a building labelled Housing, another, National Bank. In between the two shores, a big ship, the SS *Freedom*, steams towards Australia.

In Chapter One, when my 'father' has a brush with a Russian soldier in a park, the decision to leave is sealed:

… [The soldier] burst into a coarse laugh, shouting to his companions, 'Come comrades, look what we have here! A Hungarian dog who thinks that by his pretty speeches he can liberate his fellow dogs!' So, thinking himself extremely witty, he burst into a fresh roar of laughter, kicked Mr Verö, saying, 'Let's see how we can tame the dog!' Mrs Verö screamed and pressed the two girls to her while they

watched the proceedings with frightened dilated eyes. Had it not been for his wife and children Verö would have landed the Russian a nice right to the chin and taken the consequences, but as it was he just had to remain passive although his heart burned within him ...

The decision had been made. They were going to leave loved ones, friends of life-long standing, the country of their birth, social life, a fair amount of wealth, and most painful, their past life. Was freedom worth all this? It was!

My almost-eleven-year-old account hardly touches on the War, far less the Holocaust. We leave solely because of Communism; the Nasty Russians were very much in vogue in 1954. I saw our lives as really starting in Australia.

Perhaps the Holocaust was too awful and too recent for me to talk about. I saw it then as unprecedented, mysterious, almost a natural disaster that we had the enormous luck to escape. It was the Unmentionable.

In reality, for a year or so after their marriage, Heddy and Gyuszi led a busy, quite comfortable life. Initially Heddy kept up her role in the Schwimmer feather business and watched Gyuszi embroil himself in the postwar recovery boom. We went to school and kindergarten, and superficially things went back to normal.

But the political situation made Heddy's keen nose twitch and lent an extra edge to her desire to leave. The home-grown Communists were becoming daily more powerful, and the Russian occupiers, so low key in the first year after liberation, were beginning to show their hand.

'I couldn't see your future, nor mine ... In my guts I couldn't bear it there any longer, and I knew that what was to come would be doubly unbearable. I felt this police state atmosphere, everyone began to be afraid. Then tighter controls here, then nationalising this, nationalising that. I felt that the noose was tightening again, like Hitler, except then it was against the Jews, now against everyone, which was easier to bear, but then again, one had to make friends with another "ism". And I didn't count after all – I wasn't a peasant or the proletariat ... once there had been a big, wealthy firm – what might they want with me now? I felt danger, really, but Daddy said, "I can always get a Government job." (They'd already offered him a quite high level ministry job.) But I said, "And then how many arses will you have to lick? You'll have to enrol in the Party and bark with the other dogs. And there'll always be more and more controls and less and less income, and they'll take away rights and earning possibilities." But he said, "From the money we have outside, we can always have parcels sent", and I said, "I'm not basing a future on parcels." '

Nothing much mattered to Gyuszi, after the camps, beyond the continuing miracle of a clean bed and enough food to eat. He thought things would work themselves out one way or the other, under Communism or Capitalism.

Heddy worked on him. He said he would not go anywhere without Jóska. So she worked on Jóska, which was easy.

'You're right,' said Jóska, 'we should leave this rotten stinking arsehole of a place. After what these bastards have done and what's yet to come, we can't go on living here. Let's get the hell out.'

And so Jóska's wife Klári was brought around, too.

There were eight years between Jóska and Gyuszi. The brothers had always got on, but after the War they forged business and personal links that were to be indissoluble. They were totally different and oddly complementary. Jóska had a streak of brilliance, a unique wit and a peripatetic, brusque personality that was endearing if you were a friend of his and infuriating if you were not. Gyuszi had a smoother surface; he was persistent and consistent. His loyalties and interests were plain – family and business. His contradictions were less obvious and dazzling, but they were there; kindness verging on sentimentality, toughness verging on ruthlessness.

The brothers became partners in every way. They fed each other emotionally, and gave each other ideas. Loyalty was their credo – to each other and to those belonging to them.

The new wives were also very different, but they, too, developed a complementarity. Klári was a quiet woman, inward to the point of secretiveness, with some inner part of her locked shut. Heddy the extrovert, the doer, warmed her. And Heddy could talk to Klári. Jóska and Klári's new baby, also called Zsuzsi or Little Zsuzsi, was fifteen months old when we left Hungary. She was a chip off her father's block – wilful, lively and utterly charming.

Even before we left, the brothers felt they had forged a strong unit; two wives, three children (two of them 'prefabricated' as Jutka joked later), with which to start a new life. We children were happy with our new aunty, uncle and baby cousin, and the women knew how much store their men set by the new alliance. We were beginning again.

Heddy made sure that she was going into the New World prepared. They could not take out Hungarian currency, so she spent what she could on portables. Three years later Jutka and I were still decked out in the tiny pleated grey skirts and white galoshes which were the height of Budapest fashion in 1948. Australian kids wore only longer tartan skirts and black gumboots.

A containerload of goods left before we did. Inside was the black and gold clock, most of Heddy's carpets, a bronze chandelier of magnificent weight, the Maria Theresa crystal chandelier and her elegant 'style' furniture from her first marriage. Some objects, assessed as valuable to the state, had to stay in the country – among them Kató's Bösendorfer grand.

How weird it all looked in our suburban red-brick bungalow in Chatswood! Our neighbours would go away saucer-eyed. I never knew whether to be proud or embarrassed.

Our family was one of the last to leave Hungary on legal passports before the Iron Curtain came down. The Communist leader Rákosi proclaimed an amnesty, encouraging the departure of some intellectuals and members of the bourgeoisie seen as troublesome to the regime. Their passports were stamped 'never to return'.

It was a tense and hazardous time. There was fear in the air again, of the knock on the door, of fortunes reversing overnight. Gyuszi 'donated' our flat to the police to ensure our safe passage from the country. Heddy and Klári made preparations to leave in secrecy, for fear of jealous neighbours.

The special passports eventually came through, but landing permits, to anywhere, were the stumbling block. Our permits for Australia came through a chance meeting on a Budapest street with a Hungarian businessman living in Australia. He charged 500 pounds for the favour, and the permits did not include Kató. She would join us after a year, if she could get out of Hungary.

There remained the business of our names. Heddy had persuaded Gyuszi to change his name; many Jews were changing their German-Jewish names to something indistinguishably Hungarian, like Varga. Gyuszi wanted to adopt us children, but the procedure was too long-winded. They

hit upon simply Magyarising our names to Varga too, ena-
bling us to leave looking as if we were his. Not wanting to
confuse us, Heddy just told us to say our name was Varga
if asked.

We left Hungary on 12 December 1948. We said goodbye
to Kató at her Tátra Street flat. Jutka and I walked down
five flights of stairs crying our eyes out, convinced we would
never see our grandmother again.

We were booked on the train to Vienna. No one was
allowed to come to the station to farewell us. Just as the
Gestapo had patrolled the railway stations during the War,
so now the AAVO, the secret police.

On the train the adults were silent, waiting for the border.
We were quiet, too, sensing their tension.

A bulky official with important moustaches and watery
eyes opened the compartment door. He scrutinised our
papers, then leaned forward to pat my head.

'And what is your name little Miss?'

I punched my fist in frustration.

'I know, I know, I know, but I've forgotten!'

The big man stared and breathed heavily. He looked from
face to face. Heddy's hands were cold, as of old.

He closed the door, walked down the corridor and off
the train. No one spoke. They watched the countryside roll
past. Austrian countryside. They hugged and kissed and
toasted the New World in apricot brandy, certain they
would never see Hungary again.

We made our way to London where Rózsika and her family
had settled. We had berths booked on the *Queen Mary*,
bound for the United States, where Heddy planned to see
János and pick up the precious hard currency that he was
minding for her. From there, Australia.

Heddy had allowed herself few farewells. She was

estranged from Baba. She persuaded herself that, apart from Kató and Pubi, who would hopefully follow us out one day, no one else really mattered.

But she wrote one farewell letter from the deck of the *Queen Mary* as it left Southampton – to the silver-haired doctor who performed the abortion in January 1945; the love affair that never was.

'Dear István,' she wrote. 'Before I leave Europe to start a new life on the other side of the world, I feel I must say goodbye to you with just a few words. I will never forget the way you cared for me. I will cherish the memory of your friendship all my life.'

Chapter Fourteen

At Sydney Airport the man who had extracted 500 pounds from us for the entry permits sent his secretary to meet us. We drove past the factories and flimsy fibro houses of Mascot, past the stinking tannery works, and into a grey and monotonous city.

We spent our first night, and the next couple of weeks, in the Brooklyn Hotel in lower George Street. Today the Brooklyn has been renovated into trendiness. In 1949 it was a sailor's dive, with stained floral carpets, dark stairs and airless corridors.

London and America had done nothing to prepare us for the Sydney of 1949; its colours were brown and drab, its buildings haphazard and unlovely, its people closed in, stiff. The men looked identical in shapeless grey suits, the women dowdy in floral dresses. Even the smells were alien; the rankness everywhere of mutton and dripping, the whiff of fish and chips.

The adults wandered the streets and ate in cheap cafes. The waitresses slopped milky tea at them without asking how they drank it. Oh, Hungary where tea came amber coloured, served deliciously with rum or lemon or both!

They looked up a few prewar Hungarian émigrés, none of whom were particularly welcoming. One man gave them coffee and some curious advice before he showed them the door. At all costs, he said, they must buy some singlets, and make wills.

Heddy felt sick with responsibility.

'For three days I was in a terrible emotional state which I tried to hide, because I thought quite simply [they] would kill me, they'd attack me, saying what have you done, where have you brought us? I was the one convinced we had to leave. But then we had to arrive too! But no one said anything, everyone kept it inside. We just looked and walked and walked, totally lost.'

Little Zsuzsi got sick, and they were in a panic to find a Hungarian-speaking doctor. They got out of the ill-smelling Brooklyn but the next hotel, a genteel establishment at Elizabeth Bay, threw them out for heating the baby's milk in the room. The third hotel, an anonymous place in Phillip Street, was more within their means.

As the only one with a little English, Heddy had to deal with the estate agents. She found herself helpless against the impenetrable Australian accent.

Rental properties were scarce. We ended up in a small holiday flat at Manly, in a liver-coloured block of four or six facing the ocean. You can still see those blocks between the glitzy high rise. I can remember a rickety back staircase, mangy sofas and grubby holiday linen.

Heddy and Klári went shopping to celebrate. In a Sydney pre-capuccino and delicatessen, they found a German grocer from whom they bought real coffee and schnitzel, and went home to cook their first meal.

At dusk, Heddy sat on the Corso and watched the ocean. She wrote to Kató:

I'm sitting here on a wooden bench, with the pines beside me. I don't look back to the miserable flat where I can hear the rats in the walls at night and the wallpaper is peeling off the walls, but at the ocean and the horizon beyond, where I see our bright future. I

don't look at how things are now, but into the
distance, where it's beautiful ...

The first weeks in Australia came close to being the biggest
trauma of our lives. It was like being born again, but without
the luxury of time to grow and learn. Knowledge had to be
acquired very fast and acted upon immediately. Small mistakes
had disastrous consequences. Every tragi-comic incident, each
tiny milestone, has gone into family legend, but defies retelling
because its poignancy derives from the first-time, do-or-die
quality of all our actions at the time.

But after the first awful months were over, the energy of
the battle gripped us, and in many ways the early years were
the best. There was no time for phantom shadows, or com-
plication. We were Carving Out A New Life, and the agenda
of each day was self-evident. My parents were relatively
young, and had the will to make this strange new country
yield them not only a living but a life. Each year brought
new achievements. In that first year, they bought a radio
and started a business. In the second, they bought a car, an
Austin A40, and dabbled in a second venture. In the third
year, they moved house, and began to have a bit of social
life. In the fourth year, they bought a Holden and went on
holiday to the Blue Mountains. By the fifth year, they were
fulfilling the migrant's dream: building their own home on
their own block of land.

They began to settle in and gained the stability, predict-
ability and prosperity that Mother had dreamed of. There
was no more war, revolution or persecution. We children
were growing up with plenty to eat, out of danger, going to
school. Gyuszi was a good husband, and, as the years went
by, an even better provider.

But the drama turned internal. The more deeply cherished
dreams of harmony, happiness, did not always turn out. In

adjusting to another life, we lost or diluted much of our former selves. And repercussions, echoes of the past, came years later to bedevil us in forms that we often did not understand, or even recognise.

When we arrived we had enough money to live on for a few months and for a deposit on a house. We found one on the border of Willoughby and Chatswood, a dark, red-brick affair with an awkward shape, but it had two bathrooms for the two families, and a largish garden.

Gyuszi and Jóska did not want to get stuck in dead-end low-paid jobs. They spent the first months walking the streets, sussing out kiosks, leather goods, dry cleaning, whatever. Almost every morning at 11 they rendezvoused with other Hungarian refugees under the Post Office clock in Martin Place, for an exchange of tips and moral support.

Eventually they bought into a clothing factory on Parramatta Road, which we always called the Becher factory, after its former owner. No one knew anything about the rag trade, but Klári had once done a course in cutting children's clothes, so she became the designer and cutter.

Heddy was to look after the three children. For the first time in her life, she was a full-time housewife, cooking and cleaning for seven. She wrote panicked letters home for recipes. The Ruszwurm confectionery course had taught her nothing about cheap family meals.

'I know we will fight again when we are together,' she wrote to Kató, 'but it doesn't matter. I need you here ... The big news here is that we have bought a radio! You can't imagine how happy we are.'

She missed Kató badly.

In November 1948, three months before we arrived in Australia, the first Holdens came into production and became an essential part of the Australian dream. When we got one, in 1953, we were thrilled. There is a photo of us hanging lovingly all over it, like any other Australian family.

Refrigerators were just coming into vogue; a few families had them, sometimes (in pride of place) in the living room, next to the sole power point.

In 1949, Menzies regained power and held onto it all through my growing years. He promised to ban the Communist Party, the promise that set the tone of the fifties. The next year, Australia joined the war against Korea.

The Snowy Mountains Hydro-Electric Scheme started up in July 1949, shortly after our arrival. Almost every week it seemed, for at least the next decade, there were pictures in the *Daily Mirror* of smiling New Australians, a mini-United Nations, out there in the wilds, forging Australia's future.

For the first time in Australia's history, wogs of every sort were swamping migrants of British stock. The Australians and the New Australians eyed each other askance. The embarrassment was reflected in the very words 'New Australian', as if we were to become Australian as quickly as possible, the 'New' a necessary but temporary appendage. It was reflected, too, in the Good Neighbour movement, a Menzies idea, which had a touchingly naive aspect, as if the neighbours being nice to you was all that was needed. Although there was something in it, in our case. I doubt if any of our three sets of neighbours in the moves we made between 1949 and 1954 were in the Good Neighbour Movement, but they were our lifeline and our passport to the 'real' or 'old' Australia.

On my first day at Manly Public, I had walked unawares into the boys' toilet and had been thrown out by some large, jeering Australian boys. I had refused to go back. Now Heddy enrolled us at Willoughby Public.

This time I invented a fantasy language as a defence against my useless Hungarian and lack of English; I inhabited my own country which was full of fascinating adventures. I'd tell Mother such plausible tales that she almost believed me – anything was possible in this God-forsaken place.

Judy, more firmly rooted in reality, suffered; she did not speak like the other girls, she was not dressed like them, her mother looked like no other mother; she did not knit or make lamingtons or wear the right sort of hats.

Yet within a few months we were moving with increasing ease between our two worlds. Our neighbours' rooms and gardens were magical stage sets into which we could wander, to learn and absorb. We just wanted to stop being different, in any way, in the shortest possible time. Within a year, as if by osmosis, we had picked up the language, and had lost all traces of accent. We trailed our battered globites home from school on hot afternoons, pretending, even to ourselves, that we were not so very different from other kids. We were so intent on mastering the present that our former lives receded, half-forgotten, certainly repressed.

But every time one of our new friends met our parents, there were awful reminders; everything about *them* – their accents, voices, clothes, laughs – marked *us* out as different. Heddy tried, for our sakes, to learn new ways. She went to Mothers' Meetings, and nodded and smiled and understood nothing. She accompanied us to birthday parties and learned to copy the shiny party hats, the streamers, the hundreds and thousands and sausage rolls, but she baulked at the red and green jelly. The photos of our children's parties look almost like those of other kids, except that we still don't look quite right; we're still a little too pristine and carefully dressed, and, well, European. A photo of Mother and us, taken somewhere in the city, shows us in matching cream corduroy coats, little cream felt hats, immaculate white shoes and socks. We are gorgeous, but all wrong.

At the end of our first year's residence Heddy applied for entry permits for Kató and Pubi.

In Hungary the Iron Curtain had been rung down heavily and there was a brisk trade in clandestine escape routes. Kató and Pubi set their plans in motion as soon as they got Heddy's coded message that the permits had arrived.

In *Seven Arrive*, I went to town.

'Vera! Run and get the mail! Hurry!' Mrs Verö's tone was urgent and her face grew a little white as her daughter hurried to get the mail. Vera came flying up the path, her face red with excitement.

'Mummy! Vienna postmark! Is it news about Granny?'

Tearing open the envelope, Mrs Verö grabbed the sheets and for a moment couldn't read because the letters danced before her eyes. She steadied herself and read the first couple of lines, then collapsed onto the ground, white and shaken. 'She's done it! Escaped. Oh, I can't believe it!' ...

'Dearest Laci and Magda,' it began. 'We're free! My companion and I managed to reach Vienna after the nightmare escape and are now resting for we were completely exhausted. It was terrible. We slept in factories, fields, one always on the watch. Guards were everywhere and once we were almost shot. The peasants who we were told to contact helped us tremendously. Once I was disguised as a deaf-mute peasant woman pretending to be taking my grandchild to see some relatives and thereby managed to go quite a long distance by train. One day we were nearly discovered when guards came to search a furniture factory but by some freak mischance they didn't look into the tiny room in which we were huddling. I am glad it is all over ...'

All this was true, more or less. Kató and Pubi were in hiding in Bratislava for weeks. We had no news until they reached Vienna.

The majestic glittering white ship slowly sailed into the busy bustling harbour while the crowd on the dock cheered and waved and a frail old woman on board strained her tear-dimmed eyes to catch a glimpse of her loved ones. In half an hour the gangplank is down, and the family is milling round her, laughing and crying for they are all reunited again.

In the books I was devouring, people had small, dainty grandmothers with tear-bedimmed eyes. When Kató sailed to Melbourne on the SS *Vollendam*, she was in reality robust, larger and louder than ever, and had the other émigrés eating out of her hand. When she spied Heddy waiting on the wharf, she bellowed, 'Heddy, there you are! My God, what have you done, you're as fat as a pig!'

And in real life, we could afford only one fare to Melbourne. Judy and I waited at Central Station, our white piqué welcome dresses ruined by the chocolate icecream we had gobbled in our excitement.

'Who the hell are the Tomp-shons?' Kató asked Heddy on the train from Melbourne. 'I got a telegram from them on the ship.' The Thompsons were our neighbours. They had lived through the tension of Kató's journey out with us. The day of her arrival they fixed a Welcome sign on our gate, adorned with a small Australian flag. Mrs Thompson borrowed Mother's keys and put flowers in every room.

The Thompsons were unbelievably kind to us. They were the first of a little band of people my parents collected around them in the early years with whom they then kept in touch for life. There was always someone, usually a neighbour, perhaps an English teacher, who was both sympathetic to and fascinated by us. We were a source of amusement, glamour and absurdity. They laughed at us and with us, and we taught them all sorts of things – paprika, sour cherry slice, opera, cinzano, and a different conversational dynamic.

The Thompsons became for us the emblem of all that was good about Australia. They were unflappable, wholesome, and a little slow – until he, in particular, had a drink. Heather Thompson invited Mother to afternoon tea and introduced her to Sao biscuits with a slab of tomato and a sprig of parsley on top and passionfruit sponge, and sat patiently through a conversation by dictionary.

'I'll never forget the night we invited them over for coffee and cake. After we'd limped through the evening, we were all exhausted from the effort. We saw them to the door. They stood there, we stood there. They wouldn't leave. I began to sweat. My English had completely dried up. Still they wouldn't go! Later I found out that in Australia the guests never open the door first. In Hungary, it's the other way around.'

Miss Leary, the elocution teacher up the road, gave them English lessons. She was straight backed, genteel and reserved. Sensing that she was about Heddy's only contact with 'a better class of person', she invited her to one of her monthly literary teas. Heddy sat among the flowered teacups and dainty sandwiches with the crusts cut off and didn't understand a word. She didn't go back. But she did try literature with Miss Leary one more time. She told her how much she liked Stefan Zweig's *Amok*. Miss Leary read it in translation.

'Did you like it?' Heddy asked her.

'No,' said Miss Leary calmly.

'It worried me, that "No," for years,' says Heddy. 'Some

years later I read it again. Perhaps because I'd been in Australia a while by then, or maybe I was just older, but I didn't like it either. It was too flowery, too fulsome ... too much in that old-fashioned, European style.'

With Kató installed at home, Heddy went to work at the Becher factory.

The factory was up a steep flight of steps from Parramatta Road. You went past Gyuszi's domain, a dark cubby hole at the top of the stairs, into a huge light room, with the machines and cutting area on one side. On the other, there was a long table covered in plastic where the workers ate lunch and morning tea. They were mostly Australian women, in hairnets and Mother Hubbards that tied at the front. There was the odd Italian or Yugoslav; they were shy and sat together. The women worked fast, their fingers flying dangerously, their feet rhythmic on the pedals, and they talked over the noise of the machines and the radio, which was always on. They kidded the foreign bosses with a sly, utterly good-natured humour.

Heddy was the 'the Mädchen für alles' – 'the how do you say it, "the Friday girl". I swept out the remnants, I helped Jóska get the orders together, I took work out to the pieceworkers ... I'd stuff, say, a hundred dresses into a suitcase, and take them out to Bankstown or wherever. I went to the beltmakers and button manufacturers – I knew all the button manufacturers, and I bought thread and patterns, all that.'

On Kató and Pubi's arrival, Jóska, Klári and Little Sue moved, first to a flat in Croydon, then to a house in Strathfield. Judy was glad to have at least an aunt and uncle here in Sydney. When the other kids described what they were doing on the weekend, she could say casually, 'I'm going to stay with my aunty in Strathfield.'

Kató took over the household reins. She cooked us wonderful things suitable for another climate and another life.

'Why, there's nothing fattening in it. Only a little butter, flour and sugar. Eat.'

She had no adjustment problems, at least none she would acknowledge. She despised the afternoon teas that Heddy arranged for her with other displaced old women.

'All the old biddies do is long for home and complain about their sons and daughters-in-law. I won't go. It does me no good.'

She was too old to pick up much English, but she got herself about on trams and buses, confident in the goodwill of others. She wasn't fazed when she ended up at Taronga Park Zoo or North Sydney instead of Chatswood; it was part of the adventure.

Dresses were brought home from the Becher factory for finishing so that she could make a bit of money. She hated being dependant. She spent hours sewing on zips and buttons, spreading thread and scraps all over the house, driving Heddy mad.

Kató spent the money on fares, little presents, and music. She still played and sang for pleasure, and made regular journeys to Palings in the city for sheet music.

'She wouldn't ask me for help. She'd go in and sing the aria she wanted, in the middle of the shop. Everyone gathered around her. Even when she was old and her voice was no longer what it was, it was still a cultured singing voice, a professional voice. All the staff laughed and flattered her and said, "Come any time, and we'll serve you. You just come and sing."'

The Becher factory permeated our lives. Boxes of Becher dresses sat about waiting for Kató to get to them. The women, including Pubi's newest wife, wore dresses made of

Becher material; the bedspreads were of Becher material. Everything revolved around Becher, which was starting to yield a living.

But once Becher was on its way, Gyuszi and Jóska were ready for a second venture. A fellow refugee, whom Gyuszi had met in Mauthausen, wanted to go into partnership making handbags. Hollywood Handbags began in the garage at Chatswood, with two sewing machines. When a neighbour complained, they moved to a room in Oxford Street.

Heddy's job was to be the travelling saleslady. She took the range to buyers in department stores and shops. She put the dozen or so bags in two large suitcases, then togged up in her best Budapest suits, got on the city buses to go around to David Jones and Farmers, Mark Foys and the shops in the city and suburbs. Whenever she got on a bus or tram, lugging the suitcases, resplendent in her grey flannel suit from Móguc ('every elegant woman in Budapest had to have one') and a smart hat, the men would leap to their feet to help her.

'They assumed I was going to Central Station to catch a train to Leura or Melbourne! I said, 'Thank you, very kind,' in my best English, thinking, "Oh yes, if only you could help me all day long." '

In the stores, she could manage 'Three weeks delivery', and 'The price is …' and 'we have this bag in black and brown', but after that she was lost. She let the buyers fill in their own order forms.

She made a daring trip to Brisbane with the two suitcases. Brisbane buyers were a cinch; these were bags with a bit of style, a hint of Europe. One clutch bag, in big grain crocodile leather, looked expensive, but wasn't; it was immensely popular.

After a year, they set up a little show area in the Oxford

Street room, and the buyers began to come to them. Heddy was relieved to put away the suitcases and go back to Becher.

★

By the time we had been in Australia perhaps two years, three important things had happened to make Heddy feel more confident. With Kató's arrival, she no longer felt marooned; her mother was in her rightful place, close by. Second, the container load of her possessions had arrived. With her furniture and objects around her, the chandeliers hung, the monogrammed linen stored, she felt more herself, less of a 'bloody reffo'.

The third was the absence of fear. She had been here for some time before she realised she felt different, and why.

'Fear had left me. I wasn't afraid any more. I *hated* that fear. I had been afraid so much, and then it stopped. If I had to pay a price for that in Australia, I didn't mind.'

Chapter Fifteen

We lived about three years in Chatswood. I felt strange in infants school, but by the time I graduated across the fence to the girls' primary I was an old hand. Life at school was a haze of sun on hot asphalt, bruised jacaranda flowers to arrange on one's fingers, secret confabulations with best friends, sweaty tunnel ball teams and occasional skirmishes with the boys' school on the other, forbidden side of the compound. A little further away was the Domestic Science Girls' High School, where most of us would one day learn to cook and sew and type.

Some lunch times, there would be meat pies from the dim grocer's shop in Willoughby Road. (Mother never did master a decent Australian-style sandwich, but nor did we acquire a taste for Vegemite and peanut butter; there were limits to our determined assimilation.) Afternoons we played with the neighbouring kids. At tow-haired Robert's up the road, I was allowed to play the Victrola; I'd watch the yellow-brown paper with the strange holes in it wind past as I trod the pedals. The lounge room had the musty smell of the rarely entered room. The carpet was dark floral and all the furniture was stiff and dark, with little doilies on everything.

Our house was on a corner. Every Sunday the Salvation Army used to park themselves at our gate and give a concert. Young girls without makeup bashed the tambourines and portly majors beat the side drums. On Sundays too, most of our neighbours straggled up the road to St James Church of England, the girls with their gloves on, the boys with their shoes shined.

I didn't really mind not being a part of that; I knew the words of many hymns anyway, from school. I had mixed feelings though when my own lot gathered at the Chatswood Town Hall twice a year for the High Holidays. We didn't have a synagogue at that stage. On the North Shore in the early fifties we were just scattered about, the odd (maybe Jewish?) foreigner, the odd reffo. But here at the Town Hall we had a recognisable face, we were a tribe. So many foreign accents all together, so many obviously Jewish people in one place! I loved and hated it. I watched everybody, I grew bored. But secretly I thought that church hymns were insipid compared to the wild wailing resonances floating down from the Town Hall stage.

★

In 1952 we moved house to Lane Cove. It was an interim measure until Dad felt confident enough to build on the piece of land he had bought further up the North Shore.

The new house was a white dolls house, neat and trim. Everything about it was little: little windows, painted green, little rooms, a neat little garden. The little man who sold it to us worked in a bank. On one side loomed Mrs Lansen's house, large and low-eaved, on the other side, an unremarkable house with a family in it so unremarkable I cannot remember them at all.

At Lane Cove it was Mrs Lansen who became our 'special' neighbour. I have no idea how old she was when we met her. She already looked old to me, wizened, with deep folding wrinkles that I loved. Her eyes were young-old; quizzical and critical, full of humorous energy.

Mrs Lansen took to us kids, although in general she did not have much truck with foreigners. She admonished and reproved us, but we knew she loved us from the start, as we did her.

We were welcome, any time, to come through her big rambling garden, past her black and menacing cat, onto her back verandah, past her husband who would be quietly making tea or working in the garden – he was a beautiful-looking man who never dared say a word – and into her inner sanctum near the fireplace.

I would sit in front of the fireplace – in my memory there was always a fire going – and listen to her prejudices and opinions for hours. Mrs Lansen's world philosophy was: Jones's was the only place to shop; one should always go on a pilgrimage there in gloves; men were fools; the Masons were up to no good, and the Catholics were worse (nuns were to be turned away with a few sharp words if they came to your door); women had all the good sense and brains cornered and should have their own careers.

She was a dreadful snob. She went endlessly on about her daughter, Esmé; Esmé's achievements at ballet, her marriage to a wealthy New Zealand grazier, her career as New Zealand's sole woman M.P. The Ballet and a Sound Schooling (private of course) had been the right grounding for Esmé's brilliant career. Mrs Lansen relished the very word Esmé – she had chosen this classy French name as an augury for her daughter's future.

Her house was strictly divided into front and back. The back verandah, inhabited by old ice chests and faded chairs and her unmarried son (who was beneath contempt) led on to the sparse kitchen, and thence to the homey dining room with the fireplace.

In the front part of the house all was strict cleanliness and stiff curtains; in her bedroom, the satin bedspread always exact, the big cupboard dark and shiny, the figurines always dusted. We were never sure whether her husband Eric was allowed to enter this temple, far less sleep there.

The lounge room was for the best teacups and special occasions. I remember a musical jug, more figurines of ballerinas, stiffly stuffed and covered chairs, and landscapes. There was a confidence about the room, a room that said, 'this is the only kind of taste, and it is Good Taste'. Nothing like the restrained European grandeur crammed into two small rooms of our place next door, but so Australian, solid, of itself.

Lane Cove had a friendly frontier quality. We were crowded and a bit dilapidated, 'camping out' till the Dream House at Killara materialised (it was another two and a half years away). We were reliant on each other. Our only other real company was Jóska and Klári and Little Sue over the 'other side' at Strathfield.

My favourite photo of that time shows us gathered for breakfast in Granny's bedroom, which was also where we ate, at the red laminex table. There are a couple of milk bottles with their silver caps off, and bits of half-eaten toast everywhere. We children are tousled in our dressing gowns, Kató is all bosom and grin, dominating her end of the table, and Mum and Dad look chubby and energetic, ready for work. The black-and-gold clock looms in a corner.

'When we were at Lane Cove,' says Heddy, 'I still felt as if I had just married again, and we were a young married couple, starting out ... So much had happened, such drastic changes in our lives – the housing problem, earning bread, the children's adjustments, the trauma of Katus coming out, then adjusting to living with her. And trying to have a bit of social life too, not just work – coming home after a long day at Becher and preparing for a party. And outings for the kids ...

we did go on outings; we used to go to Balmoral on Sundays, and you remember the little tea rooms at Church Point – that was a real treat ... and Daddy had his bridge by then. Really it was such a full, full life. And yet, funny, I remember the details of the Budapest life better. The change had such a huge impact, there were so many things to learn ... But we had a lot of determination, and a lot of trust in the future. We were happy. We were not unhappy *at all*.'

She looks at me defensively, as if to say, see, there was a time when we were all happy together. I agree with her. At that time she and Dad gave off a radiant, purposeful energy that made me feel secure and purposeful too.

But they were also working very long hours at the factory, and often things were tense. I remember the one Terrible Quarrel they had in those years. After a series of eighteen-hour days, Dad forgot their wedding anniversary, and Heddy, goaded by Kató – what kind of husband was this – took him to task. He got into one of his rare and frightening rages, and banged his way out into the street. Judy and I were terrified. Our new father's benevolence and constant good nature were articles of faith.

Later that night, I crept into the darkened lounge room where he was sitting alone and begged him to make up with Mum.

It was in Lane Cove that my memory focuses and forms some sort of continuous scenery, as opposed to the arbitrary snapshots of the Chatswood years. In Chatswood, I see the tree in which you could play games and find cicadas, I see the massed hydrangeas at the front of the garden, and its shadowy, scary parts. I see the Thompsons' dunny in the long grass in the heat, I smell the sick of vomiting in the dark, I hear the scrape of our heels as we trailed home from school and the clank of trams on Willoughby Road. But I don't see or feel me. In Lane Cove I remember a me, who came home from school, said hello to Granny, fetched a plateful of Jatz crackers from the kitchen, got out my latest Enid Blyton or Nurse Barton, and read and ate, oblivious, until my parents came home from the Becher factory.

I remember waiting, mad with impatience, each Friday for the next edition of *Girls Crystal*, and running to the newsagency to get it. My sister and I were united in the delicious weekly anticipation of Friday afternoons, as we were in the thrill of turning off the light at night in bed and turning on the radio for 'Nightbeat', stories of a hardened and cynical New York private eye: 'Dum-de-Dum-Dum-DAAAH. Night Beat ... Tales of the City.' The radio serial and the *Girls Crystal* were about all that united Judy and me; otherwise we were locked in a sibling battle of such deadly intensity that it still frightens me to think about it.

At Lane Cove, we got the Holden, we started to go on holidays to Katoomba, I listened to Jimmy Carruthers fighting for the world title, holding Dad's hand in the excitement. Granny was always there and loved us, I got my first dog for my eighth birthday, and I always had a book to read – not just from the library – Mum would buy me the next in whichever series on Anglo-Saxon female hearties was fascinating me that year. Mother says I read the newspaper wrapped around the spuds which I was sent to buy, I read the newspaper on which I was supposed to be cleaning my shoes, squatting on all fours on the floor, I read under the table at dinner time. I read about lives utterly different from mine, and kept the real world at bay.

★

The Becher factory remained our flagship right through the fifties, but after a couple of years with Hollywood

Handbags, Gyuszi and Jóska sold out. Their next venture to be run in tandem with the factory was a fish shop cum restaurant in King Sreet. Heddy was spared from Becher to help during the lunch-time rush.

She loathed the New Astro. She didn't mind the work, it was the smell. She couldn't get the smell of fish off her hands. And the place was always wet, with the ice from the oysters, the wet sliminess of fish in general.

'My Veres Pálné education, Monsieur Pierre, the piano and singing lessons had not prepared me for this! Even after Hitler, when I was sure I could put up with anything just to get out of Hungary, I hadn't quite imagined serving fish. Becher was freer; lots of different jobs, I could run around in the car. And there was something about serving – it went against the grain.'

I must have been about ten when the fish shop era started, so I remember it quite well. Downstairs, it was a noisy busy place. Behind the counter was a taciturn Greek, left over from the former owners, the loud-voiced Hungarian partners who knew something about fish, and Mum, looking rather beautiful. A long display counter ran down most of one side; on the other were booths for the quick feed customers. Downstairs was linoleum and laminex; if you wanted a more leisurely meal, you were conducted upstairs, via an old lift, to the first floor, into a shabby auditorium-like room with scraggy carpet and dull chairs. Red paper napkins, white table cloths and classier menus were the signals that you had entered a higher price bracket.

It was much like other city restaurants of that time. You got a reasonably edible feed in reasonably clean circumstances. The upstairs part never really prospered, although the downstairs fish sold steadily.

Mum and Dad did not get home from work till 6 or 7, after they had dropped Klári and Jóska home. Kató was the stable figure in our daily lives. She was at once indulgent and strict. When she laughed, it was a pure, big laugh; when she was angry, it was pure anger. We knew not to cross her. Once when Judy did, she got a single king hit that made the blood run. We always knew where we stood with Kató.

Sitting in that tiny house, around the red laminex table, or lying stretched out on the Becher-covered beds, I'd listen to the stories of her opera career in distant Hungary. In some ways I preferred her tales to my parents' stories of the war years, for theirs were full of indigestible bits of horror, even though they never told us the worst parts. My parents' stories brought up questions that had no place in the snugness and smugness of Lane Cove life, whereas Granny's tales were the stuff of daydreams.

She showed me fading sepia photographs of herself in costume, buxom and wasp-waisted, or looking strapping, dressed as a boy. Another photo, which Mother had framed and gave to me, is painted over in delicate watercolours, as was the fashion. A young Kató stands on a lyre, surrounded by pink-cheeked cherubs who lift her up to the musical heavens.

My favourite story was of Kató's rise from an impoverished girlhood in Transylvania to star of the Budapest stage; it had all the right fairytale elements.

When she was a little girl of ten in the old and cultured town of Arad, she had a longing for music but not even a piano in the house, and certainly no money for lessons. One day she read about a piano scholarship in the local paper, which was clearly not open to Jews. She decided to go to the Town Hall to ask the Mayor about it anyway.

In the town square she saw a kindly looking grey-haired man feeding the pigeons, and asked him how she might find the Mayor. 'What would you want with the Mayor, little girl?'

'I want to learn to play the piano, more than anything else, but my family is Jewish and we're poor. I think the Mayor might help me.'

The grey-haired man smiled and asked her more about herself, and promised to tell the Mayor. He did not tell her that he himself was the Mayor, but told her story around the wealthy dinner tables of the town. A benefactor was found to pay for her lessons.

The music came to her fingers, but there was nowhere to practise at home, so Kató chalked up the keys on her mother's sewing machine and practised in silence.

At fifteen, she won a scholarship to Budapest. One of her teachers was the mighty Rennebaum, who had been a pupil of Liszt himself. Kató would practise for Rennebaum all week, only to have her slam the score shut within minutes and scream, half in Hungarian, half in German, 'No good! Awful! Go home and practise some more!'

Another of her teachers, the respected Professor Hiekisch of the Music Academy, had been a friend of Wagner. Kató was seventeen when she fell in love with the professor's son, the dashing Richárd, who had ambitions to become a conductor. Both sets of parents were desolate. The professor saw no match in a poor Jewish girl from the provinces and Kató's mother saw no good coming from her deserting the faith of her fathers.

But, for a while, it was a brilliant match. They embarked on a musical career together, giving recitals, playing duets. A flier announces a concert in Vienna, with Richárd at the piano, Kató on the clarinet.

Then, a marvellous new twist. When she was already twenty-five and established as a pianist and clarinetist, Kató's voice was discovered. After only a year's training, she made her successful debut as Azucina in *Il Trovatore*, in the town of Kolozsvár. Next, a contract with the Budapest

Opera and the launch of a short but illustrious career. She sang several leading roles, including Carmen. Once, she told me, she sang with the renowned Chaliapin. Chaliapin saved his voice during rehearsals. On the opening night Kató heard its full magnificence for the first time. She was so awe-struck she missed her own cue. 'Stupid ass!' hissed the young Fritz Reiner from the conductor's box.

Even as Kató's career flourished, her husband's womanising was ruining the marriage. Finally she left him, hired a nanny for the two boys and continued with her career. Then she met Náci, left the stage and settled down.

I sensed, even then, that this fairy story had a disturbingly non-feminist ending, not that Kató ever complained.

Heddy told me another story, of the time when Kató's stage career was already in the past. Heddy was about eight years old. They were sitting in the crowded dining room at Rákoczi Street and Kató was telling her all about Carmen, and Don Jose's hopeless passion for her. Suddenly Kató grabbed a rose from a vase, arranged a chair as Don Jose and sang the famous aria of seduction full belt, swinging her hips, twirling the rose. She sang with the same abandon as if Heddy were the first night audience at the Budapest Opera.

Mum and Dad told us stories, too – especially Mum, once they judged us old enough to know a little bit about the War and the Holocaust. From this time, I remember her stories about hiding in Kisláng; the time Kató was close to capture by the gendarme, the flight in the snow to the railway station and thence towards Hódmezövásárhely; her bringing me boiled potatoes to eat on the train; how I nearly died, and so on.

These stories excited and haunted me. I always wanted to hear them, yet I was afraid to hear them. I would have much rather that the only reality was in my books about boarding school and horses and happy family life in English villages. I tried to pretend that these books, and my life at school, were all that mattered.

At the beginning of fifth class, I was sent to Artarmon Opportunity School. I was excited, but I didn't want to leave my best friend from Willoughby, Diana. Diana was a solid, amiable redhead who invited me to her house for weekends.

In my memory, all Australian houses of the fifties are dark; sparse, proper and dark. Diana's house was not as big or classy as Mrs Lansen's, but there was the same sort of master bedroom, where the double bed sat stiffly in the middle of the room, always beautifully made up in pink satin. To one side, again, the dark shiny wardrobe; to the other side, the dark shiny dressing table with the mirror. Perhaps a vase of cut crystal with artificial flowers, perhaps a Namatjira print; nothing else. These rooms were slept in, tidied, left in state all day long.

Diana and I were allowed into the lounge room to play. It was wonderfully cool in there on the hottest day. You could barely see, not that there was much to see. Two enormous armchairs, an enormous sofa, a smoking stand, a stand-up radio, a gas fire. No one came in at all during the day, so we could play at dress ups for hours. Diana's mother kept a cardboard box for us of old scarves and dresses and suits.

I went more often to her place than she to mine. Going to her place was better; there it was quiet, and we were left alone. The thing that fascinated me the most was the quiet. Diana's father rarely spoke, to anyone. He was a Rugged Australian. Diana's grandfather was shadowy, out the back or in the garden tending the tomatoes. Diana's mother spoke, but nothing extraneous. I don't think they were unhappy. There just wasn't much to say.

Nothing like my family, where they all spoke, and loudly. Always a bit louder than other people's families, always with foreign accents and God-awful grammatical mistakes and always saying things that were never said in other families. Even when they laughed, they laughed louder, at different things. Judy and I didn't believe it when our friends seemed to like our parents; we were too embarrassed by them.

When the Christmas holidays came we didn't have to be embarrassed; we were going off to the Blue Mountains where just about everyone was foreign.

What an extraordinary place the Mountains was in the fifties. Every Hungarian Jew in Sydney, and many Polish, Czech and other Jews, saw it as the *only* holiday destination. Everywhere else was too far, too bare, too flat, too Australian. In Hungary, summer holidays had been spent either in the hills beyond Budapest or at Lake Balaton. The Sydney beaches were nothing like Balaton, but in the mountains, aah, there were echoes, beauties that were recognisable, air that was crisp, smells, like pine needles, that were familiar. Beyond the Mountains was the unknown world, frontier land. The Mountains were tameable territory.

Going to the Mountains was a ceremony in itself. The Holden was piled high with feather pillows – it was ten years before we got used to little hard Australian pillows – the garlic press and decent pots and pans. When we reached Parramatta – then the end of the city – and hit the highway, we whooped for joy and sang a little verse in Hungarian that said, in effect, 'We're shitting on the world, we're on holiday!'

We'd found a duplex in Katoomba, the Blue Echo, that could accommodate both families, and thereafter went there every year. We children went riding at a mangy Blackheath riding school, and the women rested, although they continued to cook and clean. Gyuszi and Jóska went on long walks together, content with each other's company, or played cards at an establishment nicknamed the Mandlerei.

Mum was a bit snobbish about the Mandlerei. She thought that the Hungarian Jews who went there were loud and vulgar, a bit loose even. They did nothing but play cards, smoke, gossip and eat pastries on which they got fat as pigs. The morals of some of them were suspect.

The Mandlerei was a messy, sprawling wooden guest house, taken over from a sedate past to become a smoke and strudel laden outpost of Mittel Europa. It was set in glorious grounds; spreading trees bringing shade to sweating Europeans, banks of old oleanders and rhododendrons. The card tables were set out everywhere, inside and out, kids darting among them, yelling in newly acquired Australian – everyone over ten spoke strictly German, Polish or Hungarian. Black coffee was drunk all day, or soda water. No one was ever drunk. Mothers yelled at kids, husbands and wives quarrelled in public, and everything that was to be known in the émigré world could be learned in one hot afternoon spent at the Mandlerei. That's why Mother turned her nose up at it, but Dad didn't care – that's where the best bridge players were, in a delicious haze of cigar smoke.

Chapter Sixteen

In the middle of 1954 we moved into the house we had built on a battle-axe block in Killara. The move marked a transition from the innocent battles of the first five years to a more complex existence. We were no longer struggling New Australians for whom the meaning of life was to put bread on the table. We were starting to 'make it'; we were entering the established middle class and slipping into stability. It was then that some real problems emerged. This North Shore middle class that we were supposed to fit into was nothing like that of Budapest. My parents, having paused for breath, having got us to our first proper home and the first schools we were to stay at indefinitely, began, I suspect, to feel the cumulative strain of the past dozen years. And we were entering adolescence and beginning to feel, and resent, the strain of our double lives.

I hated Killara. It was middle everything; middle North Shore, middle class, middle brow – I still can't drive past it without shuddering. I don't think the full impact of being migrants in Australia hit me until we settled – or sank – into the North Shore life.

This was private school land, land of deserted streets, large jacaranda trees and tended gardens. Here was an awful quiet. Somewhere in my pre-memory must have been the streets of Budapest, for I never took to Killara – it was always alien, this silent closedness, the wooden faces of the private school kids, the repressed blanks that were their parents, even nature set up primly in lawns that were always mowed and hedges that were always clipped.

It's not that we were the only migrants. There were Hungarians next door, German Jews on the other side. But it was just little pockets here and there. And I *felt* really different, and alienated, for the first time. There was a heavy weight in the air of Sunday roasts, Church, sensible shoes, tennis lessons, correct behaviour, and snobbery. The Sillingers, in the house behind, were almost sinister in their cold-shouldering of us, and we knew that nothing we ever did would please the Grangers a couple of blocks away, who sent all their weak-eyed nose-in-the-air sons to Shore and pretended, year after year, that we didn't exist.

My refuge, at least for the first year, was school. I was in sixth class at Artarmon Opportunity. Artarmon was a relief, like a door opening into sunlight. It was only then, and only dimly, that I realised just how different I had felt from other kids. At the beginning of third class at Willoughby Public, when we all had to announce our religion for the roll call book, and everyone had droned out C of E or Presbyterian or Catholic or Methodist, there had been a collective gasp and a collective swivel of the head when I said Jewish. As far as I knew, there was not one other migrant in the class – at least no weird foreign names. At Artarmon we were all different. Being a migrant was just one of the many eccentricities around; my deskmate, Richard, for instance, who muttered to himself, never washed his ears, and did maths for a hobby. We were a little ghetto, the segregated despised class of 'bright' kids, encouraged to do all sorts of things, like write novels.

For the first time, I felt my Australian and my other self synthesising. There was someone timidly emerging, who felt she could do and say things, have some mastery over life. I was grateful and amazed. I wrote *Seven Arrive* there, and finished it with this paean:

Two years have passed and the Verö family is a very very happy one. Mrs Verö is having a cup of tea with the next door neighbour, Mrs. Smith, and they are chatting happily. Mrs Verö is talking about what a wonderful country Australia is and Mrs Smith in return is saying what a wonderful asset New Australians are to Australia. Rózsi, Clari and Penny, (the child who had made them feel welcome on their first night in the new house) are playing chasings in the garden, Vera is at a birthday party, Granny is knitting happily in her little room and Mr Verö and Mr Fehér have just caught the bus on their way to their now promising business. Both Vera and Clari had done well in school, Vera having passed her exam was now in High School and picking up rapidly, Clari in fourth and the naughtiest one in the class, and Rózsi had just started kindergarten.

The next day being fine and clear with just a few snowy scudding clouds Mrs Fehér suggested going for a drive because after all, they still didn't know much about Australia. They bundled into their new Austin A40, all the seven of them and in a couple of hours were driving along the smooth wide road passing by fields, meadows, small farms, scrub, and then into the bush ... Far away in a haze of distance the Blue Mountains loomed up against the azure sky. A hush fell over them – even Rózsi – they hardly knew why – but it was still there. Suddenly a sudden gust of dry wind stirred the dull withered brown leaves at their feet making a ghostly rustling sound. In the bright sky above a brilliantly coloured bird – red, yellow, blue, green, winged its way towards the endless blue horizon. Carefree, joyful ... free! It was symbolic. At their feet was their past life – in the shape of down-trodden withered leaves. Miserable, full of fear, forever scurrying before the merciless oncoming wind. Above was the bird – their new life. Its colours represented their feelings, brilliant colours for they were joyful feelings. Hope, happiness, honest striving; – fulfillment! The endless blue horizon was the future years.

Yes: this was Australia, their land; the land they loved. Thank You, Australia! Our land: Australia!

How much I wanted it all to come together. I was brim-full of the romantic idea, and the propaganda. I must have thought I'd wrapped it all up, because my next novelistic effort is pure Australiana, about a pioneer girl with red hair and brown eyes whose mother has an Irish brogue.

My parents probably smiled to themselves when they read *Seven Arrive*, but they were pleased and proud, too. Wasn't it proof that their gamble had paid off and their children were enjoying all the fruits of their labours?

★

Heddy loved the new house at Killara. 'I felt finally at home, away from the heavy, dragging Australian life that was so hard for me. I had my own created environment.'

She strove to make the house the best that fifties architecture and limited means could offer. It boasted a huge picture window behind which she had planned a kind of three-room formal area, fitting spaces at last for her Hungariana. Behind the plateglass window was a small sitting room where the daintier furniture, covered in a pinkish brocade, sat, together with a vitrine full of pieces of Europe. Above, eclipsing everything else, hung the Maria Theresa crystal chandelier that had survived the journey out with not a tear or pendant broken. Mother eventually sold it, as being too over the top and of the past.

A gas fireplace acted as a room divider to the main lounge room. Here was the heavy carved furniture, covered in a russet velvet, that she had acquired on marrying Feri. Our most recent acquisition, the gramophone, was there too. When I got to high school, and Mum was still working at the fish shop, I'd come home from school with a friend and listen to Beethoven's Fifth Symphony, which I'd got for my eleventh birthday, or his Violin Concerto, which I got for my twelfth. Mum was very conscious of the cultural icons, the Essentials of Good Music, the Encyclopaedias, the French lessons. Later my friends and I graduated to Sibelius and Schubert and the sophistication of Dave Brubeck and 'Take Five'. On some degenerate afternoons in our teens, we'd sneak some thick yellow advokaat in Mum's good Hungarian glasses, while we listened, transported from the sordidness of Hornsby Girls' High and its order marks, sports days and silly homework. My Australian friends thought this room, and the advokaat in crystal glasses in particular, really something.

Hornsby Girls' High knocked the little bit of stuffing I had acquired at Artarmon clean out of me. It was a school of endless strictures and platitudes, of hopelessly high corridors, fearful hours outside the headmistress's door and embarrassment in smelly changing rooms. It stank of rotten egg gas seeping from cold labs and of lunch-time oranges on wet stairs. It reeked of the transcendental boredom of assemblies and sports afternoons. It was peopled by terrifyingly eccentric, embattled teachers: Miss Rishworth of the caustic tongue and kind eye, Mrs Tendy of the tingling voice, as huge as a painted elephant, Miss Porter who blushed over rabbits in biology, Miss Collins of the weird French accent, rouged and ancient, stranded among us like some antipodean Miss Havisham. They taught us periods of Caesar and Gaul and The Ancient Mariner and the French

Revolution, and no Aborigines, none at all, except a few grateful savages, and *A Midsummer Night's Dream*, all mangled and senseless.

I detested the controlled violence of the place and its meaningless propriety. As the only selective high among a sea of private schools, Hornsby was obsessed with making us as close a clone of Nice Young Ladies as possible.

It was no accident that my little group of friends consisted of a girl recently migrated from Israel, a German girl (of Communist not Fascist background I was quick to ascertain) a girl with a Scots mother and a deprived background (a great rarity on the North Shore), a child of two liberal-lefties, equally a rarity on the North Shore, and a couple of other oddballs who would not have fitted anywhere else. We were the 'out' group, the weird ones. Everyone else, it seemed to us, went home to neat houses and gardens with unexceptional parents who went to the Club (Golf or Bowls on the North Shore) or Church, or both. Everyone else seemed to think that living on the North Shore in the fifties was just fine.

I took up a routine; giggling meetings with friends on Gordon Station, last minute Latin homework on the train, the hated hours of school, hanging around the station again, eating icecream and chocolate sauce in the milk bar, then home through the deserted streets, beguiled, despite myself, by the smell of burning leaves or the brilliance of jacarandas. I usually walked home by myself because I had made no friends with the neighbouring kids. We were friendly only with the Rowes, our next 'special' neighbours – we went to their place for Sunday lunches of cold lamb and salad while they became enamoured of Mum's sour cherry slice – but their kids were younger than me, and went to Abbotsleigh Ladies College.

I was totally reliant on my school friends; on the notes

and whispered confidences, and the long afternoons at each other's places when we discovered Bach or Shaw or a Great Truth. Mostly though, we gossiped, giggled and were everything to each other. I clung to them because I felt that the world was falling apart around me.

Mother was puzzled by the change that came over me. I seemed to change overnight from a relatively tractable 'nice' child to a sullen monster. It wasn't just that I hated my school. Until then she and Gyuszi had been the Promethean heroes of my existence and the source of all love. But now I was falling from their grace, and they were tumbling off my pedestal. I felt that nothing was sure or certain about the present, the future was problematic, and the past had terrible, insoluble mysteries in it, which were somehow – I didn't know how – the key.

I was entering a particularly troubled adolescence in which sexuality, Jewishness and migrantship were key problems. The Holocaust loomed over it all, still the Unmentionable, but carrying with it such nightmare images and implications that I became resentful. I was only twelve, thirteen, fourteen; how was I to understand it? Why was I burdened with it in my past when my schoolmates' nightmares had no parallel in reality? It wasn't fair.

I didn't talk about such matters to anyone, except a little to my best friend. Her parents were Polish Jews who had left Poland just before the War started. Their families had been wiped out. We never talked about the details of our families' experiences. But we had a special understanding; there were things we knew that our other friends didn't. There were no awkward pauses, as when other friends asked you questions: where you'd come from, when you'd arrived, were you ...? Sometimes I'd leap in ahead and tell them, in a studiedly neutral way, that I was Jewish, and that my mother had been in hiding and my father in concentration camps and that he had lost nearly all his family. It was a way of saying, you need to know this about me: but now beware. Ask no more questions, and be careful what you say to me.

Apart from my best friend, I recoiled from seeking out girls with similar backgrounds, although I knew there were at least two others in my year. It was *my* nightmare. They were probably more normal. They were leading happy lives, as I was supposed to. Their parents no doubt had put it all successfully behind them, as my parents tried to. Besides, who was I to say that my parents had *not* put it all behind them? All the outward signs of success were there. They worked hard, they led a healthy social life, mostly but not exclusively with other Hungarian Jewish refugees, they were becoming financially secure, we were doing well at school.

But my internal debate never stopped. I never wanted it to stop, because it was more real to me than what was actually going on. While I caught the train to go to another boring school day, or hung around the milk bar in the afternoon debating whether to walk home now or ask Mum to pick me up, I also debated Good and Evil, Nazis and Jews. The evil, active Nazis, the passive, good Jews. But if it was true that the Jews went like lambs to the slaughter, there was nothing good about that passivity; it was cowardly, shameful, petty.

In those days the dominant image in the popular consciousness was of the naked line-up of people waiting to be gassed to death. I did know that there were other stories: my parents and most of their friends, if I'd cared to ask, had stories of individual courage and resourcefulness and good luck. But they were just individuals, here and there. Where were the leaders, the heroes who said this does not have to happen, this *will* not happen?

I had heard something of the Warsaw ghetto uprising, but that was all, and that had failed. I fantasised that I would have been such a leader, or at the least I would have set an example with my courage and idealism. But I wasn't in the least sure of my fantasy. It was more likely that I would be a coward, that I would not be able to stand hunger, far less any real pain. And if I worked in some underground, alongside, say, the Maquis, and I was captured, how long would I last under torture? A day, maybe two? In this fantasy I'd try to prolong the time: if I lasted more than two days, maybe I would become used to it, and then stoic endurance would set in – I would never betray my friends.

And what about the Nazis? Were they demonic force, evil incarnate? I didn't believe that. I was sure then (as I still am) that there is no such thing as pure evil. Even when I was quite little I thought that Heaven and Hell were silly ideas. I suspected that the Nazis were ordinary men dressed up in jackboots who killed a lot of people. But that made it far worse. They were ordinary people capable of extraordinary evil. That made the world senseless, disgusting. Perhaps that's why so many people went passively to their deaths; they had ceased to *want to understand* the world they lived in. If you no longer want to understand, you may no longer want to live. That made sense to me.

I thought I understood the wish to die better than the drive to survival. But I was scared and ashamed of feeling like that. I felt guilty about my thoughts and kept quiet about them.

My friends and I all became interested in religion at fourteen or so. We were at that stage of adolescence when we were confusing religion with sex, in our efforts to deal with the unnameable yearnings coursing through us. And Billy

Graham was in town; there was a religious fever in the air.

Some of my friends, who saw themselves as sophisticated and enlightened, assured me they did not believe that the Jews, collectively, had killed Christ. Nonetheless, they thought it would be rather a coup to convert a Jew, and engaged me in earnest discussions. I balked amiably at the Trinity, an extraordinary concept to an outsider, and they were equally puzzled as to why I would want to remain a Jew when I was leaning towards unbelief.

'No, it's not a religion, well that's only a small part of it.' I laboured at an explanation. 'It's most certainly not a race ... What was it then? I could never explain it, even to myself. 'Well, there's a shared history,' I'd say lamely, 'a certain sense of humour, it's more a cultural thing really ...'

It wasn't enough to fend them off, so I went to a Billy Graham meeting to oblige them. I even had a momentary frisson as the lights glared and the crowd roared and a mass of people surged up the aisle towards salvation. But the next morning at Gordon Station nobody looked different for having been saved, and I went back to poking fun at the Trinity and my friends' efforts to explain it. Besides, no self-respecting Jew believed in Hell after death – we knew there were plenty of hells offering here on earth.

But I did make one cross-cultural stab at religion. I had only the faintest, musical, emotional notions about Judaism, born of the twice-yearly High Holidays. I knew that there was a lot of mumbo jumbo and those embarrassing dietary laws (everyone persisted in being amazed that we ate pork, whereas all the Jews I knew did). But I also knew that we believed in one God, and that there was no complicated doctrinal nonsense about Him, and I was proud of that.

It was enough to begin to pray. I prayed every night for a couple of months, with an adolescent fervour that tried to match that of my newly Billy-Grahamed friends. In the

Anglo world of books and pictures I'd seen, golden-haired children knelt at their mother's knee, lisping 'Now I lay me down to sleep', and equally golden haired young women (Meg, perhaps, in *The Family At Misrule?*) slipped into church and knelt on the cool flagstones, praying with a modest fervour in times of trial. So I, too, knelt by the bed with my hands correctly folded, and prayed hard.

It leaked out somehow. The adults came to know about it. One night Dad intervened. This normally non-interventionist dispenser of treats and affection actually intervened. An ancient duty called him. As I knelt one night, hands folded, the door opened, and he stood looking at me in a shaft of light in the doorway.

'Susan,' he said gravely, 'Jews do not kneel.' He shut the door quietly behind him.

*

In the mid-fifties my parents led the archetypal life of the middle European migrant. They threw themselves at the new world with enthusiasm, chased opportunity, and enjoyed a competitive camaraderie with other Hungarian émigrés. Who was going to make it big? Who was going to get the balance right – assimilate with these bland Australians without disappearing altogether, retain their Jewishness without standing out too much, put the past behind without wiping it out altogether?

The last was the hardest balance. There was an unspoken complicity between the survivors 'to put it behind them'. To dwell was morbid, self-defeating. 'We knew each other's stories. We talked about it a bit at first; where were you – Mauthausen, Auschwitz – in hiding? ... who'd lost their family. But then we stopped. And people in our circle were fairly intelligent; they didn't go on about the things they'd left behind, the comfortable life; it wasn't "sympathique". And besides, it was all over, finished. For many years, it never occurred to me that I'd go back, or that I'd even want to. Our passports had said "never to return" and I'd accepted that. It was final. Much later, circumstances changed, and so did we.'

When I was in my first year at Hornsby Girls, Kató became seriously ill.

As Heddy talks about Kató's illness, she is close to tears, but I can tell that she has dealt with it. I realise I have not.

For the first eighteen months or so at Killara, Kató was quite happy. She was pleased to be back with us; while the house was being built we had rented rooms in Gordon, and she had boarded with Pubi (who was between wives) in a room at the Cross. When she rejoined us, she had a room of her own with a built-in cupboard, a built-in radiator and space for her big chair, and a piano with the black-and-gold clock installed on top.

She cooked for us, pottered in the garden, and waited the long hours for everyone to come home. Then she'd treat us, over and over, to tales of her past life and glories. One night, after a long day at Becher, Heddy burst out, 'Enough Katus! Gyuszi has heard that story not once, but a thousand times!'

Gyuszi looked up mildly.

'I? Never. Tell me again Katus.'

Later, in the bedroom, he said to Heddy, 'She's alone all day long. What's it to me to listen one more time?'

I used to go into Kató's room to listen to the music the clock made, and to practise the piano. I was taking lessons, desultorily, from a Hungarian friend of my parents who had given up a promising career to emigrate. Now she taught kids piano, and every now and again she gave a ten-minute recital on the ABC in a weekly slot before the news. This spot was filled with émigrés who had given up promising careers somewhere else.

Kató started to fall down when out in the garden, and couldn't get up. It was some time before muscular dystrophy was diagnosed. She lost the use of her legs, then progressively, most of her other functions. At first, she could still get out to the kitchen to help with the cooking, then she had to be carried there, then came the wheelchair. If there were visitors, she would be wheeled out to see them and she would regain some of her old force and spark for a while, but she was growing listless and apathetic. We came to realise that she was dying.

I spent the year preceding Kató's death pretending to myself that nothing much was happening. I found going into her room harder and harder. My piano practice fell away. I couldn't deal with the pain and decay. It was hard to watch my large vigorous grandmother becoming ever thinner and smaller. Even her eyes sank and got smaller. Her skin, which had always smelled lovely, grew pasty and smelled different. The vast prow of her bosom sank and shrank under the shapeless house gown she took to wearing – Kató who had always looked grand in dark silk dresses with white lace collars, and whom I had never thought of as fat, because she was magnificent.

I watched her become ashamed of her new unrecognisable body and of her helplessness. I saw not just her self-confidence ripped from her, but her self-recognition. I could not bear her suffering and I ran away from her.

Heddy stopped working to nurse Kató once she became helpless. Singlehanded, she would roll the inert body from the bed, wash her, comb her hair, roll on her stockings, put on her housecoat, sit her on the commode, and prop her onto the big chair, where she would sit all day long.

'Sometimes she fell when I was trying to lift her from the bed onto her chair, and we'd both end up helpless on the floor, flailing about on top of each other. But instead of feeling desperate, we began to laugh. We still laughed together.'

They laughed over a newspaper item Kató found when she was reading the paper while Heddy was cleaning her room; as the illness wore on, Heddy had to turn the pages for her. Kató read out a gossip item on Zsa Zsa Gabor, Zsa Zsa who even at thirteen was stealing boyfriends at the Budapest skating rink.

'See Katus, you made a mistake raising me to be a nice young lady.' Heddy grinned. 'Look where it's got me – the fish shop, and Becher. And look at Zsa Zsa – what her mother raised her for – and look where she is now!'

'You're right,' Kató said, and laughed.

For close to two years, life revolved around Kató's illness. She went into hospital for two brief periods, but each time Heddy brought her home. The third time, Kató stopped the ambulance men at the front door and took a good look around.

'I won't be coming back,' she said, matter of fact. 'No, don't say anything. You know as well as I it's better for both of us if I die. I don't want to live any more.'

Ten days later, she was dead.

Everything changed for us when Kató died, although I didn't register much at the time. She was the vast, bold backdrop to our lives, in primary colours. Nothing could go totally wrong for any of us while she was there; her vision wouldn't let it. Once she died, it seems to me now, everything was up for grabs.

Chapter Seventeen

I have told Heddy that I want to stop the taping around 1960, when our story becomes more internal, becomes another story. Even as she talks about the turbulent late fifties after Kató's death, when Judy and I were locked in battle with her and each other, she stops telling me stories and starts to explain and justify and complain. And I can no longer be a good listener. I have become a participant, impassioned and confused.

'Until you were thirteen, fourteen,' Mother says, 'I must say you were a joy. I really enjoyed motherhood.'

I remember it as earlier. I think it was around twelve, and I was sitting (as I still did) on her lap in the kitchen, and it dawned on me that my parents were not gods, that I disagreed with them on a host of things, and that life was going to get a lot more complicated.

I concealed the discovery fairly well for another year or two. But by mid-adolescence the gap between words and deeds was widening. By sixteen, I'd marshalled a hefty row of principles against the combined weight of their pragmatism. At seventeen, I was bunkered down behind enemy lines and the gunfire was constant. Not long after I turned eighteen, I left home, pretending it was only for a few months, but never came back.

None of us ever quite got over it. I'd withdrawn

unconditional love and didn't have a clue what to give them instead. Unconditional love had been the coinage of our intercourse. Baser coin wouldn't do.

'You always won, in the end,' Heddy says. 'We always supported what you did.'

If I won any battles with her, it wasn't a separate or distinct victory, but a skirmish gained at the dead of night. They were bloody little victories, standing on my hind legs as the lioness roared. We tussled over love as over a piece of bloodied meat.

Around that time Mother's approval moved permanently out of reach, and we entered that bleak territory where neither of us was capable of expressing a love useful to the other.

When Heddy talks about her relationship with Kató, she paints a picture of robust affection and mutual support, and I can't gainsay it from my memory. Their natures had no foreign element. They might fight and disagree, but their visions didn't jar.

My sister and I had another element. Perhaps the dreamer, the retiring and rigid in our dead father lodged in us. Mother saw such elements as raw material for shaping. The men in her care seemed to bloom, but not us. Feri was much 'improved' before he died.

But for me, hanging on to that different inner element, hanging on to 'otherness' seemed essential for survival.

With men, women have to acknowledge otherness. Their difference is so obvious that there's a heavily marked white line between you and those other beings who share your bed or house. But between women the boundaries are not clear. And with girl children! Certainly with my mother and her girl children whom she had protected with her life during the War, the boundaries were paper thin, invisible.

I think of the summer of 1948, our last summer in Hungary. Heddy was frantic with preparations and had no time for our summer holidays. She sent us to a kind of summer camp, to a children's institution outside Budapest where we would be well looked after and get our dose of fresh air. I remember a cavernous building with long corridors and grounds with big iron gates. On weekends Heddy visited us, and each time Jutka cried and pleaded to be taken home. Her sense of abandonment, being abandoned *again*, was acute. I think I was almost as miserable, but strangely passive. I'd lead my older sister from the gates, saying there was nothing we could do. I felt no power to change things. I had to wait, a bit player in the wings, until Heddy was ready to take me onto the stage of her life again.

★

What *was* it all about those years when I fell from grace? A handful of incidents, of dust. It seemed then such a long fall, and a final one; the feeling of awful division, of starting to pretend that everything was all right. It was the war years for me. Starting to lead a double life.

What was there? Big fights about my rebelliousness at school, then, in my late teens and early twenties, over a series of 'unsuitable' suitors and friends. Mother and Dad wanted me to mix with 'normal' healthy teenagers, go out with nice boys. The whole point of coming to Australia was that we would all henceforth lead a normal life.

But by the time we settled down to the anonymous 'normal' suburban life in Killara, it was too late. Judy and I had been born into an earthquake and grew up in upheaval. The 'normal' life that Mother had worked so hard to achieve came only when our inner selves were already habituated to tension and anxiety.

We were not particularly happy children, despite the good fortune of our placid North Shore life. We resented having to appreciate everything. We had far too much to appreciate, far more than other children.

And Mother, in turn, resented the very trouble-free life she had created for us. We failed to see our life from her perspective.

I knew, in a confused way, that my parents had suffered during the War, and that there was some extra intensity and obsession in our relationships with each other that had to do with the past. I understood that what I had to do to make it up to them was to be a happy, well-behaved child. It was that simple.

It was also impossible, except on the surface. My self concept was so bound up with the past that I had trouble distinguishing the heroine or coward of those terrible war scenes in my mind from the heroine or coward on the school playground. Besides, a betrayal of a friend, failing a maths test, being rude to my parents, they weren't the *real* measure of anything. I had to prepare myself for when the real test came for my generation.

I had no idea that there were thousands like me, thinking the same obsessive thoughts, in the Americas, in Canada, in Australia, wherever the survivors and their children had gone. I didn't realise I was not the only child deeply ambivalent about my parents, guilty at causing them any further pain, not giving my own pain any legitimacy because I had never 'really suffered' as they had. Even now, as I read the accounts of others of the second generation, I compare myself guiltily to those who were 'good' children, who clove loyally to their scarred parents. Judy and I rebelled at the hidden agenda. We resented the obligation their suffering imposed on us, yet, fascinated, were drawn to it against our will.

Like many adolescents I tried to distance myself from my parents' way of life, and, if not from Jewishness, from things Jewish. I was scared of getting stuck in the past. I was going to be a proper New Australian – forward-looking, polyglot; and a new kind of Jew – proud of who I was, but cosmopolitan, picking my friends and lifestyle by preference alone. Even the question of going out with Jewish boys was loaded for me. Would there be any new worlds opening up if I went out with them? I'd be trapped in the world of obedient Jewish boys destined to become doctors.

Perhaps if I had not run away so hard, I might have worked out some things I am only now beginning to see.

One thing I could not understand was Mother's relationship to things, and her passion for order. I could not understand the intense anxiety my disordered life aroused in her. But I begin to see. What are one of the first signs of a disintegrating life? When your possessions, the objects of most familiarity in your life, are taken away, or sold off, or have to be hidden. What are the signs of your life reintegrating? When you get back the first stick of furniture and can put your own linen on your own bed again. Or so it was for Heddy.

Only recently have I started to think of Heddy and myself as part of something bigger. I was struck by a story of a survivor whose parents perished in Auschwitz. To the last, this man's parents were obsessed that he, their only son, should locate and reclaim the family belongings in storage. Their obsession had nothing to do with materialism in its ordinary meaning. It was more to do with the sense of self people lose when on the run. Their identity, so rooted in the things they have chosen, accumulated, inherited, is flung away. The fight to regain those things is correspondingly intense.

When I was growing up Heddy's anxiety about disorder

induced only anxiety in me, followed by guilt and resentment. What did it matter, in the larger scheme of things, if your shoes hadn't been put away, or if you'd lost your belt or if there was left-over food in your room? Especially to her, after what she'd been through? I knew other mothers nagged about these things but there was a special quality in her of strong emotion, almost a moral disgust.

I became her antithesis; vague, impractical in the extreme. My personal life shunned an ordered future.

I knew my choices would not please her, but I had not counted on the intensity of her grief, rage and disappointment. There was a mad disproportion to it all that lent a surreal quality to our conflict. When I got married at twenty-five, we were still at each other hammer and tongs.

Mother brings up that day as an example of the bad influence of my friends. She reminds me bitterly that B, who was going through a madcap hippy phase, arrived three hours early, carrying her guitar and in bare feet. Heddy was beside herself.

'B was a really bad influence on you. She nearly ruined the wedding!'

'B?' I gasp. 'But she's totally harmless. She didn't have any particular influence ...'

'Oh, yes. The way she behaved ... the way she dressed ... So irresponsible.' Her face is grim.

What really ruined the wedding was our conflict, both in general and about how the wedding should be staged, and my own doubts about getting married at all. But that little incident was about threatening disorder. And disorder for Mother meant, still means, genuine distress, a threat to the way she's struggled to live her life.

It has taken me a long time to work out that her distress doesn't necessarily mean that I've done something wrong.

These days, I watch myself accumulating ever more

things, and taking great pleasure in them. I think they mean that my life is beginning to acquire a little more, dare I say it, stability and substance. Perhaps I am beginning to let the Heddy in me out.

★

I notice, and not for the first time, that Mother glows when she talks of the war years, whereas her face fades and strains when we get to the present. And it's not just the healing effect of time. Back then, the stage was large, and irrational forces dictated events. The fight was against great odds, not against members of your own family – their mere words, rebuffs, or perverse behaviour. Now the wars are subtle and small and there never is a clear victory. Fighting your loved ones over well-worn territory. Fighting, in a way, over the outcome of those big years.

Mother says, 'Your father's depressed. He won't talk. It's all those things he's been pushing away for a long time.' (And I immediately think, now is it his wife and two children and the family he lost at Auschwitz coming back to haunt him, or is it that his two adopted daughters, chosen by destiny to 'make it up to him' have yet again failed to do so? – although one is just a scaled down version of the other.)

Mother says, 'He's going through a bad period, just as I did a while back, when I had to pull myself up against all the odds.' (And I remember the panic I felt then, thinking she wasn't really coping with my living with Anne. But she said it wasn't that at all, but the way I treated her. She had not suffered to be treated so badly by me.)

'I realised, years later, that you were leading a double life,' Mother says.

Sitting on the fence, double life, make a choice, you can't

have it both ways, why don't you go and live in a garret if you're such a socialist, hypocrite, liar, coward, who do you think you are? What do you think you're doing?

I copped it from the other lot, too. I never looked right, for one. Too middle class. An acquaintance has an image of me sitting in dingy Push pubs, crying into my drink, immaculate in white. Never really comfortable in the rather fierce intellectual armour on offer. And I'd still bring home the rather marginal men I'd acquire, each a different symbol of what I was looking for, and hope – for what? Hostile politeness on both sides was the most to be hoped for.

Declare your colours, join us, and submit to *our* initiation rights to adulthood, each side said. No, I thought, I don't have to choose. To choose is to deny, to miss out. I'd rather not belong than choose. You have to belong, both sides said, and that means choice and sacrifice. No, I said, my sacrifice is not to belong. When you say or imply that, both sides eye you with a bit of contempt. Gutless, they say. Lonely, I say.

During my late teens and twenties, I did indeed lead a double life, but of a sort more ludicrous than sinister. I busied myself giving each side a little of what I thought they wanted.

My wedding was my supreme effort to reconcile everything and everyone. The problem was how to get married, as tradition and part of me wanted, yet how not get married, at least not properly, as my radical friends and the radical part of me demanded.

It was the late sixties, in the days before wedding celebrants in parks; the choice was church or registry office. My principles didn't allow for church or synagogue, so we had a registry office wedding and got pissed with a couple of friends, and a few days later we staged a fake white wedding presided over by a retired Methodist minister who was happy to quote Bertrand Russell rather than God.

Yet we prepared for this charade almost as if it were to be at the Elizabeth Street synagogue or St Marks, Darling Point. I co-operated, surlily, as mother recreated the pre-wedding rituals of prewar Europe. Part of me enjoyed it; part of me rejoiced in the atavistic call. We all knew it was thoroughly compromised: not in a synagogue, the wrong kind of daughter getting married rather late to the wrong kind of man. But at least it was a wedding.

The unsuspecting guests thought it was lovely, with just a few modern and eccentric touches, as befitting the groom and me. Then we threw a big party for friends from my other life at the down-at-heel Italian restaurant in Parramatta Road which had once housed the Becher factory.

There were too many layers of pretence even before the marriage started, and not long afterwards it began to go down hill. And after that, the gusto went out of the double or rather the tandem life, although I continued to make desultory attempts to keep them at least in sight of each other for some years.

★

I feel depression coming on, the same one that seemed to settle then on everything.

As I approach the anniversary of my new love, and new happiness, all I can hear is Mother's disappointment (unvoiced) that it is not all over, and her hope that there may yet be (although time is running out) a 'normal' life for me. I can't tell any more whether it's her genuine voice – because we speak of nothing like this – or one wholly imagined by me as an instrument of my own destruction.

I take refuge in nothingness.

I see only a mess of endless detail, and love and happiness are just two irksome details I can't bear to look at. Better, far better, the dogs that haven't been walked, the bread that hasn't been bought, and will the school shoes wait till next term? Are these not, after all, perfectly legitimate concerns that most people (sorry, women) think about most of the time. And isn't thinking about them the badge of normality?

But my version of practicality is obsession. Dogs, milk and shoes parade in mad circles. Happiness is far too big a responsibility; better to think about milk. While one waits for either the new holocaust, or transforming happiness (it doesn't really matter which), it is best to withdraw and conserve one's energy.

Depression is such an easy lull. Familiar, unconditional, deep. But then anger and despair – the undersides of sweet depression – start coming out of their dark corners. Voices that aren't mine start up; at least I don't know if they're mine, or worse still, I don't care whether they're mine or not. The little whisper that is my mother's voice, that says she is not happy with me, swells into my own roar, commanding me to live as little as possible, thereby offending no one. DO NOT BE, BUT IF YOU INSIST, BE BLAND.

I start waking in the night, planning my own defeats and retreats. I elaborate my plans at first light. I convince myself that my friends don't ring me and that my lover knows nothing and cannot be my friend either. That the attempt to live rather than just survive is a fruitless one for the likes of me.

★

We've arrived at 1960, the end of the interviews. My high school years are over and Heddy is forty-four, nearly my age now. I come away from the last session in her long dining room feeling flat.

I decide to have lunch with her. She is going overseas soon. I'll discuss our planned meeting in Budapest in a few months, when she will show me all the places she has talked about. And then, gently, I'll tell her what's been on my mind; that when she says I led a double life as an adolescent and a young woman, pretending to be a dutiful and loving daughter, and at the same time pursuing my own objectives, it was not deliberate deceit but because I thought they couldn't cope with how I wanted to be. (Not that I knew how that was.)

But within minutes I am yelling, gesticulating.

'Don't yell,' she says mildly. 'You are mostly angry with yourself.'

I keep arguing and erupting, but after a while I realise that we're not really breaking new ground. We do this kind of thing maybe once every eighteen months, usually when our relationship is superficially calm, polite, and emptier than usual. My mad flow of words is to say, listen, listen to a version of my life that is different from yours. Not that my life has been good or meaningful, but your version makes it plain silly. It's just one long litany of foolish wilful actions that have made you unhappy, and as you point out, didn't make me happy either. Happiness, I say wildly, is not the point, or at least not the whole point.

She's saying to me, but that's all I saw of you; YOU HURT ME. And I say, you know there's much more to me and you didn't take it up; YOU HURT ME. We're competing for time: Listen to how you made me feel.

After a while, the zing goes out of it for me. But she wants to go on, and I think, well it's her chance, let her go on a while yet. Eventually she says, 'You'll really be angry when I say this and you'll probably explode, but I often think that you'll only be free of me when I die.'

I'm not angry at all. I give her a little pat, at a loss for what to say.

When it's time to go I hug her, and I tell her I love her,

as I often do after such encounters. I mean it, but it's also an attempt (usually futile) to forestall the bleak into-herself look she gets as she shuts the gate on me.

We're better with each other for a few days before she leaves for overseas. We were ourselves in each other's presence for a while; at loggerheads, uncomprehending, but close.

Part IV
Return

'I'm Robi, you know me'

Chapter Eighteen

Even before we have left Austria, Hungary begins to shock me. I am shocked by how soon we are at the border – how small these momentous European countries are! And at the border, I am shocked by my unawaited rush of fear. My fear has nothing to do with the present. A pimply-faced young man barely glances at my passport and smiles at me when he sees 'Australian'.

Anne and I had planned a romantic trip down the Danube past fairytale castles, but the river is too dry. At the last minute we are transferred to an old and dirty bus, with a mixture of officiousness and arrogance I instantly recognise as Hungarian.

Budapest. It is the middle of a hot August day. A taxi takes us down the long streets of Pest, curiously empty, rancid in the heat. The streets are dingy and crumbling, the people ill-dressed and podgy. Compared to charming, civilised Vienna, which we left only three hours ago, this is a ramshackle, threadbare mess of a city.

I'm instantly depressed, but my depression has a strong element of shame in it. I'm not really a stranger here. It's a proprietal embarrassment I feel … what's become of the place? It's not really *my* place, but the minute I'm here, I feel a kind of responsibility for it. Every piece of falling plaster, every dirty pavement hurts me.

Mother's old school friend, Irén, has offered us her flat until we find one to rent. She is all apology for the lift that doesn't work, the vagaries of the toilet and the ancient stove, the condition of the stairs. Things, if anything, she says, are worse since the Communist House and Street Committees have broken down – nothing has yet replaced them.

An ancient relative arrives from across town. In her white plastic bag she has brought a few peaches, some biscuits and a tin of sardines.

We walk, through listless streets and a dog-eared park, to the riverbank, the fabled Dunapart. It's a hazy day, the water is low and dirty, and huge trucks are parked all along the embankment. In the park parallel to the river, groups of men play chess or cards. Others stand behind them, kibbitsing.

Great slabs of cement have come off the buildings, especially the postwar ones, exposing crumbling brick and formwork and twisted bits of metal. The balconies look as if they're hanging in the air, but people are sitting sunning themselves, regardless.

We search the length of a dismal boulevard for a cafe where the television and games machines aren't roaring. I think bitterly of what I have heard of the fabulous cafes of Budapest. We drink coffee in a State-run barn where the red tablecloths bear the marks of a hundred meals and the high-back chairs are of nasty green velveteen. Some miserable-looking sweets and parfaits sweat behind glass. The place is empty apart from a young couple with rucksacks by the door.

In the dingy Metro, stands and stalls everywhere with obscure things for sale. The potential buyers don't look much better off than the desperate sellers of socks, cheap books, porno magazines and cans of peas.

What are we going to do in this God-awful place for ten whole weeks?

Ten weeks – time to look for a flat, settle in a little. Heddy is due in a month's time and then we will go to all the places that are so far only names in my imagination: Rákoczi Street where she was born, Rózsadomb of the apricot and pear trees and the golden girlhood, the various flats of The Fall, Pozsonyi Road, scene of triumphant young matronhood, then the sites of the war years – Dobogókö, Kisláng, Szeged, Hódmezövásárhely. But I cannot imagine what magic wand she might wave to recreate these places for me as they once were, or as she once saw them.

I am appalled at the things this city makes me feel, this city that I don't even remember. I have only one clear cameo from childhood – standing on the balcony at Pozsonyi Road, watching a bent man shuffle down the street, a cap pulled low over his eyes. I was certain he was a 'bogey man' come to get me because I had been bad.

But I am discovering that there are different sorts of memory. I remember the feel and smell of certain places, the feel of certain people on the streets. I catch myself compulsively watching them. There is a certain kind of face, the eyes cold, the expression flat and wary, and I recoil with a feeling horribly like fear. I catch myself looking, always looking. Which ones? Which ones were the killers, which colluded with the killing? Which ones were indifferent? Which were our friends?

I shake myself. This is madness – racism in reverse. Sometimes, when someone smiles or makes a joke, the fear and distaste evaporate like bad air, but then I am at it again, walking the streets, watching.

It is St Stephen's Day, the national day in honour of the saintly king who founded modern Hungary; thus the near-empty streets. Anyone who can has gone to the country.

Today will see big celebrations. The Catholicism that has run deep and suppressed in this country will today be open and splendid.

For forty years under the Communists, St Stephen's Day was called Constitution Day. Street names are changing back, too; some still have their Communist names with a red line drawn through them, others already have their former names. The older generation is exultant that it has lived long enough to see the world of its youth reinstated – at least in names.

Outside Buda castle, on a large green space, a dozen folklore troupes are assembling, each representing a different region. Their costumes are dazzling in their variety – bizarrely rich, simple, simply pretty. The broad peasant women sweat under their weight of skirts and aprons and headdresses. The men, elegant in their black and silver boleros, lounge under the trees and kid the women.

I am fascinated by the half-familiar lilt of the music, but uneasy, too. Elsewhere, anywhere else probably, I'd be seeing the picturesque; here I sense a resurgent nationalism that makes my flesh creep.

In the midst of the crowds, my purse is snatched. Suddenly I'm just a tourist again, a mug with a bag too full of American dollars, panicked at losing my American Express card.

We find the nearest police station and I am ushered in to the man in charge. My heart stops. I have never met him, but I 'know' him instantly. He is a lumbering man, swarthy and moustachioed. He has a portentous air, as if his bit of power gives him unending satisfaction. He is probably country born, ill-educated and stupid. I know all this about him before he even opens his mouth. Something like fear passes through me.

He dislikes me as instantly as I fear and dislike him. He

seems affronted that I bother reporting this theft; he is certain I am pulling the wool over his eyes.

I try to be polite because I have been warned about men like him, but I am not obsequious enough, or not formal enough. Perhaps I have shown a certain Australian friendliness.

He jots something down on a scrap of paper, making it clear that I am not worthy of an official form. We are soon at an impasse over my name and address. He insists on the English form of both, then comes to grief over them.

'I cannot understand your Hungarian,' he says heavily. 'You will have to wait till I get an interpreter.'

'My Hungarian is good enough to give you my name and address and some details!'

'But madam, what if I get something wrong? What if I find your wallet and send it to the wrong address, all the way to Australia, what would you say then, madam?'

'But I've told you, I will be here in Budapest for several weeks; I have an address and phone number here, right here in town. Let me give you that and then I can go.'

'An interpreter will be here in a couple of hours. You will have to wait until he arrives.' He eyes me with sly triumph.

I go out to the waiting room, defeated and angry. A younger, more sympathetic cop goes to intercede. The boss strides out, all menace and glower.

'Do you know the meaning of "aggressive?"'

' Yes, I understand the word but *I'm* not the one being aggressive! I can see I'm wasting my time.'

'You have chosen, madam,' he says importantly.

I sweep out onto the street, trembling.

But I have left my coat in his office. Anne wants to go back to fetch it and give him a piece of her mind. I won't let her; I can't let that man know he has got under my skin. I politely ask the young policeman to get my coat.

Hours later I am still shaken, although I don't know why.

A trivial incident, I tell myself, shake it off. I begin to cry.

'They killed my father,' I find myself saying. 'They killed my father'.

I say it over and over. I can't stop myself.

Nightfall. There will be celebratory fireworks for St Stephen's day. Irén who has lent us her flat, has invited us to her sister's in Buda to see them.

Irén and her sister are cultivated, kindly old women, 'Philo-Semites' – a term used here for people who like or defend Jews. Tonight I find the term as appalling as its opposite.

I had been looking forward to visiting these Philo-Semitic ladies. Now I dread them especially. I'm in tears again. I can't explain it to Anne. I just say, 'I'm afraid here. I wish I weren't here. I'm afraid of this place.'

The old ladies greet us warmly; they treat me so naturally, as the daughter of an old friend. They settle us down to watch the fireworks, clucking over the dangers of the new nationalism. We discuss the theft of the purse – so much of it in Budapest, they say; now that there is freedom, there is also more chaos in its wake …

As the fireworks wheel overhead – we have quite a good view from the sixth floor flat on hilly Buda – the ladies bring up the topic of the Stalinist years, and what happened to them and their kind. In 1950, 80 000 of the intelligentsia and the bourgeoisie were ordered from their homes and hauled out of Budapest overnight, carrying only a suitcase. They were sent to obscure villages and collective farms, forbidden their normal 'bourgeois' occupations. Irén's wage supported the entire family; her job as a laboratory technician was classified as manual labour.

'It was just like what happened to the Jews,' her sister says. 'I saw what happened to them, I was in a village during the War.'

I don't say more and worse happened to the Jews; it would be ungraciously competitive. I understand what she has offered – an exchange of sufferings, a kind of sharing. These women are saying, we are not outsiders, we have some understanding.

We make our way home through the holiday crowds. I feel a bit calmer. What else did I expect? I'm not here as a tourist. I've set this up.

★

I am meeting cousin Robi today, Baba's son. The rendezvous is at Gerbeaud, a Budapest landmark. It has been the city's most elegant coffee house since the turn of the century, kept that way under State control as a kind of cultural icon. Today its little marble tables and Louis chairs in green plush are as much occupied by Hungarians as German and American tourists, although some of the Hungarians are just back for a visit like me; you can tell instantly by the cut of their clothes and their up-to-date hairstyles. Why, there's Nellie Vida of Double Bay, sleek and chic, holding court like a returning monarch.

Robi walks towards us, looking more like an ageing Latin lover than someone's relative. He has a version of the Hiekisch matinee-idol looks, but there is something about the eyes that connects him to Mother. I last saw him more than twenty years ago; he was looking a bit Elvis Presleyish then and slimmer, which made him seem taller. At that time he was just another relative I had to meet. He had nothing to do with my life in Australia, or with anything that interested me then. He didn't look as if he read books.

Although we have never met, Rózsi, his second wife, is the first to recognise me. I have the look of my mother about me, she says, even though I am fair-haired and skinned and mother is dark and olive skinned. It's in the angle of the head she says, and something about the smile.

We start on the pleasantries but they only last a minute or two. Virtually without pause, Robi starts claiming me. He begins to talk about Kisláng where we were in hiding in 1944. He reminds me that he was there with us and he remembers it. He brings it up almost as a badge of honour, proof irrefutable of belonging.

He remembers my mother deciding to leave the village, ready to go on the borrowed cart, and his mother, in a panic of indecision, pulling him off the cart at the last moment. He remembers me, very small and nearly dead until medicine was procured for me.

He remembers my grandmother, and her smell. Her 'illat', he calls it, a beautiful Hungarian word, more to do with 'essence' or 'fragrance' than smell. I remember her illat too. How many other people in the world remember it?

But there is more to come. He remembers the CLOCK! I am reluctant to believe it. The same one? The black-and-gold one? I tell him I have it in my living room. *She* left it to me. He looks satisfied.

I am bowled over by his instant appeal to my emotional world. How does he know where it is located? No Australian man, no matter how close, would have the presumption, far less the knowledge. He is binding me, reluctant, to him with hoops of steel.

'Your mother is the only person in the world I'm afraid of,' says Robi.

'Me too.'

We laugh conspiratorially.

'She's strong,' we say ruefully, 'and grandmother was even stronger!'

But there's no edge in our voices when we talk of Kató.

In our eyes her strength was all grandmotherly benevolence, a huge enveloping breast, a fragrance. But with Heddy, the indulgent laughter is tinged with resentment and fear.

'When I pick her up at the airport, I'm always quaking,' Robi says. 'What's she going to say now that I've taken up smoking again?'

'Aah, I'm one up on you there. I've finally given up, so she can't get me on that one ...'

The things this stranger and I are talking about! And how aware he is of mother's family snobberies – the way she divides off the Hiekisch half-brothers as 'not as good' as she and Pali – lacking in the required solidity, perseverance and ambition. 'Your mother always says to me, "you're being a wayward Hiekisch", but I'm not, not inside, although I know I behave like one at times.'

'No you don't darling, you're quite different,' says Rózsi and pats his hand.

We talk on. One moment we have a lot to say, then nothing. We know nothing and everything about each other. After an hour of this intimacy and strangeness, my head is swimming and I am deathly tired.

★

Not far from our flat is a little supermarket where we can get fresh bread rolls every morning. It is a shabby, ill-lit imitation of a Western supermarket but I like it better. Nothing is glossy and packaged, and the sole checkout girl (a middle-aged woman in a Mother Hubbard) knows everyone. All around me I hear arguments and intimacies and complaints that the bread isn't fresh, that the price of the cheese is up since yesterday.

The shoppers bring their own plastic bags to carry their purchases home; otherwise they have to buy a bag for ten forint. And every forint is precious people say, in these changing times with price rises by the hour, after so many years when at least the price of bread and milk and sausage remained the same, year in year out. At least, people sigh, you knew where you were. You could plan.

Wonderful warm smells blast from a nearby butcher shop. Hot sausages for sale. You get a hunk of sausage on a hunk of bread, a splotch of mustard, all on a bit of paper, and you eat it standing up at dingy counters, then drop the paper on the floor at your feet. Delicious.

At night we watch television. The formal 'official' language used in the media and newspapers is hard for me to understand; it is full of words I've never heard. How officious, how self-important this sort of Hungarian sounds, how power-hungry. Far more than in English, social difference and cultural gaps seem entrenched in the language itself, in a frank and barbaric way.

My Hungarian is stuck at a five-year-old level so I can only make out a bit. There is cholera in Rumania from pollution of the rivers. There are nationalistic rumblings over the Transylvanian question. It is a 'question' again now. For forty years it was all submerged in the Communist brotherhood.

In some ways, politics here remind me of Australia. Two small populations of whom no one takes much notice, with the same sort of rooster-personalties strutting a small stage, absorbed in their bickering. But in Australia the decisions taken rarely result in cataclysmic changes, whereas this Hungary seems, just as much as in the past, a place of consequences, repercussions and barely hidden brutalities.

★

We have been invited out to Sunday lunch at Robi and Rózsi's. Their flat is in outer or New Pest, about fifty minutes drive through countryish bits interspersed with vast blocks of flats and some factories. Some of the new flats don't look too bad but they will in five years time. Their block looks like a housing estate anywhere, no more or less cheerful, no more or less neglected. They tell me it is middle-level housing; there's better and there's a great deal worse.

Inside it's light and comfortable, and for all the world like any flat in Sydney's western suburbs, down to the big television and the bright green fish tank. The bathroom is smaller, the kitchen utensils less sophisticated, and as in most Hungarian households, even pre-Communism, the lounge room and main bedroom double up. There are two smaller rooms as well, one for his mother, one for her daughter.

They're very proud of the flat and worried at the same time that it will look like nothing to my rich western eyes. But I'm impressed. There's a caravan outside, too, which they use quite frequently for country trips. Not bad for Communism, even with a bit of help from the West.

The first thing I see on entering the lounge room is a sepia photo on the wall of my grandmother. Our grandmother, as important to him as she is to me. This man really is my cousin. I've come half way round the world to search things out, to dig up the past, and here it is on the wall, present, real, not remote. Australia is remote. This is the only world that ever existed.

I realise properly for the first time that I actually share my grandmother with this man of fifty, in this neat flat on a housing estate in outer Budapest, and with that woman of fifty-four, Pubi's daughter in Canada, with the groomed, slim, rich American style. We are all alive. These scattered people over the globe, a cousin here and a cousin there; I share something with them in fact. Why have I not understood this before? It's not as if I haven't met them before. It just wasn't real then.

I have assumed that my forgotten childhood here was a clean slate, that I had shared it with no one. Had I in some sense deliberately forgotten or not taken into account everything that had happened before my 'rebirth' in Australia?

I had thought my childhood really began in the asphalt playground of Willoughby Public, searching for perfect blue jacaranda flowers on the hot black tar. Yet this stranger who is already jarringly close, who knows so much and nothing about me, has just driven me past the faded splendours of Budapest's big pleasure park. 'We were here together,' he says, casually, confidently. The place has a feel, a smell about it as close to me as skin, yet I remember nothing. But I know he's right. We have been here together and we got on. That's the level he's calling to me on. Here I am, he says. Robi. You know me.

Over lunch the photos come out. There's a whole album of us in Australia which belonged to Robi's father Baba. Baba who quarrelled with Kató over his third wife, and who only reconciled with Heddy after Kató was dead.

I remember meeting Baba only once, on my first visit in the sixties. He lived in a cramped flat – the same one where Mother asked for refuge in 1944 before fleeing Budapest. He looked to me then a disappointed fading man, crowded by an unpleasant wife – and by hundreds of cactuses, which were his hobby and passion. His face lit up with some of his old tough gaiety only when he talked of them. I could see Mother thirsting for any glimpse of the old Baba, laughing immoderately and with relief at the slightest sign of his legendary wit.

In the album there are pictures of me and Judy on our first visit here, and of both our weddings and of the house in Bellevue Hill. All the Australian pictures look glossy and unreal.

Here's a picture of Robi as a baby. I've got the same picture in Australia, I exclaim. I remind myself of the peasant who once gave me a bed in a village in Guatemala, or was it Costa Rica, who exclaimed in wonder that my watch, which came from Australia, told *exactly the same time* as the one he'd bought only twenty miles away in the nearest town. He'd made an unexpected, illuminating connection. So have I.

Robi understands. You weren't open to this last time you were here, he says. You didn't want to know. No, I say lamely, I was younger then. I came because I was asked to come, not because I wanted to.

★

Budapest is built on top of hot springs; it is dotted with bath houses and swimming baths, some dating back to the Turkish occupation of the sixteenth century. Our favourite is the Király; its bath house is a lowish, domed structure, pure Turkish, while the main building is a classical eight-eenth-century two-storey building of endearingly intimate proportions. Inside, the Király is a mixture of every imagi-nable style, including the 1960s.

As soon as we enter the baths, there is a mystical feeling of rituals long established, of partaking of something good with many others, past and present.

The Király operates on alternate women's and men's days, so there is no problem with nakedness. I am enchanted by how comfortable the women are without their clothes, how they walk around as if in their own bathrooms. There are no ideal bodies here. Breasts sag, rumps spread, thighs dimple, stomachs fold, and no one looks ashamed.

Once undressed, you put on a weird little apron which covers nothing, and go down a staircase to the steam bath. You must first shower; while the Király is dilapidated and shabby by Western standards, hygiene is strict.

The steam bath is covered by a big dome, with little openings letting in prisms of light. Women loll in the warm water, stroll over to the cold; they do their exercises, they scrub their backs, swim a little gentle breaststroke. Mostly they sit at the edge, moving their legs and arms softly and slowly in the warmth, and chat. Most are elderly women. They talk to each other of children, dogs, shopping, prices, food. In the sauna area, one old woman is talking of her cats. When her auditor leaves for her massage, she switches to me without missing a beat.

The prismic haze, the Rembrandt faces, the Rubens bodies, the strong smell of metal in the water, the homeyness of the chat ... I am soothed, intrigued, and for the first time since I've been in Budapest, properly relaxed.

After another shower you wrap yourself in a clean white sheet and go upstairs to a long airy room, a magic room, like a nursery for adults. There are comfortable white beds with blue blankets on them. On these, clad toga-like in their sheets, women doze, read, apply their body creams, knit. At one end of the room, there are foot massages and pedicures, at the other, body massages. As you wait, half dozing, for your number to be called, you hear the plop and swoosh of the massage, and the comfortable chat rolls on and on.

The woman giving me my pedicure whistles over my feet. '*You've* been able to afford good shoes,' she says with good-natured envy. Then she gives me a caustic caricature of each of Hungary's politicians, post-Communism.

'No better than the last lot,' she says. 'Idiots, to a man.'

Chapter Nineteen

Right in the middle of our first meeting at Gerbeaud's, Robi offered to take me to the Jewish cemetery. I was puzzled, and a bit affronted. Why did he want to take me there?

I had never thought of Robi as Jewish. I always assumed that he identified more with the Christian side of the family. Yet he is half Jew, half Christian, on both sides; enough to make him just another little Jew boy in hiding in Kisláng, along with the rest of us.

I see then, that his offer to take me to the cemetery is a serious business, a call to kinship.

Our first stop is at Baba's grave in the Christian section. Baba was always officially Christian, unlike Pubi who changed according to wives.

In the Jewish section, Robi takes me first to a memorial to the Martyrs of Fertőrákos. At the base, Heddy has affixed a plaque with Feri's name on it.

On a nearby clearing there are perhaps twenty tall plain columns, with names of the dead inscribed on both sides, top to bottom. They are divided between those who died within Hungary and those who died in Mauthausen, Auschwitz, Russia or other places. Some names are scratched on or written in pencil beside the long neat rows. At the bottom of one column is another plaque, reading rather curiously, 'Julius Varga, Sydney, for his family in Paks.'

Next Robi finds the grave of my grandfather Náci. I tell him the story of Náci's burial in 1944; how Mother was in a frenzy of fear lest the Arrow Cross round her up at the grave side. I can only just imagine that fear now. The cemetery is beautiful. Wild roses scramble over the graves and monuments. It is very quiet.

On my grandfather's grave, there's a line for Pali who died in Russia. 'For my son,' my grandmother had had inscribed from Australia, 'who died in another country.'

Robi drives the car down narrow lanes till he finds the Schwimmer family vault. He puts stones on the graves of people neither of us know or remember. My father is not here of course, but in some mass pit in Fertörákos. My mother has added an inscription for him on the vault, with the phrase 'a martyr's death', as was the convention.

All these plaques and memorials were done years later when we'd settled and become comfortable in Australia, and Hungary had become thinkable again. Robi himself has done some of it; Dad sends him money from Australia to look after the various graves.

The main pilgrimages over, he has more graves to show me; great uncles, a cousin's child who died very young. He shows me graves he has nothing to do with looking after. He is very familiar with the place.

'Why do you know so much about it – where all the graves are?' I ask. 'Why is it so important to you?'

He's not offended by the question, as I half fear.

'It's my way of keeping in touch with you. It may sound funny, but I'm scared you'll think it's only for the financial support that I want to stay in touch. You are all important to me. The graves are my, sort of … job.'

'You felt left behind when we left.'

'Yes.'

It's very hot in the car, and a long way back into the city. Robi stops at Rákoczi Street, the fabled street of mother's early childhood. It's a broad and noisy thoroughfare. Robi points to a handsome old pile on the corner. There, he says, that's where they were, but I have my doubts – she has never mentioned a corner.

We go into one of those awful Budapest coffee houses that are a cross between Communist chic and sixties Liverpool. I devour stale cake, coffee and a beer. We talk some more, sometimes strangers, sometimes intimates. I take one of his cigarettes.

'Don't tell,' I say conspiratorially. He shakes his head and smiles at me, pleased.

★

In Hungary, I know almost no Christian Hungarians. Here in Budapest I feel my Jewishness going before me, regardless of my irreligion, in a way it never would in Australia.

When Ilonka, daughter of one of Mother's Christian friends, invites me to tea, I find myself excited and a bit apprehensive. Will we meet as normal strangers meet, will some sense of difference, of history, hang between us?

She is a pale woman with crooked teeth, slight and childlike, very serious. She is a computer analyst, her husband is an electrical engineer who earns precious hard currency on projects in Third World countries. They live comfortably in a large modern flat overlooking the city.

Ilonka is at pains to explain that this lifestyle is the result of very hard work and good luck.

'You'd be surprised,' she says, seeing my eyes roam, 'if you went out to my kitchen. You'd see jars and jars of pickled cauliflowers – I'm pickling them because they're cheap now and we'll have them through winter. We never go on holidays to the West. We go on camping trips to Slovakia; it's a conscious decision so we can live like this.'

In this household the talk is all of politics. The seventeen-year-old is as eager to discuss them as his parents. By the time he was born in the mid-seventies, the political atmosphere was far more liberal; his generation, his mother says, is the first to think 'normally'.

'The rest of us, even my other son, who is only a few years older, are tainted; we've all been afraid.'

Ilonka turns again and again to the topic of anti-Semitism. The question worries her deeply; she feels a need to explain things to me. She talks in terms of historical tendencies and consequences. I can see in her the reverse of the prejudices she despises. She is this strange European phenomenon, a Philo-Semite. 'After the Communists took over in 1948,' she says, 'the anti-Communist opposition was divided. There were the rural-based poet-peasant types, and the urban intellectuals, among whom were a lot of Jews. We were supporters of the city-based strand, the Free Democrats. We still are. Once the Communists fell, the split between the two got wider. In the recent elections, The MDF (the conservative country strand) used anti-Semitism very effectively against the Free Democrats. When the MDF won, we were devastated. Sometimes I can't sleep at nights for worry. We have got rid of Communism, but now the country is in the hands of mediocrities at best, rascals at worst.'

Ilonka's eyes are tense as she talks of the last forty years. She has lived through the War, the 56 revolution, the Stalinist years, and now the Communist fall. I can see that she has been under extraordinary strain – of being at once a woman, a bourgeoise, an intellectual, a mother.

Politically, historically, she is saying, we are allies, friends. Yes. But I have an uneasy feeling that I am here not out of friendship but as a matter of principle. She is extending me every hospitality – except that of the eyes. When I talk, her eyes are blank.

★

We've been here two weeks. The smelly heat continues and we're restless to get out of the city, so we decide to go to Pécs, a biggish town in the south. I take my interview notes with me on the train, so as to make a list of all the places to see with Mother when she arrives.

Strange how I thought I'd have to winkle out the past, but it comes at me in all sorts of ways, all over the place, unbidden. We'd already decided on Pécs when I remembered it was where Mum and Dad spent their honeymoon in 1946. And on the journey south the express train stops only once, at a place called Dombóvár. Absorbed in my notes, I barely look up. It's a big dreary-looking country railway station. Later I realise that back in 1944, on our flight from Kisláng, we spent a freezing night in Dombóvár, right there on the railway platform, waiting for a train that would take us further away from the front and nearer safety. In 1990 I pass through, oblivious, eating bread and kolbász like an old hand, and reading the wrong part of my notes.

We wander through Pécs, an old university town virtually undamaged by the War, and stumble across the synagogue. It is surprisingly large. Inside, the carved women's galleries are painted in rich ochres and blues.

An old Jew at the door fusses over us, making sure that we have the right information sheets. I am almost relieved to see him. I am never relieved to see a Jew in Australia. But here I scan faces, automatically looking for them. Looking for Jews. Where are they? How many left? Do they skulk, try not to look Jewish? Or do they hold their heads even higher? Above all, where are they? I know there are hardly any left in the provinces.

Now here is one in the flesh at the door of the synagogue, and even though he is a pedantic old fellow, I am pleased to see him. I don't mind him fussing. He asks if my family comes from Pécs, he'd be sure to know them. If I let him, he'd talk a long time.

I ask him how many Jews there were in Pécs, and how many left. Forty thousand once, he says, about three to four hundred now. The Rabbi from Budapest comes down every now and again to hold a service, as he does for Szeged. The wooden women's galleries are not used any more. There's a small chapel at the side used for every day.

The information sheet says there is a quotation engraved on the ark: 'Those who trust in the Lord will not be disappointed.' Bullshit, I think, look what happened to the trusting and the Godless alike. Nonetheless, I mutter the first line of the only Hebrew prayer I know – 'Hear O Israel, the Lord our God, the Lord is One' – more out of pity for those poor trusting buggers than to any merciless God.

★

Budapest is in its sixteenth consecutive day of humid August heat. It is as hot as a Sydney day in January but smells worse. I have my period. I am depressed. I long for Australia.

We lunch at a restaurant that takes credit cards, a ritzed-up place, part imitation English, part Hungariana-hunting kitsch. It's crowded with new Hungarian businessmen wooing wealthier, glossier West German businessmen. Procuring Western capital is now the only game in town.

At night, on the Lenin Körút, the ring-road around old Budapest, we peer into the courtyards which can be entered from passages off the main boulevard. Once past the little display windows and stinking garbage bins that crowd the passage, you see the old apartment houses. Some have been renovated, and how beautiful they are. I think of how beautiful all Budapest could be, with some money for plaster and paint.

Yesterday we were in Isabella Street, where Mother was miserable in her late teens. On the corner of Isabella and Andrássy Avenue, Budapest's most prestigious thoroughfare, I found the famous Lukács, one of the few old coffee houses still going. The grand old Avenue and the Lukács have much the same faded, abused dignity. In the coffee house, the gilt is coming off the fake eighteenth-century seats and the service is slow, but the icecream! I 'know' the strawberry icecream, just as I 'knew' that policeman. My tongue is three years old again.

Mother and Dad arrive in a few days. I'm feeling sick and fluey; maybe it's apprehension. How will Heddy be? How will I react? Three weeks together, day in day out, with me dragging her back into her past. Will she show the strain? Will I?

An art show opening – a retrospective for a Hungarian sculptor who lived thirty years in exile in Paris. It doesn't feel much different from art shows in Australia. The crowd drinks, greets, eats, circulates and gossips, but the atmosphere is more serious and subdued. They take their intellectualism weightily here.

I look at a collection of photos of the artist's early life, and ask Vera, Mother's old school friend who has invited us, whether he was Jewish. 'Of course,' she says almost scornfully, as if I've failed to pick up on something basic.

The nation's President, Árpád Göncz, is here, not to open

the exhibition, just to mingle. The Government has appointed him from the opposition Free Democrats as a conciliatory gesture. He has been a playwright and translator and has spent time in gaol under the Communists. He is now an old man, immensely popular.

The President has a delightfully gentle manner. An old woman, a cleaner in the building, goes up to him with a bunch of flowers. 'I'm just an old pensioner from Székesfehérvár,' she says. He grins at her. 'And I'm just an old pensioner from Budapest.' From his lips it does not sound forced.

Vera points out people in the crowd to me, many from her circle – a writer here, an artist there. Half a dozen people who were in gaol under the Communists. It becomes clear to me that this is a gathering of the clans, those who were in opposition to the old regime, who are now almost equally opposed to the new. This is the Urban Intellectual Strand of opposition that Ilonka, our hostess of a few days ago, was talking about. And the President is here to reassure his old mates that his loyalties are with them.

I suspect, too, that his very presence at the exhibition of a Jewish sculptor is an act of subtle Philo-Semitism, a signal to the rest of the country. As I begin to grasp the subtleties of political life in the post-Communist world, I find it awful that the Jews should once again need friends and protectors. I think of 1943, when Hungary's Jews still thought themselves safe because Kállay, or some other prominent politician, was their friend.

On the way home, Vera talks about the President with unreserved affection. He was in prison at the same time as her own husband. Then, almost casually, she mentions my father.

'He was in labour camp with my husband at one stage. No, not at Fertörákos, before that, nearer Budapest. I met him a couple of times. He was a big, tall man, whiteskinned, rather awkward, quiet, and very shy.'

That is all, but even that has been a nice surprise. Someone who knew him, and remembers him. It seems to me at times that he was so unassuming – even his departure from the world was quiet – that he might have vanished altogether, even from the memory of others.

★

Heddy and Gyuszi have arrived; they're settling in at the Forum Hotel on the Dunapart. Mother starts holding court immediately. Relatives and friends are on the phone, sending flowers. The rituals of her visits are well-established; since the seventies, she has been coming back every two or three years. But she tells everyone she will be less available this time. She and I have things to do.

Tomorrow we start going to all the places on my list.

She seems ebullient. If she is apprehensive, she is not showing it.

She arrives at the flat to pick me up, and stops in wonder at the door.

'To think that you are actually living here, and I'm coming to one of these courtyards to pick you up ...'

She has brought a serviette full of 'pogácsa', my favourite savoury scones, purloined from the hotel's magnificent breakfast.

We take a taxi to Rákoczi Street. Robi was right, it is the big seven-storey building on the corner. Rather grandiose without; inside, it is impressive in its severity and mass, its staying power. The tiles of the internal walkways are shiny with age but not really worn. The wrought-iron railings, spiralling up the seven storeys, are as sturdy as ever. The lift well and the elaborate main staircase are still magnificent, despite the dirt and the nasty orange lift installed in the sixties. Outside almost every flat there are pots of green.

I don't have to prompt Mother. I just follow her around, scribbling makeshift notes. Everything is evocative for her, from the barber shop around the corner where Náci went for his daily shave, to the concierge's cubby from which the stately Mr S, the concierge, would operate the lift late at night, but only if you tipped him generously. Which leads her on to the under-concierge, a much lowlier creature who washed the floors, took away the garbage and beat his little son every night in a drunken rage. Heddy and her friends let little Pista into their games because they felt sorry for him. Years later, she tells me, pausing solemnly at the doorway, she heard that the boy had ended his own life.

On the fourth floor, where the family lived, every flat has a memory. That's where the mysterious Mrs M lived, she says, with her half-crazy son, neither of whom spoke to anyone. Everyone was afraid of them. There the flat of the Ts, a handsome pair, with a pretty daughter who impressed the whole building by marrying a Frenchman and going off to live in Paris.

We are coming to her old front door. She stops at a window, her hand on the sill, her voice trembling.

'I was here, watching father about to beat Baba with the tennis racquet. How I cried because Baba was going to get hurt!'

A dumpy old woman in a housecoat answers the door. Mother has her spiel ready. We have come all the way from Australia; she lived here as a child. I am her daughter, curious about the past. Does she mind if we come in, just for a few minutes. The old woman eyes Mother shrewdly, sussing her out. They are about the same age, although Mother looks as if she has stepped out of another world. But they understand each other very quickly. The old woman ushers us in.

'I've lived alone since 1943. My husband did not come back.' She does not need to say from where. The phrase 'did not come back' is common parlance among Jews.

We start with the central room, the room that was bursting with the dining table, the vitrines, the giant palm and the clock. It is large, airier than I expected, with deep bay windows onto Luther Street. In its present incarnation it is filled with an assortment of unrelated items; some fairly decent old paintings, some dreadful wood-veneer and formica furniture from the fifties and sixties, lots of beds, and bits and pieces, odds and ends randomly placed.

As we wander from room to room I try to adjust my mental images to what I actually see, but it's hard in the midst of the babble. Mother is full of memories, offered randomly to me, herself, the stranger. The old woman embarks on a counter-narrative of her life, her memories. She, too, offers them at random. They often talk over each other, but neither seems to mind. War, death, furniture, children, funny stories, calamity, nostalgia, higgledy-piggledy.

Mother stops at the bay windows in the living room. 'I watched my grandmother's funeral procession from here. I wasn't allowed to go. They thought me too young. Mother wore a long heavy black veil which frightened me.'

I think of Kató's funeral procession, which Judy and I watched from St Leonards Station. We were considered too young to go.

On the way to the kitchen we go through the maid's room, which in my imagination was even smaller and meaner than it really is.

The old woman is in the midst of making preserves. 'Still the same,' Heddy says, pointing to the ruby and amber jars in the pantry. 'Yes,' the old woman says, 'we start in May as always, and go through to the holidays in September.'

Mother imitates Kató leaning out of the kitchen window at ten each morning yelling, 'Heddy, Pali, come and get your lángos before they go cold!'

This sets the old woman off.

'My mother made us lángos too, but with jam on them. What a childhood we had in the village where I was raised ...'

She tells us about her parents in the village who were taken away to concentration camp, about the sisters and husband also killed, the children raised on her own, the age and sex of the grandchildren, the long hardships of life ever since the War.

But Mother is too absorbed in her own experience to really listen and I am numbed by the uninhibited torrent of memory. When we leave, the old woman's voice floats after us; she is barely aware that there is no one to talk to any more.

We stop at the door where Heddy's favourite uncle, Béla, lived. An elderly man arrives at the door with his shopping, and lets us in. The flat is small and dark and looks like a grubby second hand shop with its clutter of beds and boxes and newspapers, a cheap holy picture on the wall. A gloomy kitchen is stuffed with mysterious paraphernalia.

Mother recalls the days of Uncle Béla and Aunt Irén, when the flat was spotless, the white-painted furniture scrubbed within an inch of fading away altogether. The present inmate takes no offence at the implied insult to his housekeeping for within minutes he too is away on his life story. His wife, who died last year, his daughter-in-law also dead, leaving two small children, his lodger, who is nothing but aggravation, the hot water that broke down three months ago and is still to be fixed.

Is it a Hungarian characteristic, I wonder in a daze, to

compete for the spotlight, to always have the greater tragedy, the most to complain of? Maybe I have been listening
to only a slightly different Jewish version all these years ...
Part of me hates this all-too-ready emotional laundering.
Then again, part of me wallows in it. I've not been in Hungary a month, but the other day when I watched a British
drama on television, with everyone repressed and restrained
and only hinting at things, they did seem, compared to this
lot, unbearably po-faced.

We leave the building. Only a block away is the People's
Opera House, built to supplement the Opera House on
Andrássy Avenue. It was here that mother saw Pavlova,
from the number two box. She steers me on, to the little
park nearby where Kató took her children for their ritual
dose of air and exercise. It's bigger and prettier than her
memory of it, but she says the trees have all grown, along
with her.

Then she wants to walk the route to school, first to the
Máthiás Gymnasium, where she and the maid dropped Pali
off, then on to her primary school. She points some things
out to me, but her mind is busy with the life at Rákoczi
Street, what a good, full life it was.

'But how we paid, later, for Gundel's restaurant and the
Gerbeaud cakes, and violets on Sundays.'

Chapter Twenty

'You're nicer in Budapest,' says Heddy. I've just made her laugh, telling her about that grotty butcher shop where the hot sausage and mustard tasted so delicious.

'Budapest does you good,' she says.

'I enjoy Budapest,' I mutter, embarrassed; which doesn't quite convey the complexity of what I feel.

We are on our way to her old school, the Veres Pálné Gymnasium, a handsome, three-storey building in an old-fashioned part of town. For years now it has been a co-educational State school.

Outside the school she stops and points to the wide, curved windows of an apartment building opposite.

'A young couple lived in that flat. Newlyweds. So romantic! Pali knew them. It was a brilliant match. Their parents furnished the apartment for them. Every morning we kids used to hang around here, just to get a glimpse of the bride opening the curtains. She had a gorgeous satin peignoir – a wonderful apricot. Ooh, how they exercised our imaginations! How late would they get up today?'

She tells me about her first day at Veres Pálné. Kató accompanied her, both of them dressed to kill. All the children were lined up ceremoniously to give bouquets to the teachers.

'But it's hardly changed!' I exclaim. A few days before she arrived I'd seen little girls in best dresses and snowy ankle socks carrying bouquets wrapped in cellophane for the teacher and, afterwards, parents, also dressed up, treating their children to a celebratory meal, the waiters making a special fuss of the kids for their big day.

'It has nice aspects, this traditionalism,' I say.

'Not when it descends into crazy nationalism, as it usually does here,' Mother says tartly.

I am intrigued to find her, in this context, the more cynical, the more suspicious.

In the school library, the librarians, old girls themselves, produce the photos and year books for 1933–4. Mother goes through the rows of her classmates. I have looked at similar photographs in Bellevue Hill, while she enumerated who died in the War, who of natural causes, who had what love affair, who was loved/hated by the other girls. But now some of the faces have entered my world. There's Irén, who loaned us her flat – noble looking and friendly-eyed even at seventeen; there's Vera who took me to the art opening; there's Klári whom I met just yesterday.

'That's Juci Schwarz,' Mother says. 'She died young. Feri and I used to play cards with her and her husband. They were so fond of him.'

Such little scraps about him, scrounged here and there.

We are on a corner near the Danube where the traffic roars off the Chain Bridge, past two grotesquely magnificent twin apartment houses named the Klotild Palace. Heddy pauses, sniffs the air like a hunting dog.

'Kató's music school; you know, where she was a scholarship student, where Rennebaum was her teacher. It's not far from here, I'm sure of it.'

She turns right, decisively right and heads off. I trot behind, flagging but impressed. I am reminded of hot afternoons in Sydney when I trailed sulkily behind her on some shopping expedition for boring clothes or shoes, while she, intent and purposeful, charged on.

The villa at Rózsadomb in the Buda hills is pretty – much nicer, and smaller, than I expected. You can still picture how it was although the central staircase has been removed and it has been divided into six flats. The big, light rooms are still there, the handsomely designed ceilings, and there are pretty Grecian-style doors, set deep.

The first flat has the former entrance door, framed in a stone arch. Such a neat little couple live here; she sprightly, white-haired, sixtyish, he spruce and smooth, his shirt ironed to a painful degree. Conscientious civil servants, early retirement. Their apartment – the former lounge, dining room and half the hallway – is spic and span, just like them.

Mother showers them with praise, almost as if they have kept the flame alight. Yes, they sigh, the area has gone so far downhill that Rózsadomb – 'Rosemount' – has been nicknamed 'Rubbish Mound'.

'You were right to leave,' they say. 'We wanted to go, after 56, but we couldn't leave our parents. We love our country, but it has given us nothing.'

'I have never regretted leaving here.' Mother's voice takes on a significant tone. 'Finally in Australia I got the acceptance I never had in my birthplace.'

Two minutes later, still talking of Hungary, she calls it 'home'.

The neat little couple take us around the house, introducing us to the various tenants. The upstairs tenant, an ex-architect, is the only one, apart from themselves, they intimate, truly able to appreciate the quondam splendours of the villa. He is an urbane, elderly man with old-world manners and volumes of Goethe on his shelves. He lives in one long large room with views over the city.

'This was once the boys' room,' Mother says. 'On Sunday mornings they'd let me in and we'd have pillow fights, just as if we were still little kids. But that was sixty years ago ...' She sighs.

'Impossible my dear Madam,' smiles the old gentleman, 'forty years, at most!' He gives a little bow, and they're getting on famously.

Mother wants to see a flat at the back of the house, but our guides chorus, 'You shouldn't go in, you'll be upset. He's real lumpen-proletariat, dirty.' She takes no notice. We are in a dark room, once the other half of the old dining room and part of the kitchen. A grubby old man in pyjama top and tracksuit greets us.

'Yes, you can come in. Not that there's much to see. I live here alone. My wife's dead. See how dark it is, and no bathroom. I've just had an operation. I can barely walk. I need a bathroom more than ever. But there's nothing but a sink and a toilet. I've asked and begged but I won't see it in my lifetime.'

'I lived here as a child,' Mother says. 'My father built the house.'

Fear spurts into the old man's eyes. He begins to whine.

'What will happen to me then, honoured madam? I have nowhere else to go.'

He is pleading with her as if she has already reclaimed the property and is the new authority.

'Nothing will happen. Live here in peace. I'm just looking at a bit of my past, then I'm going back to Australia.'

By the time the tour is finished we are on terms of intimacy with our guides – that special intimacy you can only have with people you are unlikely to see again. Mother looks for the slope where she and Pali and Cézar spilled and thrilled on the sled. She tells them about Pali, and how he died in Russia. She cries a little.

She says she will send them photos of how the house once was, and the man with the immaculate shirt drives us back to the hotel in a clean little red car, almost new.

I feel I have just had a small lesson in the caste, class manners and economic circumstances of current Hungarian life. I have seen Rózsadomb and mother in situ. I am satisfied but exhausted. Mother is satisfied and blazing with energy.

★

Robi is driving us to Kisláng. Kisláng, the high noon of Mother's memories.

She says she's been careful what to wear today because she doesn't want to stand out. She sighs, thinking back.

'When I was last there, the whole purpose of every day was to sink into the background, not to be noticed.'

How hard that must have been for her, I think with wry affection, she who dominates most of her encounters! And as for today, she might as well not bother, she'll stand out like dog's balls whatever she wears.

On the way down, she encourages Robi to tell jokes, do funny accents, and pisses herself laughing. She likes bringing out his father in him. And he is so pleased to be pleasing her. I laugh too, but I don't always understand everything. This part of their relationship is based on their knowledge of Hungary, Hungarianness. There are a lot of jokes about peasants who suddenly have more money than they've been used to and who ape 'Western' ways – the extraordinary uses to which they put their new bathrooms – jokes about policemen who are little Hitlers and so forth. It is a black humour of national self-sendup which reminds me eerily of Jewish humour. I can see why there was greater assimilation here than anywhere else in Central Europe. I get glimpses, still, of how a symbiosis, a love-hate operates for both Jew and Gentile.

As we get closer to Kisláng, Mother becomes serious.

'You know the whole reason for leaving Hungary was to be rid of the fear, for once and for all.'

I can better comprehend what she says now. Here fear is a currency, a constant undercurrent. But the other side of that, I think wistfully, is that there is more colour and density to life here than any life I have lived in Australia.

'You know when I was really afraid?' asks Robi. 'During the 56 Revolution. When the Arrow Cross brought out their old uniforms. They used to sing (in rhyming slang): "Don't be scared Yids / This time not as far as Auschwitz."

'A friend of mine told me it wasn't the right time to mention to anyone that I was part-Jewish. I said to him, "and you're a piece of shit, that you'd deny it at such a time, when you're as much a half-breed as me."'

I have heard the argument, from the few who admit they were once Communists or even Communist sympathisers, that 56 was really a counter-revolution, a front behind which all the rightist and Fascist elements regrouped, waiting to take over power. That the Russian invasion at least stopped that happening. It's not an argument I've heard from Robi though, who hates the Communists mightily.

I'm thinking about this and watching a rich landscape out of the window. It's green and flat, wildflowers by the side of the road. We are deep into the countryside, on a small uneven road. A horse-drawn cart goes by. Suddenly Robi and Mother say, 'Kisláng!'

And here we are in the place of anxiety and terror, of near death for me, the location of stories that have excited my imagination for decades.

It's an ordinary little village, two streets crossing each other. There is a town hall, a few pretty old houses, mostly deserted, among the uglier new ones. The long, flat village road makes me think of the time Heddy saw Kató sitting on a cart, the gendarme at her side, the time when she thought all was lost.

We look for the house where the six of us were hiding. Robi recognises the ditch where, as a three-year-old, he saw a dead soldier, gun still in hand, his body inflated and huge.

But the house itself looks all wrong – too new. We ask an old woman nearby.

'Aah yes,' she says, 'I remember, a few houses down, there were some Israelites, down here from Budapest.' She looks at us with shrewd eyes. Mother nods, and says, 'We were here in 1944.'

The old woman is deliberately using a word of tact and respect, Mother tells me afterwards, in saying 'Israelite' rather than Jew. In Hungarian the very word 'Jew' has a derogatory connotation.

Soon she and Mother are discussing their ages and their aches and pains. This bent old woman is five years younger than Heddy of the erect back, coiffed hair and elegant shirt and skirt, but they find a tone with each other easily. It's something I admire in Mother; her disarming directness, her ease with intimacy.

We go down the only other street, past a tiny picture show, and a fly-blown espresso which is still officially classified Third Class Business according to a spotty sign on the wall. We ask the bored girls in the 'presso about the old dispensary where the chemist lived, but they are too young to remember anything. There is not much else in the street, except a crude monument to the Russian liberators, now splattered with mud.

Then we notice, behind a new house built in front of it, the old house where the six of us were in hiding. In the messy yard a young woman is hanging out the washing, a couple of kids at her heels.

Yes, she remembers the Fehérs; the old man ended up hanging himself. She sings a snatch of song he used to sing, which mother completes. They reminisce about his prodigious drinking, his eye for women.

Behind the new house, all is as it once was; the pigs snorting in their pen, the pigeons shitting in the decaying eves, the chooks strutting and pecking, the well with a bucket, still in use. Robi is transfixed by the well.

'That's the well where the German soldier came and snatched the bucket from me. God I was frightened ...'

'It smells exactly the same,' says Mother, sniffing the odorous air.

We drive out of Kisláng. There are luscious blue-black plums on the trees lining the road as we leave, but we do not stop.

We drive through a hazy countryside, the road lined with poplars, towards the railway station at Kiscéripuszta, fourteen kilometres away. We last made this journey on horse and cart in deep snow.

'I cried when you left,' says Robi to Heddy. 'I so wanted to go with you, and your instinct was to take me, wasn't it? You know, it just flashed upon me that my life might have turned out entirely different if I had gone with you on that cart.'

The railway station is very quiet. In the middle of the deserted waiting room sits a white-tiled enamel stove.

'We waited and waited here in such suspense,' Mother says. 'That stove wasn't working. Would there be a train, when would it come, was it just a rumour that a train was running ...'

She gives a little grunt of pain and heads for the car.

We stop at a tiny village near the railway station. A few houses, a laden apple tree, a garden gone wild, a few people staring at the strangers. Robi points to the swifts circling overhead, preparing for flight.

★

I started to sneeze on the way back from Kisláng, and now I'm in bed with the 'flu, brought on by stress no doubt; Kisláng itself, day after intensive day with Mother, a mess of emotions.

It makes me wonder, this getting sick now, straight after seeing the village. Ever since that time in Kisláng when Heddy so feared for my life, my illnesses have never been 'normally' conducted. Even when it's only a cold, she worries immoderately, and I am always irritated and cranky with her. Yet I don't reject her attentions entirely; somehow the illness binds us closer together. Once again, things are anxious, grey and close, as in those earliest times.

Now, just as she would in Sydney, she arrives at the flat, bearing medicine and goodies. And just as we would in Sydney, we misunderstand each other and quarrel.

Anne says it's just the way she says things.

So many doors and hallways and windows, so many curious faces as Mother tells her story. My name is ... I live in Australia ... this was my first married home ... this is where my mother lived ... this is where my child was born ... this is where my husband lived with his mother before we were married ... my daughter, she remembers nothing ... she is curious about the past ... would you mind very much if we came in, just for a few minutes?

Usually the faces welcome. They are curious about our past too, or eager to tell their own, or they're just happy with a bit of unexpected company. Sometimes they are suspicious. Just who is this over-animated elderly woman and her anxious-eyed complaisant middle-aged daughter. What do they want? One tiny old lady, frail and a bit mad under her blonde Andrews Sisters coiffure, believes we want her flat back. She is sure that I am taking notes as evidence. She wants to produce papers to show that the flat is irrevocably hers. I try to reassure her and put my notebook away. Another is willing and welcoming until I ask to take a photograph. Then she takes fright. I put the camera away.

All these visits are in one small area, in the thirteenth district near the river. All the places I have heard about in the dining room at Bellevue Hill, on all those hours of tape, are within a stone's throw of each other.

The flat at 32 Pozsonyi Road, where Heddy lived, with major interruptions, between 1938 and 1948, is our focal point. Just two streets away is the block of flats that Feri bought when the War began, to guard against catastrophe. Another block and a street crossing to the flat where Kató and Náci settled once their worst times were over. These flats became a Jewish House in 1944.

Another three blocks, and we are looking at the grand old apartment block that housed Grandmother Schwimmer and my father before he married Heddy.

Yet another old woman lets us in. Budapest is full of old women keeping house for their daughters or daughters-in-law who are out earning income.

When we go into the room that was once my father's, I have a curious feeling. I feel it as it once was, as *his* room. He read and thought here. In that corner was the funny bachelor's wrought-iron reading lamp that is now mine. I imagine I can feel him around me, benign and quiet. This is the man who trembled with excitement when I was born. I tremble now, in his room. The feeling lasts for seconds, then someone starts talking and it is gone.

We can't see the whole flat, as it's been divided in two and there is no one home in the other half. But it doesn't matter; I've felt its ponderous simplicity, its bourgeois heaviness, seen the graceful curve in which the big windows sit. I can sense how it must have been when the family came up from the country to set up here in Budapest. I can feel them.

The day, like others before it, has felt like a speedy newsreel ... so fast through time, events, emotions. And Mother feels speeded up too – each place a large slice of her life, re-served. She tells them all, the curious, the bemused, her personal dramas in each locale, her grand scenes. Such an upfront, public way she has chosen to handle these meetings. But perhaps these scenes *are* her ... perhaps there is no choice in the matter. And almost everyone joins in – tells their life story in return, in fast-frame. It is I who am out of sync.

★

It's the eve of Rosh Hashonah, the Jewish New Year. In recent times, if Gyuszi is overseas on business, he likes to be in Budapest rather than a strange city.

We meet outside the synagogue for the evening service as if it is the only synagogue we have ever been to. There is an extraordinary familiarity about it all.

The synagogue is large and handsome in an eclectic Moorish style, but half in ruins. Word is that Tony Curtis – ex Kertész, ex? (so many Jews changed their German-Jewish names for something Hungarian sounding like Varga or Kertész) – is going to put money into restoring it in honour of his father.

Up in the women's gallery, Mother and I can't see Dad to wave to him as we do in Rose Bay, and the synagogue is larger and older, but otherwise how much the same it is!

The old ladies in their clumsy best suits with bits of lace on their heads, peering at their prayerbooks, the respectable matrons with their hair specially done, the teenage girls with their proud, dreamy profiles, the awkward group of boys lounging at the doors, lying in wait.

Downstairs the men are gossiping, ruminating, singing, swaying on the balls of their feet, tugging at their prayer shawls, cupping their chins. Archetypal poses, the same as those I have watched at the other end of the earth, year after year.

The Rabbi starts his sermon with the topical reference beloved of men of religion everywhere: a newspaper report that the local skinheads have been beating up gypsies because they are not True Christian Hungarians. They vow to go on wreaking havoc among all those who are not True Christian Hungarians. Everyone in the congregation knows who they mean.

★

Mum wants me to turn up at the end of her reunion lunch with some 'girls' from the Veres Pálné school, so that she can show me off to them. I feel a bit silly. Here am I, with a rocky life, several liaisons, married and divorced, forty-six years old, now some time into my relationship with Anne, being introduced to a group of seventy-three-year-olds as a daughter.

'Here's my daughter,' Mum says, even before I enter the room. I'm all smiles and charm as I come in. I'm doing my bit.

There's Klári Németh, who used to own a pharmacy, casting me longing looks, so I go and sit next to her. She's a small, square woman with nondescript frizzy hair and her nose and mouth all fallen in together, and it's immediately apparent that she is the soul of simplicity and kindness, so I settle down to listen to her.

'I always loved your mother, dear, from when we first met at school. She was such a sunny creature, and so good at sport. A big girl, but it suited her. So well distributed. All my family took to her when she came to visit us at the pharmacy ... My father knew she liked peaches, and once, when he knew she was coming in, he kept aside a lovely juicy peach, just for her. She ate it straight away – how she enjoyed it – and the juice ran all down her uniform. She's always amazed I remember that ...

'Your father, yes, he was tall, a bit stooped. He absolutely adored her, and why wouldn't he? The way he looked at her!

'Have you seen the pharmacy that was ours? It was my mother and father's before me. The Government took it away years ago. Irén's father, the judge, used to come in to chat ... I loved being a chemist. I miss it so much now I'm retired. The part I loved best was mixing the drugs and powders together, getting it just right. I really enjoyed the responsibility – as far as I know, I never made a mistake, not one.

'Yes dear, there is talk now of giving the pharmacies back to their original owners, if they were qualified chemists. It would be wonderful, after all these years. I've applied for all the papers, but who knows, they say one thing one day, another the next. No, no I couldn't run it myself any more, I'm too old and tired. It would be something for my grandchildren.

'I still have my father's title of ownership and his qualifications, all inscribed on parchment, but I'm not sure whether to produce it. It's in our old name, Neuremberger – we changed our name years ago – but there's so much anti-Semitism again now, I don't know if I should.'

I must have asked her a question about how she got

through the War because suddenly we're in horror-land again. Almost every one has a tale worthy of a bard, a book. I hear the terrible tale through in fifteen minutes. She tells it simply and understates her own bravery. She says, 'I don't know why I told you. It gives me a bad feeling to talk about it.'

We sit quietly after that. She pats my hand and looks at me lovingly. I have entered her Pantheon. I am Heddy's daughter.

Chapter Twenty-One

Outside our old flat at 32 Pozsonyi Road, Heddy points to the picture windows on the second floor.

'There were no such curtains as mine in all Budapest!'

Before she arrived, not sure of the number, I have looked up and down the street for windows big enough to fit her damned curtains. Now here they are.

Within days of being in Budapest I learned to look underneath and beyond to see this city's beauty; I'm getting practised at it. As we enter the vestibule I look beyond the clutter and see the clean square lines of a classy thirties Budapest apartment block; the daringly shaped, severe doors, the pale pink marble, the architect's name near the door, the locked wrought-iron garde-robe where Judy's baby carriage was kept.

An elderly man with intelligent eyes answers our knock. As soon as he understands our business he opens the door wide with a quiet, expansive gesture.

What have we here? This is no secondhand shop, no make-do random mix of furniture and bric-a-brac such as I now expect from nearly every Budapest home. There is a collection of ancient ceramics, souvenirs and carvings from around the world, books everywhere, some nice furniture. Evident prosperity, quiet cultivation, no show.

He is a retired government official. His wife is still working as a journalist. Her salary, and his substantial pension from the old regime, give them a level of ease that is unusual.

Within minutes of our meeting, the wife has dropped a password – Auschwitz – so we know the territory. The husband, while his friendly eyes follow us everywhere, is much more guarded.

Mother is telling me where everything was, how it was, but I really don't take much in. I am content just to be here. I feel comfortable, familiar. I could sit down in a corner and read, or go to sleep. Aah, I am in the land of pre-memory again – I *feel* this territory. I can feel myself, at three or four, watching from the balcony as the bogey man comes down the street.

The conversation floats around me – past/present, our past, their past. Mother dominates it all. Our hostess doesn't even get much in about her Auschwitz; Mother's Kisláng is the order of the day. But no one seems to mind, not even me today; I am high on the strange pleasure of being here.

In the living room, Mother and Éva Somogyi exchange histories and stories. Does Heddy by chance remember Dr B and his wife who lived below? The wife died only last year. But of course Heddy remembers Mrs B; she was a flower girl at her wedding! That's where she met her husband! How she adored him! And a discussion of the dead woman's character and marriage follows.

From there, the stream of coincidence becomes a river – or is it just that a certain sort of Budapest has never died? Of course they know Vera, of course they know the old lady who has just turned 100. So it goes, as the world gets tighter and tighter.

Mother gives them a potted version of her life, not in any necessary order: Kisláng, Rózsadomb, the first years in Australia. She reaches a kind of peroration:

'After the first sixteen years in Australia, we felt secure and settled and I had my first trip out of the country. After sixteen years, and I was going on a trip for five whole months! I actually cried for joy as I looked out of the plane window. There was Hitler, safely dead and buried and here was I, alive and well, flying out of Australia on a trip to Europe. What a moment!'

Éva Somogyi takes her cue:

'My greatest moment was when I met the Queen in London. I come from a poor Jewish country family. My mother struggled to bring us up alone. I survived Auschwitz. It's been a difficult life. Years later, in the late fifties, my husband was posted to London. We were to meet the Queen at a diplomatic gathering. Everyone was taught to curtsy, but I knew, even though I said nothing, that I wasn't going to curtsy. As a foreign national, I didn't have to. So there was I, a survivor of Auschwitz, meeting the Queen of England, and I didn't bend my knee!'

Eva's husband has been sitting quietly, listening. We ask him about his life. He has had a distinguished career, is now retired, paints and writes a little, and follows recent events with despair. He feels that his life's work is being undone.

He is the first Communist functionary I have come across, or at least the first to talk of it openly. He is still a Communist of conviction. He is restrained and modest, but staunch about what he sees as his achievements and those of Communism.

'I have worked very hard,' he says, looking us in the eye.

He shyly asks Heddy whether her husband might know a friend of his from labour camp days who now lives in Sydney. When Mother recounts the afternoon to Dad, his face lights up.

'Béla Somogyi! I remember him well! He'll know me as Gyuszi Weiss. We were together in labour camp in Poland. He was always a gentleman. And always a Communist. A man of conviction.'

Our last pilgrimage is to one of Heddy's girlhood homes, to Isabella Street, where the finances began to stablise and the carpets to come back from the pawn shop. Not a lot has changed. The building is still dilapidated, still raffishly charming. Nothing much has changed inside either – an old-fashioned unremarkable flat.

A retired couple is sitting at the eating nook in the kitchen, having lunch. The man is talkative, discursive; the woman stares and stares through owlish glasses. They are both ex-teachers, life-long Catholics, supporters of the present conservative government. Life was hard under the Communists, the man says. They had to hide their faith; there was no career advancement for people like them.

Then he turns to the present. 'The gypsies,' he says, 'there's a lot of talk about them now. They're responsible for so much crime, out of all proportion to their numbers in the population. There are decent ones among them of course. We don't dislike the gypsies here, only the evil ones, the criminals.

'People say there is anti-Semitism in this country, but there isn't really. We don't hate the Jews in general, only those who were the top dogs in the party, the Jews in the secret police, those who wanted revenge for the War. Look at the ones who dug themselves into top positions in the party. Rákosi himself for one …'

I don't trust myself to speak. But Mother keeps her cool. She debates things with him in a friendly manner. When he talks of being persecuted, she just says, 'Aah, but it depends who you are, where you are, as to when you feel persecuted by whom. Everyone's turn comes.'

★

We leave Budapest, going south to Hódmezövásárhely. On the way we stop in Paks, Gyuszi's home town. In Paks the scenario is much the same as when I was here with Dad more than twenty years ago; we visit the cemetery, then his old house, finish at the fish restaurant by the river.

The cemetery looks much better than on my first visit, when it was desolate and waist-high in paspalum. Dad is more business-like than the last time I was with him; he says *kaddish* at several graves, then goes looking for new ones that he wants to restore. Robi follows him, taking notes; he will be following up on the restoration.

'Do you know how many graves you've restored over the years?' Robi asks.

'No.'

'Twenty-four.'

At the gate the caretaker produces water and towel for us to wash our hands, and a dog-eared visitor's book. The last entry was six weeks ago, a man from Wisconsin, coming to see his grandparents' grave; three months before that, someone from Brussels. Occasionally there are visitors from Budapest.

The house where Gyuszi was born is a solid merchant's house on the main street. It is painted in flaking ochres and yellows, the flag-stoned rooms are cool, and the courtyard is full of fruit trees and ducks. There are stables at the back where Samuel Weiss once kept fine draft horses and a cart for transporting grain.

The current owner's wife is cooking Sunday lunch.

'Not much to cook these days,' she sighs, 'things are bad.'

'What,' says Dad, 'no meat on a Sunday?'

'Oh well, yes.' She smiles at him. 'There's some meatloaf.'

★

Mother and I are standing in Bercsényi Street in Hódme-zövásárhely, looking for Feri's house. Heddy knocks at the door of one very like it. The Schwimmer house? It was right next door, pulled down years ago. The bright-eyed woman remembers Mrs Schwimmer, with her snow-white hair, always standing at the top of the stairs. She was a child of eight when the labour camp was set up in the storehouse on the other side of their wall.

'The men used to gaze over that wall into our yard. My mother gave them bread and eggs, poor things. They used to pick the fruit from our trees, those they could reach.'

We are standing in a kind of miniature farmyard; three handsome black horses whinnying in the run-down stables, a haystack, a tractor, a trailer spilling over with corn husks, four yelping dogs, chooks, sensuous farmyard smells.

'Why, we were only talking of the Schwimmers the other day,' the bright-eyed woman says, 'about the rats getting into their feather store after the War, and how hard it was to get rid of them!'

Bits of old garden flourish in the farmyard. The woman picks a perfect rose and gives it to us.

'You should visit the Weiss sisters across the road. Do you remember them?'

Mother shakes her head dubiously.

'Three of them are still there. They will remember. When old Mrs Weiss, their mother, was taken away by the Nazis, she said to my mother, "Pick the apples from my tree. Don't forget to pick the apples."'

We have an appointment with a Mr Szemzö, the Schwimmer family lawyer. We have come across him by a most circuitous route. Feri's brother János died in America a few years ago, followed by his wife Margit. Their son George, wondering who to notify of his mother's death, came across the name of a man in Hódmezövásárhely, his mother's birthplace, in her address book. He sent him a death notice. The lawyer was surprised and pleased to hear from America, and wrote back. But George could no longer read or write Hungarian, so he sent the letter on to my mother in Australia, asking her to reply for him.

That is why we are knocking on Mr Szemzö's door at 3.30 on a mid-September afternoon. He ushers us into the drawing room, which has the hushed primness of provincial drawing rooms everywhere. Four huge brown velvet chairs, a large desk for his work, china figurines on lace, a very proper bookcase with some serious-looking books, a neat drinks trolley, which looks rarely used, by the door, an oil painting of Budapest on a rainy night at the turn of the century. A room almost charming in it's dullness.

Mr Szemzö sits behind the desk, courteous, assuming a quasi-professional tone. He still does a little work from home he says, to keep his mind active. He's a smallish monkeyish man, deliberate and quiet, very alert. He is over eighty but amazingly well preserved, his face unlined, his movements slow and supple.

I think about how many survivors I know who have the same healthy alertness, who look young and life-loving. Almost as if their brush with death has given them a greater than normal appetite for life. As if their sufferings have geared them up for living. It's the next generation, my generation, which is often sickly, weary of life and confused by it. We seem to carry some sense of consequence with us, some unnameable burden which the survivors have shed.

After he came home from the labour camp, Mr Szemzö's life in Hódmezövásárhely was a quiet one. It doesn't take him long to recount it. Straight after the War he did a lot of compensation cases, then he was a Public Notary until the town's sixteen lawyers were collectivised. He worked in the collective on salary until his retirement. Now he does a bit here and there for people who ask him.

Mother tells him of her first stay in Hódmezövásárhely

when, hearing of what was happening to country Jews, she fled back to Budapest. She describes her two visits to the police chief – the first to bribe him to let her stay, the second to beg him to let her go.

'He was quite decent. He didn't ask me for money the second time. Now what was his name ...'

'Benitsky,' he says instantly.

For all of them the details of this time are what counts, what sticks, not the subsequent years.

'Not that he could have protected you by then,' he adds, sadly, practically.

'We got back here in January 45,' Mother says, 'after a nightmare journey east. We were in a terrible condition. I went straight to my friends the Patzauers, you remember the Patzauers. Ilona Patzauer saw me at the gate but she didn't recognise me, not until I spoke.'

Mr Szemzö becomes quite animated.

'I got home a couple of weeks before you! I went straight to the Patzauers, too. I escaped from a camp at Miskolc and got home by Christmas, 1944. They were very kind to me as well. I stayed there for about ten days. This house was here but everything had been looted – the furniture and linen – there wasn't a pot or pan left. But I got organised and moved back in.'

I ask him about the Jews who survived, their life postwar.

'There might be thirty of us left. We kept pretty quiet, but we all know who the others are. We didn't practise religion much; it was frowned on, for one, and there weren't many opportunities. Our big thing was to fix up the cemetery. We all contribute; some money comes from emigrants abroad, too. We sold the synagogue organ – we had no more use for it – and put the money from that into the cemetery. It's pretty good now. We have a caretaker and last year we put in cement paths. We restore a different part of it each year.'

There is a story about the synagogue that he tells with some pride. The local Jews decided to sell it to the town council because it was far too big for them. But the Budapest Jewish Community intervened, claiming jurisdiction over all Hungarian synagogues. They proposed selling it for three million forint and disposing of the money as they liked. The local Jews were incensed.

'They said it is still our synagogue; we don't want to lose control. They came to me, and I looked into it. What Budapest was proposing was certainly illegal. I wrote a few letters and the big city boys caved in. We took over the sale.

'The local council has committed itself to restoring the building, inside and out. It will always look like a synagogue. The ark remains. So does the memorial in marble to the martyrs of the War.

'They will use it as a library, and we will use the old Jewish school as our synagogue – it's big enough for the twenty or so who come to Yom Kippur. I think we have negotiated something suitable and honourable.'

Mr Szemzö also says we should visit the Weiss sisters who have lived opposite the Schwimmer house all their lives. They are very old now, but they will remember a lot. He telephones them. There is evident confusion and flurry at the end of the line.

'They are here all the way from Australia,' he says to them. 'They may never come again. They don't *want* tea and cakes; just to come by for ten minutes. Yes or no?'

He puts down the phone. 'They are very frail, but go and see them now.'

At the door, he turns to me. 'When your book comes out, I would like a copy, even though I can barely read English. I saw you taking notes,' he adds approvingly, 'so I tried to be accurate.'

I like the old man, the dignified way he has handled the afternoon.

We go back to Bercsenyi Street, to the home of the Weiss sisters. A door I never expected to open; a door I never knew existed. When we walk into the low-ceilinged room, it is like a magical passing into – not another time or another world exactly, but another feeling, other presences. The three Weiss sisters greet us, all joy, as if we'd left yesterday, as if they know the present me, rather than the six-month-old baby they last saw so long ago.

Three very old, bent ladies, so neat, dainty even, their white hair freshly coiffed. So old, you couldn't really tell which of them was older than the other. All with lovely, pale old skins, soft, fine-boned hands. The one with the face of a simple young girl, all goodwill, sits next to me and repeats, every few minutes, 'Of course we knew the Schwimmers, all our lives. You have the look of your father about you', and strokes my hand and smiles into my eyes. She has on a freshly ironed apron – she looks as if she has always worn an apron.

Another sister, taller and bonier, getting about in a walking frame, peers at me kindly and joins in the chorus of welcome. 'Your father Feri and I went to school together. We used to play like gypsies among the feathers. They were just across the road!'

The third, tiniest of the sisters, is sitting on their best Biedermeier sofa in blue Chinese pyjamas. There is more worldly wisdom, more sophistication, in her face. 'I remember the Schwimmers, of course, but not as well as my sisters. I went to Budapest to study medicine, and lived there most of my life.'

The other two sisters have never married. They have lived their whole life in this house.

We are sitting in the low-ceilinged living room, on the

stiff and proper (but not graceless) provincial furniture of the mid-nineteenth century, lovingly preserved. All around the walls are paintings and pottery, almost like a gallery.

We talk and we don't talk; it's almost as if we've come home and there's not a great deal to tell us. My father is so familiar to them, the boy across the road, that they have nothing particular to say about him. And everyone knows this visit is so short – we are running late and they are so frail – that words might waste it. I think we would all be content to just sit there and smile at each other while the little lady in the apron strokes my hand quietly. But we talk, intermittently.

When Mother tells them about her sojourns in the house across the road, the two maiden sisters chorus, 'We remember, we remember.' How is it that they remember us so well, when we were here for such brief and tumultuous times in 1944 and 1945? Through Jancsó. Jancsó was a friend of theirs and on each of her visits to them over the years, even when she went up to Budapest to live, she told and retold the story of Heddy and Judy and Susan. Jancsó's love for us has kept us alive for them.

There were five sisters originally. Two were deported and 'never came back'. The two maiden sisters were deported to Vienna and put to forced labour in factories.

'What the Fascists did to us, we can't even talk about. The fear, the fear ...'

They struggled home from Austria around May 1945, around the time Heddy was preparing to return to Budapest.

'When we were deported (you were gone by then) we didn't know what to do with the furniture. Jancsó was across the road and she let us store it in your storeroom. Most of it was there when we came home, though some had been stolen. We set things up again. We've lived here ever since.'

The third sister was living in Budapest, deeply, mutually in love with a Christian army officer, unable to marry because both sets of family strongly opposed the match. During the War she worked for nothing in the Jewish hospital in the area that became the Budapest ghetto. After the War, when parental opposition no longer seemed so important, she and the soldier married and lived happily until his death. She then came home to her sisters.

In the double room that is the living quarters, there are dozens of pictures and pieces of pottery on every wall space and surface. Some crude, some good, some experimental. The sisters catch my fascinated gaze.

'Our father was passionately interested in art and culture. Most of the pots are his. He was a shoemaker by trade, but his real work was his pots. There was an artist's colony in this town in the twenties and thirties. Our father was their "patron". There was always someone here for a meal, day and night. We still have a lot of Father's pots. We have to sell one occasionally, to make a little money. We try not to sell too many.'

Some of the pots are sturdy and peasant-inspired, others graceful thirties vases, stylishly decorated. I want, very much, one of their father's pots, so that this hour, this room will always be with me. But while I am thinking about how to try to buy one, they are ahead of me, pressing not one, but three pots on me, as a gift, a memento. One is a lovely brown and yellow Grecian-inspired jug.

There is no stopping them. It's only fitting that I have them, they say, to take back to Australia with me, as a memorial to Hódmezövásárhely and to my dear father, whom I so resemble.

So we leave them, go out of their big wooden gate and out of their world. For hours afterwards I am back with them, graced by the feeling of that low-ceilinged room.

Chapter Twenty-Two

Mum and Dad are due to leave soon – Dad is waiting for the second big Holy Day of the year, the Day of Atonement, before flying out. Mum and I have seen most things together we need to see. Anne and I will stay on another three weeks.

Heddy comes by to help us pack the folk-art plates I have picked up and the pots the Weiss sisters pressed on me, then goes back to the hotel to pack her own things. We wander around the city, go to the markets. We sit for hours in our favourite coffee shop; the waitresses know us by now. We drop into the sculpture exhibition at the Ernst Museum, where Feri bought the farmyard picture for Mother as a first sign of his love.

Days like this I could live in Budapest forever.

At night I have a meal with my parents while Anne goes to a concert. Something has changed. There is a new ease, born of something shared, between Mother and me. Dad sends Anne some medicine for her cold. He says we should look after each other.

★

On the morning news I hear that the writer Csori has been asked to resign from the Writer's Union, following the furore over his remark that 'the Jews seek to assimilate the Hungarians rather than the Hungarians the Jews'. The

President, the gentle old man at the Art opening, is a member of the Writer's Union and supports the Union's stand.

Later, listening to the radio, I hear a Catholic woman philosopher attacking Csori. She makes an impassioned plea for tolerance.

Another news item: a storm over a remark in Parliament by a member of the ruling party that the opposition Free Democrats are nothing but a 'soapbox for the Jews'. Some say there has been a play on the word 'soap'.

The same day I am swimming in the Rudás baths, an echoing ruin of a place on the Danube, filled with pensioners to whom entry is free. My eye is caught by an old fellow in a baseball cap and glasses, swimming at a leisurely pace beside a large old woman with be-kohled eyes and a purple flowered cap. As I swim past them, he is giving her a recipe. I slow down to listen:

'You take two big onions my dear lady and fry them till they are transparent. Then add about twenty decagrams of mushrooms. Cook them together my dear lady, for about five or six minutes, then take them off the stove. Preheat your oven for ten minutes. Put some sour cream over your mixture, and a liberal amount of grated cheese. Cook it in the oven for about fifteen minutes. It's good, there's no meat in it, so it's reasonably cheap, and it keeps well the next day.'

Next time I swim past I've got my ear cocked for more culinary tidbits but they're on quite a different tack.

'That business about a soapbox for the Jews,' he says, 'it doesn't mean much, the word "soapbox", it's a meaningless term really. I can't see what all the fuss is about.'

He catches my eyes, mutters something to his companion in the purple flowered cap and they swim on in silence.

The next day we are invited to the house of a museum curator and her son, a young literary academic. I ask the young academic about the well-known writer who made the anti-Semitic remarks, thinking to learn a bit more about the context, but he just says irritably, carelessly, 'Oh everyone is so sensitive these days. You can't say or write a thing without being leapt on.'

Is he right? Is everyone (read me) becoming too 'sensitive'? True, I listen with a keener ear than I would in Australia, or if I lived here all the time.

But what I hear is always unexpected, unawaited. I am swimming in the baths, listening for recipes, and I hear something else. I switch on the radio to hear about Iraq and I hear a defence of the Jews. I try to get a grasp of local politics and I hear about the double meaning of 'soap'.

It looks as if Communism has been only a hiccup in the long, tragic, complex tale of Europe. Much older passions and hatreds are waiting, resurfacing.

But there are Fascists in Australia too, I remind myself, some of them Hungarian Fascists. Quite a few Arrow Cross emigrated at the same time we did, with the connivance of ASIO. And their activities over there in distant Australia are not all small beer: real war criminals, infiltration of the Liberal Party, dirty tricks, backing from the émigré clergy.

But would it have been paranoid, unnecessary, in the sunny land where nothing much really happens – at least to Europeans – to take note of everything?

★

'But there's nothing there!' Heddy said when I told her I wanted to go to Fertörákos where Feri died.

'I know, but I still want to go and have a look.'

This is the first expedition I am making off my own bat. All the others have been with Heddy, or in the wake of her memories. But I feel dubious about myself and slightly false. There is no grave at Fertörákos and I am not about to go on an elaborate search for the exact spot where my father died. I am not going to stand there and weep for a man I never knew.

Why am I going then? Would I have gone if there had been no book to write? Almost certainly not. It's part of the 'research' I tell myself lamely – that's a legitimate reason surely.

As we wander the ancient streets and courtyards of neighbouring Sopron, listening to the Austrian tourists from just across the border, the whole enterprise feels silly, manufactured. I am irritable with Anne, out of sorts. The truth is, I don't want to go. I would rather keep the image that I have in my head, of my father not getting up from his bunk, saying, 'Tell them I love them very much but that I died.' It is neat, complete, tragic. I want to leave it be.

The bus from Sopron takes us through a soft Hungarian day. Red poppies are growing wild in the yellow and green fields. My eyes are streaming from hay fever, my mind is blank.

The village has grown lengthwise so that a long, straggly main street peters out on each side into meadow and farmland. There are 'Zimmer Frei' signs on every second door and heavy-limbed middle-aged Austrians everywhere; the men have short-back-and-sides, the women fussy fifties perms. A statue in the main street commemorates the dead of World War II. I have seen its like in many Australian country towns. There is another memorial further up the street, this time in German, to the dead of World War One. I make a mental note to check out the history of the place.

It's lunchtime and the village is sleepy. Few people are out. I approach a clutch of old women.

'Forgive me the interruption,' (I have learned my Hungarian formalities), 'but perhaps you might remember a labour camp here during the Second World War?'

A buzz of memory straight away, but some disagreement.

'Yes, there was a camp, but soldiers only.'

'No, there were Jews kept up there on the hill, past that corner, where the quarry is.'

They agree that most Jews were herded into the barns of various farmhouses around the town.

The most talkative is a toothless dame with reddened cheeks, squat and small in her old-woman's uniform of kerchief and drab cardigan.

'Oh, I remember them well. There were about sixty Jews in the barn of the farm where I was working. I came close to losing my life because of them. They were always hungry and I felt sorry for them, but we weren't supposed to go near them. There was one man with a little boy. I gave him bread whenever I could. The mistress caught me and threatened to tell the Germans if I did it again. The SS would haul you away for less.'

'I was sorry for them, too,' says another woman, looking at me apologetically, 'but I was afraid. I didn't dare give them anything. They were cruel, those SS men.'

They were cruel times, I say, to show there is no need to apologise to me.

'Yes,' the toothless one cuts in, 'and everyone was frightened, even if they deny it now. But that man always looked out for me ... When he left, he gave me the carpet he used to wrap around himself and his boy to keep out the cold.'

'Do you still have it?'

'No, dearie, it was a long time ago. I had to sell it at one stage. But I know they survived because they sent me a card from Budapest at the end of 1945. But God knows what happened to the others.'

'You must have been quite a young girl then,' I say (for she could be anything between fifty and eighty).

'Oooh, well, not such a very *young* girl! I already had four children. That's why it was such a risk, with four kids

dependant on me and my husband away at war ... Do you
see that palace down there?' She points to a pretty eighteenth-century mansion a hundred metres away. 'It used to
be the bishop's palace. That's where the SS were housed.
The younger ones were the worst.'

'Yes,' says another, 'the fifteen- and sixteen-year-old kids
were the cruellest; they didn't know any better. If you go a
little further down the street, you can still see the huge
trenches they made the Jews dig.'

'Can we ask you,' they say with quiet courtesy, 'why you
are here?'

'My father died here,' I say matter of fact, and they take
their tone from me, as if we were talking about commonplace things, as in a way, we are. Here War, Fascism, Communism and death are everyday matters.

'We've had quite a few people come through,' says the
toothless one, 'looking for the places where they were, showing their friends or relatives.'

Looking for the stone quarry, I ask directions from the few
people on the street. One man says automatically that he
wasn't here during the War, another says he was away at
the front so he knows nothing. An old couple are sitting
silently by their door watching a huge pig wander down a
side street. They know. Dourly they give me instructions and
compress their lips.

At the edge of the village, opposite the gypsy camp, the
old couple said. We come to an untidy stretch of gouged
earth, white and chalky. There is nothing except a deserted
stonemason's workshop and what looks like a statue dis-
carded from the Communist era. There is nothing to show
me, one way or the other, whether thousands of labour
camp inmates were once here. The mass pit graves may be
here, they may not be. I have no idea whether my father

died here, or anywhere else within a few kilometres.

A sign tells us that Austria is just up the road and some sweaty cyclists pass by en route to the border. On the other side of the road the fields are filled with poppies. I pick a couple, in some vague association with remembrance, but all I get is a disconcerting vision of wizened little men staggering under their medals in the Anzac Day sun.

Anne wants to take my photo, and not knowing what to say, makes some clumsy joke about smiling for the camera. I can't smile, I say sourly. I am, if only a little, sad.

There's not much truth in 'sad'. Irritated, disconcerted, confused and disappointed more like it.

We catch a bus back to Sopron and hours later, grim-faced and streaming with redoubled hay fever, I pick a fight. When I calm down, we talk about reactions to death. I realise that I should have made my 'pilgrimage' on my own and allowed myself, in solitude, to feel whatever it was that I was feeling.

I think about going back there the next day, to pay my 'respects' alone. But everything has already happened in its particular form. I cannot make it happen differently.

The next day I go alone to the famous thirteenth-century synagogue in Sopron, the second oldest in Europe. In the courtyard 'the Israelite Congregation of Sopron' (all fifty of them) have erected a small memorial with a wreath, and these lines:

Remember 1640 Sopron Jews who fell,
Sacrifices to Fascism.
Hate killed them.
May love make their memory live.

It's a simple memorial before which my cynicism melts.

Inside, in front of the chipped ancient stone Ark which has survived, I pay my respects, briefly, full-heartedly, to my father, and to all the others.

★

Back in Budapest. Only a week before we leave. I take the walk to the Körút which is now etched inside me. Out of my dilapidated doorway, into a street grey with age and grime. Past the dog shit, the wine bar filled with frowzy men, the seedy cake shop of few customers, the old courtyard with the huge tree filling it with dapples, the man at the door hitching up his pyjamas. Down towards the intersection with a noisy traffic street, past the new and sparkling deli carrying with it the hopes of its owners for riches.

At the corner, the unclassifiable neo-Renaissance-Art Nouveau-Rococo building with the Star of David motifs – one of my favourites in Budapest's bizarre architectural smorgasbord. It's being renovated and turned into a bank – another capitalist dreaming. Opposite, the yellow Baroque church where the faithful gather, in increasing numbers now, for Mass. Past the cinema, then the bronze doors of the Ernst Museum, past courtyards with pot plants and washing and kids. From the apartments near the Ferenc Liszt Music School, rehearsals and scales float down to the street.

I turn the corner into the grandeur of the Körút, the Ring Road where you can catch the Metro, the bus or tram to almost anywhere. The apartment buildings sit squat over the dress shops, cake shops, stalls, offices. I am within sight of my favourite coffee shop with its oh-so-light cakes, its Biedermeier chairs and pretty, obscure oils on the walls. The waitresses wear a brown uniform with frilly cream aprons and the cream, open-toed open-heeled boots that signify Hungarian Waitress.

If we go home a slightly different way, we pass the Opera House, that great symbol of bourgeois culture, gilded and ornate, Budapest's pride and joy.

When I call to say goodbye to two of Mother's old Budapest girlfriends who have lived through so much and now watch, with a pool-side but avid interest, the new Hungary hell-bent on pursuing capitalism, neither of them is envious of my life in Australia.

'Oh, it's a mess here,' they say airily, 'but it's a damn sight more interesting than Sydney.'

★

I have asked the three sisters at Hódmezövásárhely if I can come back to see them on my own.

It is a few days before we leave Hungary entirely, and the first day of a nationwide strike. The taxi drivers have brought the country to a standstill, protesting a huge rise in the price of petrol. It is the last in a series of price rises that have left people confused and desperate. The taxi drivers, supported by truck drivers and unions and most of the country, have blockaded all the roads. Only the trains are running.

I decide to brave the blockade. I want to be with the sisters again, although I am afraid the spell of that first meeting will be broken. By now, the train carriage, the countryside, the feel of things, are all familiar to me. I am inside my own thoughts.

I reach Szeged. No buses, so I take a small slow train for the forty kilometres to Hódmezövásárhely, the same train we took on the last leg of our trek from Kisláng.

The old ladies are in a flutter of anxiety and gratitude that I have braved the blockade to come and see them. We sit down to lunch, gazing at each other with goodwill through our threadbare connection.

The youngest, the tallest one, bony in her walking frame, is the boss. She has always been the organiser. When she was young, she went out to work in the local store.

'Your father bought all the books that came in. Not just the fine literature. That too, but just about everything that came in. I could tell he read them too – he didn't just buy them.'

The middle sister, with the apron, has bright eyes, a strong voice. She is given to short, decided pronouncements.

'Your father was very shy. He didn't play much with other boys at school. He never asked a girl out. We couldn't believe it when we heard he'd married a Budapest girl – and a beautiful one, too!'

The oldest, the one who has come home from Budapest, has wise, sad eyes and a deep, resonant voice.

'The Schwimmers always kept to themselves, all of them ... they didn't say much. Your father went everywhere with his head lowered. He looked at no one. He knew what was going to happen. He understood the times he was living in. Yes my sweetheart, your father knew.'

After lunch they elaborate their themes. They are doing their best by me – they know I have come a long way. The youngest reads me a passage about the Schwimmers from a big book on local families and pauses solemnly for me to take notes. Their three pairs of eyes, shining with intelligence, beam at me.

The train back from Hódmezövásárhely is full – the strike is still going. At Szeged, the station teems with worried people and there is a rush for the doors, but in first class things are relatively quiet.

I return to a deserted Budapest. Anne greets me at the station, full of news. The shops are out of bread and milk. People have queued for these staples for hours. The relatives are appalled that I have been out and ring on the hour for news of me. There's fearful talk of blood, of people not taking it any more, of Revolution even ... Everyone is at home, glued to their television to see what will happen next.

I think of Australia where this would be just another strike. Here, it seems, any movement on the social surface and there is fear of the deepest fissure, of a bottomless gulf.

We walk home through the unnaturally quiet streets, the trams standing idle, the shops shuttered and locked. We talk of the strike, of politics, of the old ladies, of Europe.

The strike is in its third day. Demonstrations in front of Parliament. Negotiations televised all day long and into the night. Long speeches in smoke-filled rooms. God can these Hungarians talk! All the Budapest bridges are blockaded – only emergencies and ambulances are let through. Interviews with irritated tourists stranded in remote places. Kindly locals offer them food and showers. Bread is gone from the supermarkets; people buy up a dozen, two dozen loaves at a time. I am scornful at first of all the panic, then join a queue, stand for three hours.

The evening before we are due to leave, and the strike is still on. Rumour is that it will be resolved tonight. The protagonists are still mouthing at each other in the smoke-filled room.

At 10 p.m. Anne and I haven't packed a thing, still glued to our television set like everyone else. We are mesmerised, half hoping the strike will go on so we won't have to leave this strange country, not quite yet.

By 11 p.m. it looks over, the agreement signed in front of the cameras, and Robi rings to say he has checked – the roads will be cleared during the night. He can drive us to Vienna as planned.

He and Rózsi arrive early next morning and he huffs and puffs our bags into and onto his little Russian car. He is nervous and picks on Rózsi. He recovers himself as we drive through a bleak morning towards the border; enough to joke and bombast and get sentimental. How much he and I have found in common, how much he likes Anne, how he wants, more than anything, to come to Australia one day, to 'lay a single rose on my grandmother's grave'.

We sit down to a farewell lunch at the airport cafe. He whistles at the Western price for sausage and sauerkraut, tastes it and says no self-respecting Hungarian would eat it, then eats with gusto.

It's nearly time to get on the plane. We change Hungarian money into schillings to reimburse him for the petrol and so that he can have some hard currency.

'Maybe don't tell your mother that you gave me the schillings,' he says, looking worried. 'Not that there is anything wrong with it ...'

Next moment he is making gleeful plans to spend the money on his caravan.

He doesn't want to say goodbye. He rushes out to mind the car instead. I follow him out and kiss him. I have become so fond of him.

He softens a little, kisses me, bangs the car door, waves. They're gone.

Epilogue

My cousin Erika is coming to Australia for a conference called Child Survivors of the Holocaust. She wants me to go. Erika and I have met half-a-dozen times over the last dozen years but we have never discussed these things.

I am reluctant to go. What could a conference teach me? Besides, I don't remember anything about that time. I was a baby. Really, I was of the second generation.

But I go, and when, embarrassed, I tell my story, the co-ordinator of a workshop says, 'That is perhaps the worst of all, when we have no conscious memory.'

I went as a member of the second generation. I come home a member of the first. I was there.

I come home to my garden, my ordered self-created life, but I do not feel at home. I want to go back to the womb of chaos, disorder and formlessness. I want to be paralysed, ill and, ultimately, rescued. I am back in my first world.

Everything I have known and written about shifts focus. It is only a small shift, like viewing a scene through the tracery of a tree, then moving a few inches to see the panorama clear. But having made that shift, I see I have to claim a part of myself long disowned. I am excited and very frightened.

I look again, with my new eyes.

My two childhood memories of Hungary: the gate that shut, and the bogey man. Even when I was safe, clean, nourished, in the comfortable flat on Pozsonyi Road, I was convinced that someone evil and sinister would come to get me, and it was my own fault. There was nothing I could do.

The other memory – I am not so sure that I really remember this one. The big iron gates shut. The good ones, the rescuers, (Mother and Gyuszi) are on the other side, but they have decided not to rescue us. The go away. I take my older sister by the hand and say there is nothing we can do.

In my later life, these are my inner themes. They will come and get me. The rescuers will bypass me. The only way to help myself is to withdraw, and wait.

In my outer life though, I have fought, made noise, tried to frighten away the evil ones and attract the rescuers. I felt it my duty to change the way things were. But inside, I did not believe it. Inside, I was paralysed.

I did not pay attention to that silent, fatalistic, fearful child. She came to me in my depressions but I did not recognise her. I fought her off.

I know who she is now. She is a child who survived the War, at the outer edges of the Holocaust. I can trace her through who I am now. She is my fears, my sense of displacement, my omnipresent sense of threat. She is also my resilience and accommodation, my will to find meaning and to make things work.

Two words are used often to describe the personalities of child survivors: 'dissimulation and adaptation'. So it was in the postwar years, and so it remained. So it continued into the immigrant years. Changes of identity, half in one world, half in the other. A child, yet not, a Jew, yet not, an Australian, yet not.

★

I have moved to the country. We are living a couple of hours from Sydney, in a landscape soft with echoes of Europe.

302 | *Heddy and Me*

Outside my study window stands a huge and ancient gum, and in front of it, a European tree that is starting to lose its leaves for autumn.

In the hallway, among all the objects of past and present worlds, sits my grandmother's black-and-gold clock. I still play it sometimes for people who have not seen it before, and often the same look of dreamy delight comes over their faces as came over mine as a child.

I chat often with Heddy on the phone. We rarely talk about anything important, but it is comfortable chat. We like each other. We have things in common, Heddy and I.

Acknowledgements

There are, of course, innumerable works on the Second World War and the Holocaust, but not much available in English on Hungary and the Hungarian Jews. I have found three books particularly useful: Jorg K Hoensch's *A History of Modern Hungary* (Longman, 1988), *Righteous Gentile* by John Bierman, a readable account of the remarkable Raoul Wallenberg's activities (Penguin, 1982), and Randolph L Braham's impressive and exhaustive two-volume work, *The Politics of Genocide: The Destruction of the Jews of Hungary* (Columbia University Press, 1981). I am indebted to the latter two for quotes used on pp. 148 and 95–6 respectively, and to Braham for much factual material.

I want to thank those people who have, in their different ways, been important to this book: Fred Lowry, Masha Eisenberg, Robert Gordon, Keryl Egan, and last but certainly not least, Gyuszi, or Dad.

Heartfelt thanks to Jennifer Compton and Sasha Soldatow for excellent critical comment. And to Jan Kenny for her careful reading, good suggestions, and for much else.

My special love and thanks to the two people who have been essential to *Heddy and Me*: to Anne Coombs, who got me started and who saw me through with support, love and an unerring eye, and to Heddy, for having the courage.